To the family of

With the wish to feel what for me is...

Cosmos

R oot

E thos

T ravel

Echo...

CRETAN MUSIC

*Unraveling
Ariadne's Thread*

Editing: Maria Adamantidis
Proof reading: Kalliope Gourntis
Preliminary editing: Anna Bakola
Production: Atelier KERKYRA PUBLICATIONS
Cover design and page layout: Adriana Panayotopoulou
Illustrations by Eirini Koutridou
Photographs by Yiannis Bromirakis
Photo on p. 93 courtesy of Laodikis, photo on p. 151 courtesy of Ourania Xylouri
Production co-ordination: Efi Andrikopoulou

This book is accompanied by a CD entitled *Cretan Music: Unraveling Ariadne's Thread*.
For track and copyright info see CD jacket.

ISBN: 978-960-8386-52-5
© 2007 KERKYRA PUBLICATIONS LTD. - Maria Hnaraki

Kerkyra Publications, 6-8 Vlahava Street, GR-105 51 Athens
Tel. +30 210-331 4714, fax: +30 210-325 2283
www.economia.gr, sales@economia.gr, bookstore@economia.gr

Maria Hnaraki

CRETAN
music

Unraveling Ariadne's Thread

KERKYRA
publications

SUPPORTED BY

SCORE

CHORUS
Sotirios Chianis, Professor of Ethnomusicology, State University of New York............. 11
Emmanuel E. Velivasakis, President, Pancretan Association of America 13
Nikos Dimou, Author.. 15
IMPROVISATION 17
INTERLUDE 19
MAP OF CRETE 20
REHEARSAL 23
PRELUDE 24

STEP 1: ENTERING THE LABYRINTH.. 28
Thread.. 31
Meanders 32
Kronos 37
Odyssey 39
Amalthea 45
Mythologies 53

STEP 2: INTO THE LABYRINTH... 56
Minotaurs 62
Hyacinth and Zeus 67
Erotokritos and Aretousa 72

STEP 3: ARIADNE.. 76
Labyrinths.. 79
Theseus 84
Ariadne 94

STEP 4: UNRAVELING 114

    Psiloritis 116

    Erofili 118

    Zorba the Greek 121

STEP 5: AMAZING MAZES 132

    Knossos 135

    Hermes 139

    Atlas 144

    Ithaca 148

    CODA: DA CAPO AL FINE 156

ACCOMPANIMENTS 158

    LIGATURE 160

    NOTES 167

    PICTURES AT AN EXHIBITION 177

    COMPOSITIONS 186

    INDEX 187

CHORUS

*I*t is a distinct honor to introduce a most welcomed addition to the numerous volumes devoted to Cretan music. The author skillfully combines the disciplines of mythology, history, anthropology, ethnomusicology and folklore together with her own extensive fieldwork to give the reader a comprehensive overview of an extremely complex cultural phenomenon. Interrelationships that exist in a typical Cretan ensemble of instruments and voice, the repertoire, weddings and dances, and the all-important extemporaneously composed vocal distichs known as *mandinades*, are thoroughly discussed in an interesting and scholarly manner.

Professor Hnaraki's volume is destined to serve as a model for all future scholarly works on the music of Crete and Greece in general.

Dr. Sotirios Chianis, PhD
Professor of Ethnomusicology, Emeritus
Binghamton University
State University of New York

*D*r. Maria Hnaraki's suggestion that music can bring people together is well supported by her philosophical approach towards Crete, her island. She created a writing to be read by all those who love life. Crete is her palette which she skillfully uses to depict what is really worthwhile in life. Her nostalgia for the Greek island blends in with a brilliant selection of people and works, all related to Crete in ways that have led to major breakthroughs and changes, not only for the Cretans, not only for the Greeks but for the whole world.

Dr. Hnaraki's *Cretan Music: Unraveling Ariadne's Thread* is a rich writing which I salute with great pride, as it manages to appeal to different groups of people. It is in itself the proof of what she suggests, namely that we are all alike! It will give information to the historian, vital links to the researcher, pleasure to the poetry reader, clues to the philosopher, knowledge and perhaps a new awareness to all!

I congratulate all those who supported Dr. Hnaraki's "quest" and realized the importance of her project. Most of all, though, I congratulate her for the mental map she provided us with, in order to help, move and support us in our own unraveling of Ariadne's thread!

Emmanuel E. Velivasakis, P.E., F.ASCE
President
Pancretan Association of America

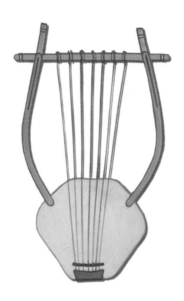

Maria Hnaraki is an artist and a scholar. Not only does she combine these two, seemingly contradictory, attributes but she excels in both.

And what is more, as an artist she creates in many forms. She is a poet, a singer, a musical performer and a teacher.

Which means she can look at any cultural phenomenon both ways: as a spectator and critic – and as a creator and performer.

And on top of all that, she is a Cretan – a quality which eludes any kind of definition. (Actually this book is an attempt to define the essence of Cretanness).

So here is a work of feeling and thought. Dealing in beauty and tragedy – two things that are indistinguishable in Greek (and Cretan) tradition. You may read it as a treatise or you may enjoy it as a performance. It is both.

Nikos Dimou
Author

IMPROVISATION

Heartfelt thanks to:
   Saint Nicolas, the traveler.
   The Cretans and the Anoyanoi, the dancers.
   Nikos Dimou, the on- and off-line spiritual father.
   Henry Glassie, the insightful.
   Ross Daly, the guru.
   Vasilis Stavrakakis and his family, the hospitable.
   Laodikis, the storyteller.
   My grandparents, the angels.
   My father, the telepathetic.
   My brother, the different.
   My sister, the teacher.
   My mother, my soul.
   Theodore, the source of inspiration.

Acknowledgments to:
   The ethnomusicologist, Sam Chianis.
   The Aerakis music family.
   The painter, Mrs. Eirini Koutridou.
   The photographer, Mr. Yiannis Bromirakis.
   The Pancretan Association and its current president, Mr. Emmanuel Velivasakis.

Last but not least, wholehearted thanks to:
   Mrs. Alexandra Vovolini-Laskaridis and her hard-working team, Mrs. Maria Adamantidis in particular.

M.H.

INTERLUDE

*T*he book you hold concerns Cretan music. It starts with a confession, and the description of a musical event. Then, five main chapters follow, each one with different numbers of subunits. Each chapter is preceded by the description of a music scene, to guide you through. An epilogue marks the end. The notes, list of sources and a glossary are for readers who wish to study certain topics further. To flavor the sound, a CD is included. Lastly, photographs serve as images, and drawings allure.

Greek words and place names have been transliterated according to the Journal of Modern Greek Studies, and a system which approximates Modern Greek spelling. Stress accents are provided for words of more than one syllable to ensure the closest possible correct pronunciation. Proper names have retained their established anglicized form or the spelling preferred by the person cited.

Purposefully and through respect to the reader, I have chosen a non-academic (by definition) but yet scholarly style to re-present a serious topic. It was not my goal to write a history of Cretan music, but rather to open pathways and supply lenses through which one may meditate on it.

Without further ado: once upon a time…

Chania

Rethymnon

WHITE
MOUNTAINS
(Madares)

Mt.
PSILORIT
(Ida)

▼ Sfakia

🏛 *Phaisto*

L I B Y A N   S E A

CRETAN SEA

Heraklion
●

▼ Anoya

🏛 *Knossos*

▼ Mirtia

🏛 *Diktaion Andron*

LASITHI MOUNTAIN RANGE

🏛 *Gortyna*

MESSARA PLAIN

● Sitia

Aghios Nikolaos
●

● **Ierapetra**

Map of Crete
● Major cities   ▼ Villages   🏛 Archaeological sites

REHEARSAL

Innocent warning confession: The theater of life.[1]

God, may You give me enlightenment, and a heart big as a boiler,
To be able to sit and think, like Daskaloyiannis.
The Daskaloyiannis Song (traditional Cretan)

"... There may be no future at all! ... I saw the airplanes passing over my head and sensed how much everything is hanging by a single thread. I have a notion that I shall soon be taking leave of this earth and I am waiting calmly, absolutely ready. And so, dismiss things 'future.' Without becoming nerve-racked, we must strive to live the present terrifying moments the world is undergoing, for we too are bound to experience them. Much patience and love are needed to endure with dignity this critical era it has been our lot to live in. I am certain that I have both these needed qualities. I beg you to have them too. Now, at moments such as these, the mettle of a human being is revealed... I begin work before daybreak; at nightfall I stop. I plunge into the sea, eat plenty of figs and grapes and in the evening glue my ears to the radio. Agony, but I am trying to tame it by working..."
Nikos Kazantzakis in *Nikos Kazantzakis: A Biography Based on his Letters*

These are Nikos Kazantzakis's words in a letter to Helen Samiou (the future Mrs. Kazantzakis), on May 15, 1941, five days before the invasion of Crete by Nazi forces. These are the words that I also apply to myself and dedicate to you, sixty five years later. My hope is for a better world. With this book, I want to show that we are all alike; that we should not engage in conflict. And I ask you: Can music and dance help us in this direction? Can they possibly unite us?

Cretan music plays on my stereo while I write. I choose music from my country, from my island, to be always present in order to remind me that I need to go on and write for the people I love, for my homeland, for the people of the world. In the end, it is to all of them that I owe my existence. Without the music, without the vivid presence of Crete, a documentation of its life is not possible. Come and discover Crete with me. I want to communicate my enthusiasm and my passion with clarity so you can smell the Greek and Cretan air, see the Greek and Cretan people, listen to their music, and envision their dance.

I talk about music and dance because they help me escape. They soothe my k a i m ó s (sorrow) and empower my identity. I believe that tradition is not something that necessarily belongs in the past and eventually dies. In this sense, I am a traditionalist: I am inspired by the past in order to walk steadily toward the future, building on a solid present.

My passion and nostalgia for my country can often reach extremes. In the end, this book is about identity, and my own undoubtedly "sounds" Cretan[2]: Writing about the music of my island feels like telling the story of my own life. In a sense, it's self-revealing.

The same tiger that follows Kazantzakis in his journey ("tiger the co-traveler" in *T a x i d é v o n d a s [Journeying]*) accompanies me as well. I can even see it on the face of that green-eyed big cat that often visits me in the early morning, scratching my window, meowing for my attention. With these thoughts, I invite you to view this book as an ethnographic life experience that will not exclude any actors or acts.

PRELUDE

*J*une 16, 2001: We are on a boat heading from Athens to Heraklion, onto Knossos and the palace of King Minos. Sailing from the Aegean to the open Cretan Sea, the wind blows against us, but the salty air is refreshing and invigorating.

As we enter Heraklion port we see the massive Koule, a sturdy tower with a winged Venetian marble lion atop it. In one of its dungeons we are to attend the inaugural performance of the *Elefthe ría - Thisía - Zoí* Concert Series *(Freedom - Sacrifice - Life* Concert Series). Soprano Anna Trocchia-Taiganides, the American wife of a Greek-American, will perform in solo voice a program of music that embraces many cultures and traditions.

The dungeon is cold, humid and dark. There is no electricity. Tea candles bring us some light and a small hole on one of the four stonewalls gives us a glimpse of the sky.

The audience for tonight's concert consists mostly of family — from my mother's side — and other Cretan, Greek, Greek-American and American friends. My father ready to record the performance. My task is to distribute the programs before the concert starts, as well as to serve the nuts and the Cretan r a k í (the Cretan version of grappa) during the break.

"Thank you for coming. It has always been my dream to sing here. I hope you will enjoy the performance," says Anna. The first part of her recital begins with a " K í r i e " which she has composed, a majestic and dignified musical piece strongly influenced by Byzantine church chanting. Songs and vocal music by the well-known composers Samuel Barber, Henry Purcell, Giacomo Puccini and G. F. Handel follow.

After the break, we get to listen to some folk songs, one by the Shona people of Zimbabwe, the Irish song "Danny Boy" and the Greek song ʿΆ r n i s i ʾ ("Denial"), by composer Mikis Theodorakis based on a poem of George Seferis. The finale comes to rivet our attention: "Amazing Grace."

A bus is waiting to take us away to a Cretan feast in the mountain village of Avdou, which took its name from an old Turkish pasha, Abdul, or from prophet Havdeu,[3] and where Anna and her husband's family have bought some houses to spend their summers. In front of the village's central church, long tables are arranged for the guests. Traditional Cretan food and delicacies have been ordered and are being prepared in a restaurant just around the corner.

The musicians are already here. They drove from Heraklion and the village of Krousonas. They are about to sit on a small wooden stage by the side of the churchyard, in front of the tables. They are setting up their microphones and testing the sound. They are all men, one l a o ú t o (large lute) player, one guitar player, one l í r a (the main folk instrument on the island of Crete) player and the singer of tonight's Cretan feast.

First come the appetizers with the bread, then the cheese and the salads. The main course — roasted meat with potatoes — follows. It is time for the musicians to start performing, so that we can all stand up and dance with a full stomach. Some of the music performed is vocal, some not. Those who are not familiar with the Cretan l í r a are amazed: The sounds coming out of such a little string instrument are so unique.

The l í r a player is seated between the two other men, the one playing the l a o ú t o and the other the guitar. These instruments do not seem to surprise the audience as much as the Cretan l í r a does. The l a o ú t o looks to them like most of the large lutes found in the eastern Mediterranean. The guitar, on the other hand, is definitely familiar to all, replacing in tonight's performance the second l a o ú t o, which is traditionally present.

Dimitris Vererakis performs dance melodies on the l í r a. The l a o ú t o and the guitar players keep the rhythm. A solo melodic invitation by the l í r a player invites all to start dancing: My cousin with his family stands up first. Next, he invites me and I join the dance with more family members.

The dances we perform are dragging or leaping, slow or fast, moving in a counterclockwise rotation or danced by couples. They are Cretan and Greek, with an exception of a special order made by my cousin's father, who comes from the region around the Black Sea — what we call Pontos. In all dances we smile because we are happy to be together: Our Greek and American relatives, our friends, all our guests unite in dance.

My cousin is the first to start and lead each dance. After all, it is "his" feast. He arranged and organized the event in honor of his wife's recital and of all those who were able to attend. At the head of the circle, he performs numerous leaps, turns and acrobatic movements. He is the one who has paid the musicians, who constantly throws extra money to the stage and who orders the songs he wishes to be performed.

When my cousin invites me to be the lead dancer, I break away and begin to execute complicated steps consisting of whirls, turns and lively jumps. Then I go back to join the circle and invite somebody else to come up to the front position and be the leader.

On this particular night, we have the chance to dance with Americans and teach them how to dance. They do pretty well. However, my relatives, especially the ones who came from villages and not from the town or the city, carefully observe them dancing and comment on how I, in particular, dance well because I have "natural" movements: Cretan dancing is in my veins, they say.

The singing of Dimitris Vererakis, the l í r a player, is definitely of an oriental nature, with a specific and deliberate use of a certain nasal quality. A m á n - a m á n (for mercy's sake! woe is me!) is an exclamatory expression he often uses to begin improvising.

As he is a Cretan, it is natural for him to know how to perform proverbial couplets, m a n d i n á d e s. Due to my extensive research, my passion and love of Cretan music, and the fact that I am a Cretan in opposition to my cousin and his family who are Greek-American, I already know by heart and I can sing many of the m a n d i n á d e s performed by the musicians: In a sense, I am able to communicate with them, but also to judge them.

During the whole event, I get the chance to do some fieldwork. I introduce myself to the musicians and talk to them about my research. I write down their phone numbers as they show willingness to assist me. They inform me they have some other scheduled performances over the summer, which I plan to attend. My cousin invites them to the United States to perform at his annual party.

The dancing continues until the early morning hours: Tonight's central, most astonishing as well as observed dancer is my grandmother, born on February 13, 1913. Since she was a child, she had problems with her vision. She had to quit school and stay at home. Several years ago, she became blind in both eyes. Now all she can see is shadows. Despite this, my almost ninety-year-old grandmother Christina, my mother's mom, still dances at wedding feasts and other occasions. Her presence is full of energy and power and is an inspiration to us all.[4]

She knows by heart and indeed possesses the dancing steps so well, that she is able to lead a dance by herself and create lines of amazing labyrinth formations: In this book, dancing is a central element. The labyrinth is an essential symbol since the Minoan era in Crete: It has shaped the way Cretans think of themselves as well as the way others think of them.

As you read this, imagine making your way through a labyrinth where nothing is linear. My goal is not to perplex you, but to a-muse you. Inspired by Clifford Geertz and Henry Glassie,[5] my goal is to reach you.

Time is a central concept and has a different feeling or sense in the Greek and Cretan culture. Greek and Cretan time is — as the labyrinth is — "ancient" in both character and nature, another symbol that accompanies us in the labyrinth and plays a very significant role in the formation of the Greek and the Cretan identity: Historical and contemporary time shape who the Greek and Cretan people are and how they behave.

In other words, this book moves in both space and time. The space is the labyrinth. It is also the geography, the world in which we find Greece and then Crete. On the island of Crete we trace the specific places I talk about and examine, such as the village of Anoya. Since my goal is not to examine all music performed in Crete but, instead, draw upon specific phenomena and musicians, I call my study phenomenological.

I investigate the complexity of Cretan musical identity by looking into its genres and aesthetics. Moreover, I intend to answer the following question: What is Cretan musical identity and how does it work? Following initial participant observation on my part, I rely on the musicians themselves who perform in Crete nowadays to provide candid answers to my questions. I then look into how they simultaneously separate themselves from and perceive themselves as a part of a specific musical tradition. In order to do so I observe and participate in music and dance performances.

This book consists of five chapters, which I call steps: They recall the very popular Cretan dance p e n d o z á l i s (p é n d e means five, z á l a means steps; thus, a five-step dance). P e n d o z á l i s usually follows a slow dance (s i g a n ó s), which then accelerates. These well-known, traditional Cretan lyrics accompany p e n d o z á l i s: "With the perfumes of May, the red cherries, look how the Cretan young girls dance!" This is not a coincidence: I was born in a May and I choose to, as much as possible, dance in a crazy p e n d o z á l i s mood.

Today, what we find in Greece generally and in Crete specifically is an amalgam of mythology shaped by places, but more so by people, in both time and space. Mythology is the world of myth and musicology the world of music. It is this interplay of time and music that I wish to present in the beginning of each step, which opens with a mythology and a musicology, viewed always through ethnic lenses, so that my observations are at once ethnomythological and ethnomusicological.[6]

In the center of a circle, the labyrinth, lies the island of Crete and its music: It blossoms and dies, according to Heraclitus's idea of acme and decline. Also, in the center of this circle, lies the main idea: We are what we think we are. The stereotypical Cretan l í r a player and his music are in the center of this study as well, like Zorba the Greek — Zorba the Cretan.

Vasilis Stavrakakis, with his singing of *E r o t ók r i t o s* and his mandolin, an instrument of Venetian origin, moves us from the center of the circle westward, whereas Laodikis, the Syrian percussionist, takes us south. It is in this part of our circle that we trace the North African and Middle-Eastern influences on Cretan music. Ross Daly then carries us to the east, having us complete a semi-circle, as he particularly studies and occasionally even performs and collaborates with eastern and Asian musicians.

Ross Daly crosses borders. Through his musical experiments and distinct talent he brings Cretan music to the rest of the world. Through him, as we move north, and then west again, we are able to complete one circle. However, we continue moving, as Cretan musical time in my view is not linear, but akin to a labyrinth: It is a continuous mixture of past and present.

Time is responsible for bringing together on the island of Crete the three musicians I examine. Time, placed around the Cretan musical circle, moves counterclockwise like Greek and Cretan dancing. Time runs and everything repeats itself. Time, in the end, is what created what you are about to read.

step *1*

Entering the labyrinth

STEP 1: ENTERING THE LABYRINTH

*Y*ou are about to enter the palace of Knossos. The thread to guide and help you orient yourselves is the story of Kronos, who does not manage, in the end, to eat his child. Thus, Zeus, with the help of the nutritious milk of Amalthea, grows up strong. This Odyssey is to always be remembered and repeated.

> "Demon"
>
> The time's wheel turns like a demon:
> I am just a lit candle in the winds' eddy.
>
> The only way to encounter Death:
> When He comes, be worthless.[7]
>   Stavrakakis, *Sti díni ton anémo*

Time to bring together Ross Daly and Vasilis Stavrakakis, our two main protagonists. In the summer of 2001, while I was conducting field research, the compact disc *Sti díni ton anémo (In the Winds' Whirlpool)* was released, with lyrics and music by Mitsos Stavrakakis, Vasilis's first cousin. Vasilis is the main singer on the compact disc. Ross Daly orchestrates the pieces and he plays the *líra*, the *oúti*, and the saz (long-necked type of lute).

> "Light Blue and Green"
>
> A light blue and green seashore in your eyes roars:
> Whoever enters and does not drown will have stories to tell.
>
> Over the sunset the sun touched your lips:
> Now the sky is on fire and the evening burns.[8]
>   Stavrakakis, *Sti díni ton anémo*

As Mitsos comments in the compact disc liner notes, the melodies and the lyrics of this work, dressed in everyday attire, have already been performed several times, for small and big audiences, on formal and informal occasions. Now, in "Sunday clothes," they decide to go for a walk, invited or not, in private or public. They are nervous and embarrassed, hesitant as teenagers, fearful of the society.

> Kondiliés (Cretan musical phrases)
> Sometimes fate makes people blind:
> They sing in other tunes than the ones the *líra* plays.[9]
>   Stavrakakis, *Sti díni ton anémo*

Time perplexes these melodies: Birth comes first. Melodies become adults, capable of further stepping into the musical passages, with elegance and decisiveness. They eventually meet with impatient Skironas and Procrustes. Some melodies Skironas overlooks and Procrustes neglects. Most of them Procrustes does not even think of laying on his bench. Others, however, he handles with sensitivity and understanding, with respect to their form and inner context.

'Manousáki' (Narcissus)
Before tear, some joy inhabits:
Before laughter, a strangely sad silence.[10]
   Stavrakakis, *Sti díni ton anémo*

Ross Daly, an Irishman, collaborates with the Stavrakakis family of Armanoya. He plays the l í r a, but also the Middle Eastern saz and the o ú t i. To the melodies he orchestrates, Daly chooses to add the sounds of the f l o g é r a (fife), the l a o ú t o (large lute) and the b e n d í r (frame drum). The lyrics are well known, Cretan distich m a n d i n á d e s that deal with traditional themes such as life, death, time, fate, love, pain, relationships, solitude, bravery and survival. The recording is made at a local studio in the city of Heraklion, Crete.

Because Cretan music is basically a social phenomenon, in this book I investigate its identity and question its aesthetics: What is Cretan music? Let us now consider the p e n d o z á l i s, the Cretan five-step dance.

Thread

My passion for music and dance springs from the need to express myself. It is a passion rooted in my blood when, as a child, I performed dances at social gatherings and various music and dance events in Crete. This passion certainly grew larger when I left Crete and moved as a student to Athens. It certainly reached its most extreme, when I decided to continue my studies and professional life in the United States. Listening to music from Crete and dancing to it stimulates my identity. Writing these accounts feels like dancing a tango with Marta Savigliano. As she chooses to explore her Argentinean identity, I also invite you to watch me wander into music and dance realities.

Like Zorba in Kazantzakis's novel, whom I identify with, I choose to dance rather than cry. In other words, I choose to show you who I am, who the Greek and Cretan people are through "our" participation in music and dance. In the process of trying to discover who I am and how I came to be what I think I am, I realized that I am a special case (as we all are). Though of course I carry a Greek passport, I almost never identify myself as a Greek, but as a Cretan. At the same time, even though I feel more Cretan than Greek, I can also trace in myself several Middle Eastern characteristics. Maybe this is because my maternal grandfather came to Crete from Ephesus, Asia Minor, after the Greek uprooting of 1922. Whatever the case may be with my past, the point I am trying to make here is that one's social and cultural identity is shaped locally.

The same things happen all over the world, but in different ways. In this sense, Cretan musical identities are shaped according to local and socio-cultural conditions on the island. In all circumstances, which in my case involve music and dance, there are always ideals,[11] departures,[12] and varieties,[13] which I do not regard as negative.

Moreover, I believe Cretans, as well as other people of the world, are products of many influences (in my case, specifically Arabic, Turkish, and Venetian and generally Middle Eastern and Mediterranean). To show that, I intend to follow in this book a multidisciplinary approach by looking into the history, the literature, and the arts on the island of Crete, as well as their impact on Cretan music.

In this initial step of the book, I would like to begin a historical overview of the Greek-Cretan cultural and musical history, because I assert we cannot explain the present or look to the future without the past. So I will talk about a people, specific people, in past, present, and future time. In the third step, I focus on three people in particular on the island of Crete. By looking into individual musicians I intend to show how we are all linked to larger communal processes that may be, for instance, historical or social.

Music and dance on the island of Crete reflect identity — mine, yours, ours. Music and dance, as I see life, challenge boundaries. And I agree with Martin Stokes when he says — in *Ethnicity, Identity and Music: The Musical Construction of Place* — that a strong sense of identity can be put into play through music by performing it, dancing to it, listening to it, or even thinking about it: Because music provides us with an opportunity to observe and engage with it as a vital form of social creativity.

Meanders

Music is created socially just as culture is created socially. Because I am part of a specific society and culture, I am also socially and culturally shaped.

Knowledge depends on our experiences. Whether I acknowledge a theoretical orientation or not, I surely possess one. Throughout my writings, I may exclude or forget to clearly point out some of my theoretical influences. I suppose this is because some ideas have so become part of my active thinking that I feel unable to separate the two. I do not purposefully choose to highlight some scholars, works and ideas and "neglect" others.

I examine in my study songs, dances and musical processes of individuals and community members. I rely on a defined geographical area, but at the same time, I am also interested in the smaller units within this area (a particular case is my more thorough study of music and dances on the Cretan village of Anoya "Speaking Without Words: Cretan dance at Weddings as Expression, Dialogue, and Communication") as well as the relationship of Crete to Greece and to the rest of the world. I talk about specific musicians from the village of Anoya, as well as Cretan and Greek people in general.

Music and dance events are artistic expressions of the people (locals and non-locals) who participate in them. In the stories I tell here, I do not intend to exclude any performers. By looking closely at the way people choose to express themselves during occasions where music and dance are performed, I attempt to share with you true narrations. Moreover, I look into something that, I assert, happens all over the world in different ways. Music and dance events are art for the people of Crete as pottery is art for the "heroes" of Henry Glassie's *The Spirit of Folk Art* and *The Potter's Art.*

Through these music and dance events, both public and social in nature, the people of Crete articulate their community beliefs and represent their Cretan identity. Because music and dance are a form of language,[14] a form of communication through which people express ideas about their culture and society, their analysis provides another mode through which to understand social processes.

Deeply interested in literature and poetry especially, convinced that novels and poems contain strong truths, I do not purposefully exclude any such works that I judge important to my present document. Rather, I have selected to review and make use of literature and poetry related to the island of Crete.[15] Moreover, I am also interested in any other craft, such as architecture, for example, or even cooking, as long as it can help me support and illustrate my arguments and ideas.

The Cretan culture is molded by the interaction of the locals with each other and the rest of the world. In all these relationships, individuals are linked to larger communal processes, both historical and socio-cultural.

The main method that frames my realities is fieldwork, the purposeful and intense immersion into the daily life of Cretan society. The tool I use to get to the core of things is the description of particular events and circumstances. Analysis of songs and their lyrics follows so I can analyze the main issues and topics discussed in this book. Thus, what I am building here is an ethnography based on real people and situations, inspired and motivated by literature and philosophy.

The theoretical orientation I follow in my book is phenomenology. My goal is an accurate, as much as it is possible, first-hand account of the Cretan phenomenon.[16] To achieve all the goals I propose, and to answer the research questions that I suggest in my study, I look for small details that explain big issues, as a phenomenological study does. In addition, I examine particularly the roles of multiple worlds, near and distant at the same time. Phenomenology is a useful tool because it allows me to describe the expressive condition of performing-for-others, in other words, of being-for-others. Furthermore, it helps me describe one's consciousness of others, namely, the inter-subjective field. In addition, I use phenomenology to understand the relationships between the local and the global, their representation, role and nature on various performance occasions.

Acting as a phenomenologist, I initially conduct broad observational research to investigate what questions may be important to my work. How do Cretans visualize themselves locally and as part of the world's body, and how does the world welcome Cretans? Having done that, I am then very much interested in the details that come out of feedback questions and interviews.

While examining issues important to my writings, I also adopt relativism, the concept that everything is acceptable since it is possible. I use relativism as a way of talking about multiple vantage points and different interpretations of reality. I oftentimes make use of my field notes and interviews that I have transcribed and translated, as well as of the life histories of the main musicians to illustrate these points.

In the philosophical context of relativity, I also add that of Heraclitus on "fluidity." According to him, "everything flows and nothing remains stable. All gives way and nothing is fixed," to use Willis Barnstone's translation in *To Touch the Sky*. In the same Heraclitian sense, everything has a peak and a downfall, and this is absolutely natural.[17] Throughout this book, I view music on the island of Crete as something that constantly changes, that is flexible and able to move in many directions.

Case studies of Cretan musical ensembles, of individual events, as well as of specific musicians (in other words, life histories that reveal the personality of the artist and not merely give her or his biographical information) illustrate specific points I make throughout. For these purposes, current studies on ethnographic writing are important.[18]

A model for my ethnography is anthropologist Michael Herzfeld's book *A Place in History: Monumental and Social Time in a Cretan Town*.[19] Whereas Herzfeld examines a particular city in Crete, Rethymnon, using cultural and historical notions, I am more specific in my study by providing a history of music as well as of dance performances through historical, anthropological, ethnomusicological and cultural lenses as well.

In his book, Michael Herzfeld examines questions confronting conservators and citizens as they negotiate the "ownership" of history: Who defines the past? To whom does the past belong? What is "traditional" and how is this determined? In the same sense, in my book, I look more generally at the island of Crete and more specifically into its music and dance phenomena, investigating notions of belonging. My question is: Who defines what Cretan traditional music is? To answer such a question, I also examine the history of the island of Crete and take into consideration past Arab, Venetian, and Turkish occupation.

I emphasize the importance of history because I maintain that who we are today is shaped to a great extent by who we were in the past. Therefore, attached to the realm of relativism are ideas that deal with the notions of time. Besides time, which is the subject of history, space is also important here. In this spirit, I comment on the actual geographical position of Crete, an island that lies somewhere between the East and the West. Crete is part of Europe, but at the same time has been influenced through the ages by great Middle Eastern traditions.[20] In this sense, it is interesting to see how geographical borders do not always strictly follow a population's movement.

It is not easy to put borders on a sea, the Mediterranean, and divide it into East and West.[21] However, we occasionally need to do this for analytical purposes. I much prefer the term eastern Mediterranean to the so called Near and Middle Eastern. My concept of Eastern Mediterranean countries includes Turkey, Syria, Cyprus, Lebanon, Palestine, Israel, Egypt, Libya, Greece and Italy. That does not mean, however, that I do not recognize influences and dialogic relationships among nearby regions such as the South of France and Spain, Tunisia, Algeria, Morocco, Azerbaijan, Afghanistan, India, or even "The Balkans." Instead I like to view them all as a pan-Mediterranean whole.

The massive Koule – an imposing Venetian tower at the entrance of Heraklion harbor

Michael Herzfeld successfully manages, in my opinion, to depict the unbelievable turbulence of the East-West division. In his eyes, Greeks struggle to keep the two apart, but their difficulties in this regard are predetermined. Thus, Greece has an ambiguous, complex historical relationship to Europe and "western" culture. "Modern" Greeks: As writer Nikos Dimou suggests in his *Apology of an Anti-Hellene* (in Greek), Europe asked them to be European, while foreign Greek lovers asked them to be ancient Greek. And as Herzfeld has noted in *Anthropology Through the Looking-Glass*, one should not forget that Greece today needs to put the word "modern" or "contemporary" in front of it in order to convince its "admirers" that in Greece one can find people who are still alive.

Herodotus foresaw the tension between East and West as they expanded geographically on his attempt to map the world, facing geographical diversity. He was mostly interested in the Mediterranean area and fascinated by its "material culture," but he had a vision of a unified globe, split between East and West. Without knowing it, Herodotus, was among the first to talk about time and space, history (time foregrounded) and geography (space foregrounded).

While talking here about ideas of authenticity, locality, identity, ethnicity, and nationality, the notion of stereotypes arises, including that of *Zorba the Greek*, written in 1953 by a Cretan, Nikos Kazantzakis. Zorba has become a symbol of the Greek, if not the Cretan, identity. Is Zorba indeed Cretan and Greek? In other words, do we create stereotypes and symbols based on our cultural and social backgrounds?[22] In our case, can music be seen as a symbolic mechanism as well?[23]

In *Anthropology Through the Looking-Glass*, Herzfeld takes anthropology itself as an ethnographic object and unites the two levels of theoretical anthropology and Greek ethnography (anthropological fieldwork combined with theory). By doing so, he manages to offer a methodology for the discipline of anthropology (auto-anthropology) for studying a nation (not only Greeks) usefully. In the same sense, by studying Cretan culture not only anthropologically, but folkloristically as well as ethnomusicologically, I also wish to contribute to a more general sense of viewing music and dance phenomena on the island of Crete and any other place in the world.

My deeper goal and another reason for my writings is to show, as Herodotus attempted long before me, how diverse people are and how this diversity should not be a threat to unity, but instead a way to respect and accept all that is different. By illustrating how "complex" an identity (in my case, the Cretan) might be, I may contribute to another way of viewing and conducting contemporary ethnographic practice.

In other words, contemporary ethnographers should make use of history to show how identities are shaped. The cultures around the Mediterranean are complex in that they incorporate many elements that cannot be taken as "pure." Greeks and Turks for example, use the same terms for dances, such as z e i m b é k (i k o),[24] often uttering the same expressions, such as a m á n - a m á n . Borders can thus be bridged and ethnographers can surely do their part toward this end.

You now have the thread and a strong sense of the labyrinth's architecture. The story of time comes next.

Kronos

My fieldwork employs close and sustained interaction with the people I study, the Cretans, and immersion into their life, music performances, and culture. Moreover, I view fieldwork as a life process. Once in the game, I cannot now merely enjoy or have fun at a Cretan music performance or anything related to Cretan culture. Imprisoned, always thinking and analyzing, I try to find things that I could possibly make use of now or in the future. This way, my fieldwork continues every day, every moment, even when not in the field.

When I say "field," I do not mean Greece, Crete or the village of Anoya alone. The field is something I always carry with me; therefore, it may be everywhere that I, as a body, can also be (corporeal fieldwork). At the same time, it may also travel to wherever I, as a mind, spirit, and soul, can travel to as well. In this sense, the "field" exists for me in both time and space, in either time or space, but also out of time and space. The "field" has the same notion that "home" has for me; thus "my field" is also "my home."

My past experiences could have been called "fieldwork" if, at that point in time, I had clearly conceived what the idea of fieldwork ("conscious" fieldwork[25]) is. Technically speaking, this happened only after I came to the United States and "theorized" on the task. Memory may be a tricky place to drag up elements from and reconstruct realities, but at the same time, I admire the signs it leaves on me and I trust it. Therefore, I cannot ignore my past and I do not intend to do so, because it is part of what has shaped me up to now; in other words, it is part of my being.[26]

Having said this, I base my book on the most conscious fieldwork I conducted in person in the summers of 2000 and 2001. I also take into consideration my 1998 field research, which focused on dances performed during weddings. During the fieldwork of these past three summers, I recorded music events, interviewed musicians and locals, videotaped music performances of various contexts, recorded concerts and conversations, collected brochures, newspapers and other articles, took field notes and photos. I also met and talked with people I consider to be my friends. I always took part in these music and dance events, not only because I enjoy dancing, but because not to have done so would have been interpreted as unsociable and improper behavior in Crete.

During the summer of 2000 in particular, I met with many musicians. I established friendships with them as well as with people from the Arabic and the Cretan-Turkish Union on the island. I attended many performances. I read about the history of the island. I visited record stores and I also conducted some interviews. I also listened to the gossip and the comments coming from the people. I was interested in knowing their opinion and I believe this is one of the best ways of getting it. I kept listening to local radio stations as much as possible and watching the special shows of Cretan music on the local television stations.

The product of my fieldwork and my research is an ethnography. Etymologically, ethnography is a compound word derived from the Greek noun é t h n o s (nation, people) and the Greek verb g r á f o (to write). Thus, ethnography is writing about nations and people. We should not forget, however, that there is always a person, the ethnographer, who does the writing. And I am the one who plays this role here.[27] As a result, my ethnography is a combination of multiple voices, of the Greek and Cretan people as well as mine.[28]

According to my ethnographic opinion and understanding, ethnography is an *honest* experience that stems from living with the people who are the focus of the ethnographic work. And this experience is the result of what we call ethnographic research or fieldwork. Folklorist Henry Glassie embraces Dell Hymes's words for ethnography as a) *bearing* (writing, bringing forth, not hiding, very forthright, direct; a gift that you make from one person to another), b) *honorable* (truthful, factual, no lies), c) *witness* ("I myself have seen"), d) *to do something human* (for people).

In *The Spirit of Folk Art*, Glassie adds his own tone to the above definition by looking at ethnography as a wonderful challenge to have an art without lies. For him, ethnographic texts are creative art, products of art. And honesty and personal witnessing, as general ethnographic principles, apply to my book.

My ethnography is influenced by the concept of the realistic philosophy of existentialism, colorfully illustrated by Henry Glassie in that work. By following it, I am replacing abstractions with intelligent people, with real individuals in actual situations. In the same context, I view music and dance events in Crete as actions among groups of people who need to communicate. Therefore, my ethnography is responsible for showing how the creators will reach out to make connections between people; how creators and groups become mutually united and shaped by the creative act.

So I realize that my ethnography does not point only to truth, but to understanding as well. I can be honest or fraudulent through it. I am using scientific techniques toward philosophical ends. All I do is argue. My philosophical goal is an ethnography that comes out of the specific culture I study. My own culture distorts and changes my thoughts. My own culture is my own philosophical tradition and through it the reader may know me, because I am also a part of this story.

Through my ethnography, I can rethink who I am as well. That is why I am building it on a reflective reality.[29] For me, ethnography functions simultaneously as the study of others but also of myself.[30] Anthropologist Claude Levi-Strauss is an excellent example of such a self-study. He feels the burdens of traveling. He feels dislocated. His work *Tristes Tropiques* is a meditation on ethnography. Viewed through these lenses, my ethnography, without necessarily being an autobiography, encompasses autobiographical elements.

I feel I have the privilege of being both an insider and an outsider to the specific culture I study. Because I grew up in Crete, I have a great deal of experiences. But I have lived in other places of the world, including the United States. Therefore, my whole identity as an ethnographer is peculiar. I have been living in the United States for almost ten years, and like Levi-Strauss, I feel dislocated. Of course, I travel to my country every year, but at the same time, I feel I belong in two places. The opportunity of studying and living abroad makes me understand how significant and unique my culture is because I have the chance to compare and contrast it with another.

The notion of home thus has a dual dimension for me (as the "field" does). As I am trying to see who I am and how I am still being shaped, I am also trying to investigate how my roots were created and how people mold truths.

In each part of Crete, even if in a very small village, there are elements that give particular color to its culture and identity.[31] Being Cretan gives me many advantages as an "insider" (such as the knowledge of the local dialect of the language), but at the same time, for the people of Anoya, I am an "outsider" because I come from another part of the island, where the manners and the behaviors of the people differ from the ones observed there.

Many of the people I worked and still work with were and are curious to find out why I am so interested in attending music and dance events. When I tell them that I am an ethnomusicologist and explain my project to them, they ask me, for instance, as happened once in Anoya, whether I know Harvard University and Michael Herzfeld, the anthropologist who had come to their village in the past and had participated in local events. I thus have to explain the term ethnomusicology to them, for they are accustomed to the term "folklore" (l a o g r a f í a, in Greek), but not to the discipline of ethnomusicology.

I always introduce myself as a Cretan, but people tend to refer to me as the researcher from the United States. Many believe I am a journalist or a writer. Others show interest in knowing exactly what I am going to include in my book and how I am going to fill up so many pages about their music and dance. Several write down material (such as m a n d i n á d e s) or hand over videotapes and recordings. Others just seem interested in reading my document when it is complete.

As a result, I expect my ethnography to be a lifeline to reality, a link to the real world. I want it to allow us to improve our lives, to teach us about how to be better. I am not claiming that there is a way to do ethnography or that there is a rule for every single thing. Surely though, every ethnography, including mine, communicates, speaks, and therefore, must be clear.

At this point, my book should enable you to see worlds in a text as a result of honest "I-witnessing."[32] My writings, imbued with pure love and passion (and an intellectual plan), should be able to tell you a story, or multiple stories, of and about real people like you and me.

Once more, this is a trip in time, where past, present and future, constantly joyous and playful, dance the p e n d o z á l i s. And in these meanders, where Kronos decides to become the solo dance figure, I again warn you that, honoring in this way my Cretan predecessor Epimenides: "All Cretans are liars, and I am a Cretan."[33]

Odyssey

If you disassemble Greece, you will be left in the end with an olive tree, a vineyard and a ship.
Which means: with that many things you can remake it.
　　　　　Odysseus Elytis, O *m i k r ó s　n a f t í l o s (The Young Navigator)*

To be Greek means a lot. I distinguish three: language, tradition, landscape. Greekness… For me it is not a concept; it is a sensation. I feel Greek exactly as I could feel, for example, Cretan.
　　　　　Nikos Dimou, *A p o l o y í a　e n ó s　a n t h é l l i n a (Apology of an Anti-Hellene)*

As I have already stated, I am teaching you a dance that expresses and speaks of who we are. I am currently showing you its first, maze-like step. In the meanders we are in, always with the help of the thread I have handed to you, we try to see more clearly who the Greek and Cretan people are and, by extension, who you and I are. To look at an ethnographic present, to build a future, we need to take a sharp look at the past. Thus, here, I attempt to give you my photographic story of Odysseus, the Greek hero who travels through time to keep us still in trouble.

The geographical position of Greece has always been and still is a peculiar one, because it lies between the so-called East and West. The study of folklore (as a discipline) in Greece developed when the Greek nation was trying to establish itself. Because of Greece's geographical position, Greek identity is something unique as well as fragile.

Greek people geographically belong to the West, yet at the same time, there are also many eastern elements that characterize them. These elements we trace in Greek music as well, something that keeps bothering me as my work progresses.

Such "problems" may very well apply not only to the Greek, but to all Mediterranean cultures as well.[34] Scholars who do not mind burdening themselves and "getting in trouble," find these Mediterranean musical areas, given their complex socio-political and historical background, ideal for studying, as attested in Italian ethnomusicologist Tulia Magrini's work. They view Greece as a particularly challenging region of the Mediterranean in this regard.[35]

I base the work that follows on dual notions, couples, oppositions, or antitheses, otherwise called d i s i m í e s, or binarisms. Heraclitus worked on such notions when he talked about two antithetical forces always co-existing.[36] Michael Herzfeld, in turn, grasps these concepts in his ethnographies as well, and he often writes and comments on them. Greece, when viewed in time (ancient and modern) and in space (East and West), offers us excellent twin dimensions for studying.

Among the first to illustrate the burdens of moving between East and West was Homer. As his protagonist, he selected Odysseus, who left his island, Ithaca, to join the fight for the beautiful Helen of Troy. The blind poet described conflicts and personal quests that were brought up in a world, which was eastern and western at the same time. His Odyssey is not merely a legend. Even today, it particularly puzzles and confuses Greece. Yet, Greeks fight to balance within them the doubtful sweetness of such an arranged marriage between the East and the West.

Undoubtedly, each nation, not to say each individual, reaches a point when the identity question surfaces. This is the case with the Greek nation when, after almost 400 years under Ottoman rule,[37] asks itself: "Who am I?" This is the case with what I study as well. In Greek and Cretan music, I constantly hear sounds that take me to the East and I see instruments that look "exotic."

In Greece, East and West meet all the time. As proposed by Herzfeld in *Cultural Intimacy and the Social Production of Indifference,* the Greeks struggle to keep East and West apart, but the task is predetermined. Greece has an extraordinarily ambiguous, complex historical relationship to the idea of Europe and what we call "Western culture."

These ideas apply to music as well. Ross Daly recalls feasts in Crete, in Heraklion more specifically, up until even the 1960s: "...they did not play many Cretan pieces... they were always playing European... you cannot say it was bad

"Bucolic traffic" in the mountainous regions of Crete

they did this thing, no, that is how these people used to survive…" He goes further in his biography of the famous Cretan artist Nikos Xylouris: "Nikos Xylouris himself once told me that whenever, as a young man, he had reason to go from his village of Anoya to the city of Heraklion, if he happened to have his l í r a with him, he would deliberately avoid the central avenues, preferring instead the narrow alleyways, so as to avoid being made fun of because he played the l í r a, the instrument of 'uncouth' villagers. At this time the people of the urban center of Heraklion were very concerned with pretending to be 'European' and 'modern.' "

To find my own identity, I search for my parents' roots. And I shall do the same for the Greek nation. Its father is an ancient, strong, heroic man, something like a classical statue of Zeus in white marble, with fine details and precise meters. Its mother, on the other hand, seems relaxed, magical, erotic, a belly dancer in the blurred harem of fate. What is going on here? Who does that child resemble?[38]

To echo Herzfeld, the two parents represent allusions to two different periods of Greek history, the one recalling the glories of the classical era and the other recalling the more recent Byzantine and Ottoman periods. Cretans from the village of Anoya honor Zeus in a feast devoted to him. On July 6, 2001, they composed and performed m a n d i n á d e s in his honor. At the same time, the mother was present in the lyrics of the songs, with ideas of fate and images of life left in the hands of destiny.

I do not wish to view Greece as the passive cultural, spiritual, and intellectual ancestor of the Europeans. At the same time, however, I do not deny ancient Greece. I feel that the Greek nation constantly, even today, tries to reach upwards and creates an excellent prototype of European culture. It dreams of being incorporated harmoniously into a civilized West. But perhaps this is precisely where its nightmare also lies.

In contemporary Greek thought, the ancient Greek tradition is prominent. Tourists from all over the world visit the famous Greek antiquities and come to meet the marvelous ancient Greek world. "Modern" Greeks are in a state of confusion. As Nikos Kazantzakis puts it in *Taxidévondas*: "What has the double-descended modern Greek taken from his father, what from his mother? He is clever and shallow, with no metaphysical anxieties, and, yet, when he begins to sing, a universal grieving leaps up from his oriental bowels and breaks the crust of Greek logic."

According to Herzfeld, Greece is symbolically both holy and polluted. It is holy in that it is the mythic ancestor of western culture and it is tainted by Ottoman culture, the embodiment of barbarism and evil. And, as Magrini proposes, the history of western culture is permeated by references to its sacred roots in ancient Greece. Yet, what happened in Greece after the collapse of the Byzantine Empire and under the long dominion of Ottoman Empire has been generally overlooked, as if the "contamination" places Greece outside "our" world.

So what happens to a nation when all these "sins" fall upon it? It reacts and decides to dress up its eastern elements with western clothes. From now on, it does not drink "Turkish coffee," but "Greek." Ted Petrides — a Greek-American musicologist and dance researcher — believes that it looks for the roots of t s i f t e t é l i (belly dance) — a mainly solo female (often characterized as "erotic") dance — in ancient Greek fertility dances. In other words, as Herzfeld concludes in "Within and Without: The category of 'Female' in the Ethnography of Rural Greece", Greece, as a modern nation-state, encourages western identity that represses connections to all things non-Greek, especially Turkish and female.

We can trace the aforementioned ideas in literature as well. In *Zorba the Greek*, Nikos Kazantzakis wants his eternal Έλλινας (Greek, Hellene) to be nothing different than the Greek race itself, a marvelous synthesis of both East and West. In his writings, Kazantzakis brings up Homeric qualities. He creates his own epic poem *Odyssey*, a vision of the fatherland, as literary scholar and Kazantzakis translator Kimon Friar believes. Through this work, he reunites the individual Greek Odysseus to the eternal elements of his nation. In order to contest Homer, the poet of poets, Kazantzakis, like a contemporary Odysseus, who loves adventurous wanderings and the boundless field of conceptualization, returns to his own Ithaca, Crete, a few days after his death.

Moreover, with "Zorba," Kazantzakis embraces both the western as well as the eastern. The protagonist wants to get rich, but at the same time, acts very irresponsibly. He abandons rationality to live in madness. He rejects mind in favor of heart, in Peter Bien's view. Everyone is overwhelmed by an inexorable, tragic, destructive fate.

Kazantzakis's vision, besides being Greek with all the implications that this term may carry, is definitely "Cretan" as well. Crete, for Kazantzakis, is a synthesis that he always pursues. He feels neither European, nor ancient Greek, nor eastern. He breathes another air, a composition of all these forces and its components that empower and make him proud and brave. The glance that dares to look at life and death nakedly, Kazantzakis names Cretan[39]. As reporter and writer Nikos Psilakis has noted,[40] it is the exact same look of the Minoan who stares at the scared bull, just before his dangerous leap.

Kazantzakis was born in 1883, when the Ottomans occupied Crete and the monuments of the Venetian presence were still prevalent. He recalled the muezzin's voice pouring out of the mosques. He saw Muslims and Christians drinking together.[41] From this world, he moved on to a French school, where he met up with the West. Back in Crete, he lived and fought in his own unique way. The official church turned its back to him provocatively: While still alive, he was stigmatized with excommunication.

Nurtured by both East and West, he attempts to deal creatively with the Greek-Cretan identity confusion. He seems to constantly be asking himself this question: What is Greekness and what is Cretanness? How should a Greek act when faced with evil? How can we be patient? How can Greece have a nationalism rooted in both its ancient heritage and its contemporary reality? What does being human mean?

In Kazantzakis's *Buddha* and *Askitikí* (*Ascetics*), eastern religious and spiritual ideas are dominant. We are a modest letter, a syllable, one word from the gigantic Odyssey. All we do is fight, struggle, and get burnt. Our "new" ten commandments, as well as our "new" credo urge us to believe in one God: Akrita, Diyenis. And who is that Akritas Diyenis, the biracial knight of the border (ά κ ρ ο), δ ι γ ε ν ί ς meaning "of two races"? The main hero of a Greek folk song category, in whose face, over the Ottoman rule, the Greek nation sees its savior.

Kazantzakis attempts to respond to identity issues. The early Greek folklorists, on the other hand, see it as their task to establish a discipline based on the idea that there is an undeniable cultural continuity between the modern Greeks and their linguistic ancestors. Using folklore for nationalistic purposes, as the vehicle for political ideology, they try to define cultural identity.[42] It is in this spirit that the first students of modern Greek folklore demonstrate cultural continuity through time. Similarly, Greek folklore tries not only to preserve a tradition, but also to defend it against everybody who doubts its indissoluble unity with its ancient past.[43]

Greek folk song collections aim at a preservation as well as a dissemination of the musical culture that is Greek. The "Society for the Dissemination of National Music" actively records music throughout mainland Greece and the islands, while the "Greek Folklore Research Center of the Academy of Athens," publishes collections of song texts and musical transcriptions of folk songs.

Since 1955, performing Cretan music with a violin has been "forbidden", the result of a nationalistic and purity policy adopted by Greek folklorists. The violin, imported to Crete from Italy during Venetian domination, was viewed as a foreign instrument unrelated to the Cretan musical tradition, while the l í r a was chosen as the heir and symbol of uncontaminated musical folklore. In this process of remodeling Greek musical folk culture, Tulia Magrini notes, the l í r a, which was present in the Byzantine period and whose name evokes classical Greece,[44] could be accepted.

To remodel the Cretan culture, people chose a musical symbol to reconnect present reality to a remote past. According to ethnomusicologist Bruno Nettl, that is a unique, particular role of music in associating a society's present with its past. The insistence with which the stereotype of the l í r a player was and is still presented in documents about Crete reveals that what is evoked by this image is considered necessary to disseminate a new sense of the history.[45] Since then, the l í r a has become the musical symbol of Cretan ethnic identity and the l í r a player a hero.

There is no question, therefore, why the identity question was and still is so prominent for Greeks. Today, Greeks and Cretans are once again puzzled and confused. The dream of a unified Europe came true in January 2002. The present era of globalization asks them for a brave and very intense look in the mirror.[46] Apart from prejudices and names, it calls on them to discover that we are all humans; everything else is superficial.

'A r o m a   K r í t i s (Aroma of Crete) is the title of a Michalis Kallergis's compact disc. Its cover consists of a composite image in an orange background. The l í r a player is on the left, in black clothes, playing his instrument; to his right, an image of a l í r a and a wooden knife, traditionally a symbol of bravery and manliness;[47] in the background, a windmill, coastal, whitewashed houses, the ruins of the palace of Knossos and the disc of Phaistos.

The image speaks of a juxtaposition that too easily joins the glorious Minoan past and present to imply, in Nettl's view, an expected and welcomed continuity. In his book *Between East and West* (in Greek) the great Greek painter Yiannis Tsarouhis recalls an inscription on the wall of Kazantzakis's house on the island of Aegina that says: "one extreme."[48] Kazantzakis's reply is: "I am an Arab, not a Greek." In his smart, *Ironic Modern Greek Lexicon*, Nikos Dimou today defines who the Greek is by using thirty-one substantives: twenty-five of those are Turkish words, three Albanian, two Italian and one Slavic.

Amalthea

> There stands Crete, an island in the sea. It is beautiful and fertile, surrounded by the sea,
> having a large population and ninety towns.
>
> Homer, Odyssey

Throughout the ages, due to its position, the island of Crete has served as a for many cultures. Historical glances into Heraklion, the capital of the island, and into the Cretan village of Anoya, in relation always to the music and dance events that take place there, help us see how locals perceive themselves as part of the rest of the world, even as part of Crete and Greece itself.

> "How beautiful Crete is," he murmured, "how beautiful! Ah! If only I were an eagle,
> to admire the whole of Crete from an airy height!"
>
> Kazantzakis, Freedom or Death

Crossroads is a label that may very well apply to any and all places. In the case of Crete, however, this crossroad scheme is, by nature and geography, unique. Crete, an island at the southernmost part of Greece serves as a connecting link between East and West. In other words, Crete, the "bride" of the Mediterranean, is a cultural crossroads that connects Greece to the rest of the world.

Here I am selecting historical information that I believe is helpful for the purposes of this work. The points I draw upon reflect how Cretan history has been shaped by the presence of various ethnic and cultural groups on the island through its very early existence. Therefore, I am presenting to you a "critical"[49] history of the island of Crete.

> Captain Michalis raised his glance to the massive Kule, a strong, thickly built tower to the right of the harbor entrance with the winged marble lion of Venice on its front. Megalokastro was entirely surrounded by walls and fierce, battlemented towers, which had been built by its Christian masters in the heyday of ancient Venice and had been slaked with Venetian, Turkish and Greek blood.
>
> Kazantzakis, Freedom or Death

Around the sixth century, the Byzantines built the first walls and named the capital city of Crete, Kastro (Castle). Later, the Arabs built a tall wall around the city and circled it with a ditch (h a n d á k i, in Arabic, al-khandaq) for greater security. Kastro then became "Fortress of the Ditch," namely Handakas. Its port served as a great commercial center and its name was Big Castle (Megalo Kastro) until the Venetians changed it to Candia. Under Ottoman rule it was named Kantiyie, but the people called it Handakas, Hora and Megalo Kastro. In 1822, when the high commissioner was Mihail Afentoulief, the city got the name Heraklion.

> Crete, my beautiful island, island of paradise,
> On your right, you hold an anchor, and on your left, another,
> You play the l í r a to them, so that they can once more dance.
>
> Yiannis Markopoulos, K r í t i (Crete)[50]

Islands are places surrounded by water. Islanders are people who cannot live far away from the sea. Salt water is a source of life to them. And sea is the mother of travel. Islands have to be independent in the sense that they may be, due to adverse weather conditions, isolated. And islanders need to be good sailors like Odysseus so that they can travel to other lands, when Zeus and time allow. Cretans have been known since ancient times to be both good sailors and travelers.

Crete is, geographically speaking, a peculiar place. Isolated, the island preserves several cultural traditions. It also embraces multiple influences from both the East and the West.

These peculiarities, that are forged by Crete's geographical position and historical path, provide a potential that exceeds the limits of the island, a phenomenon that one cannot observe, at least to the same degree, in the history of other big islands of the Mediterranean. In the Hellenistic era and until Roman conquest, Crete, abandoning its introversion, was energetically involved in the historical fermentations of the Eastern Mediterranean.[51]

It was in Crete that the first great civilization established itself, five thousand years ago. It was there that Amalthea offered her milk to Zeus, the father of the gods, so that he could grow up strong. Because of this Cretan goat, many more myths followed. Crete, winner in the battle with Kronos, still offers its milk to people who live there and elsewhere.[52]

The Neolithic and the Minoan Cretan era started in 6100 B.C. and continued to 1000 B.C. At that time, Crete mainly dealt with imports and exports. Relationships between the islanders and other regions were welcomed and encouraged. The island held the name Keftiou, according to Egyptian sources of 3000 B.C. [53]

Dance was an indispensable element of ceremonies in Minoan Crete, as one can see in many of the representations on rings and on several wall paintings in the palace of Knossos. Dancing in Crete of that time was usually a sacred, holy act that took place as a calling and invocation of the deity. Homer recalled Daedalus and his dance for Ariadne, whereas Lucian (Loukianos) maintained that most of the dances in classical antiquity had their origins in Crete: g e r a n ó s or g é r a n o s, ó r m o s, and v o t r y d ó n.

The Greek civilization (1100-300 B.C.) followed the Cretan. It spread from Macedonia to the shores of Libya, and from Asia Minor to Lower (K á t o) Italy and Sicily. The intrusion of a variety of eastern themes and motifs upon the art of the seventh century gave this period the name "Easternized". Since then, Cretan cities have been characterized by a constant tension between the feeling of their geographical unity and their deep consciousness of their autonomy. The crystallization of social and political structures during the classical era (500-323 B.C.) proceeded with a profound conservationism, which, combined with the relevant isolation of Crete, was regarded as a basic characteristic of its history.

At that same time, Attic[54] sources cited Cretans for their love of folk sayings and proverbs. Civilians were spiritually interested mainly in music, combined with poetry and dance, that served the educational ideals of their war-oriented society. Among the Cretan rhythms and dances, known all over Greece, were the war dance p y r r h í c h e (pirríchi), the o r s í t e s, the h y p ó r c h e m a, and the e p i k r é d i o s. Zeno was a famous Cretan dancer.

The Hellenistic era followed from 323 to 67 B.C. Since the first century B.C. and until the fifth century A.D., Crete

Bebo Fountain in Heraklion, on Vitsentzos Kornaros square; an amalgam of Roman, Venetian and Turkish architecture, for leisurely moments

was R o m a i k í (Roman). The Byzantine period was followed by the conquest by the Arabs during the third decade of the ninth century (between 826 and 828 A.D.). The Arabs that conquered Crete originally came from Spain, specifically from Andalusia. A monk advised them to switch army stations and indicated a place in Crete where, after they fortified it with a defensive ditch, they built their capital, Handax.

The Arabs had no reason — political, religious, or financial — to convert all Christians into servants, and, in truth, they did not do so in any of the regions they conquered. Older speculations of Arabs imposing extensive slaughters, violent conversions, and disasters upon Cretans are not acceptable nowadays, at least not to the degree that they have been stated over the years.

On March 7, 961, Handax fell and Crete rejoined the Byzantine Empire for 250 more years. Many Russians, Slavs, and Armenians established themselves on the island. One can trace this through the various place-names that survive to the present (for example, Rousohoria, Sklavopoula, and Armenoi). In August 1204, the Venetians and the marquis of Momferatos signed an agreement, known as the Refutation of Crete: Vonifatios sold Crete to the Venetians. When, in October 1204, the Partitio Romaniae was officially signed, the Venetians "owned" Crete. In 1206, Erikos Peskatore, the so-called count of Malta, disembarked with small forces on Crete and conquered it. Thus, a period of Venetian rule started in Crete that lasted approximately 450 years.[55]

Despite the Venetian feuds, many Italian and Jewish merchants inhabited the cities.[56] Conversely, the population in the villages was almost purely Greek. It is characteristic that Handakas is mentioned in the Venetian manuscripts either as the *anima* (soul) of Venice or *alia civitas Venetiarum apud Levantem* (namely, as "the other Venice of the East").

On September 16, 1669, Crete fell into the hands of the Ottomans. It remained there until 1898. Under the Ottoman rule,[57] more than 60,000 Cretans were forced to convert to Islam.[58] Therefore, a population was made Cretan in origin, language and customs but Muslim in religious beliefs. These were the very famous T o u r k o k r í t e s (Turkish-Cretans). Some of them accepted Islam, but secretly kept their Christian beliefs. They were the so-called K r y p t o c h r i s t i a n o í (Crypto-Christians).

Having inherited a rich spiritual and artistic treasure and assimilating "foreign" influences, Cretans succeeded in composing and mixing the innovative techniques from Europe with Byzantine forms. They became the bearers and carriers of a wonderful process that led to the creation of "another" Cretan civilization. Here are just a few of the major artistic figures influencing this period of Cretan history: in literature, Hortatsis and Kornaros; in painting, Damaskinos, Theofanis the Cretan (Kris), and Domenicus Theotokopoulos, also known as El Greco (The Greek); and, in music, Frangiskos Leontaritis.

The Egyptian rule of Crete (1830-1840) was fair and treated both Muslims and Christians with equality.[59] In 1840, the island again became part of the Ottoman Empire. After a period of bloody and heroic uprising, the Ottomans gave up the island in 1898. Crete then became an independent state under a high commissioner, Prince George, the younger brother of the new King of Greece. Nobody was satisfied with this compromise. In 1905, Eleftherios Venizelos, the Cretan Prime Minister of Greece, forced Prince George to retire. He became a national leader and spoke of the need for concord and harmony between Christians and Muslims, of peace and unity as the ultimate goal. Finally, on May 30, 1913, Crete became part of Greece.

In 1923, the island took part in the exchange of populations, whereby the Muslim element left and Greek refugees from Asia Minor came in. In 1941, Crete stood once more in the limelight of world history. In May, Nazi parachutists landed in Maleme, Chania. After 10 days of desperate and bloody fighting with British and Greek troops in the so-called "Battle of Crete," Nazi forces occupied the island. It became free and independent again in 1944.

> Wherever I go I carry with me soil from Psiloritis,
> To spread it so that the whole world becomes Crete.
> M a n d i n á d a

The highest mountain in Crete is Psiloritis, Ida,[60] the place where, according to ancient Greek mythology, Dias (Zeus) was born.[61] The mountain of Psiloritis in central Crete has been for centuries a shelter and a stronghold of revolution. High on the north part of Psiloritis, at about 750 meters altitude, lies the village of Anoya (usually also named as Axika Anoya or Xiganoya), which was founded in the thirteenth century. The village was destroyed by the Ottomans in 1821 and 1826, and by the Nazis in 1944, but each time its inhabitants rebuilt it. Nothing, however, destroyed the values of the people living there.

Anoya is part of the province of Mylopotamos in the prefecture of Rethymnon. Its name derives from its position (á n o means upper; a n ó y i means loft). The first dwellers came from the neighboring village Axos and this is why today Anoya is also called Axika Anoya. People of the village hold the opinion that they are immediate descendants of the ancient inhabitants of Crete (K o u r í t e s) and I d é o n 'A n d r o (the cave where Zeus was born and which is in the mountain of Psiloritis).

Anoya is 56 kilometers from Rethymnon and 35 from Heraklion (two of the biggest coastal cities in Crete; the first to the west of the village, the second to its east). Its residents are mostly shepherds, farmers, and professionals. The village became a municipality in 1947 for its service during World War II and under the Nazi occupation. It currently has about 3,500 inhabitants.

Anoya is situated on a rocky ledge. In the central square of the village stands a monument dedicated to the most important moments of Crete's past: to the fight for independence of 1821; the slaughter in the cloister of Arkadi in 1866; the war against the Nazis in 1941-44. The narrow streets of the old village lead to abrupt hills. In the village there are many squares with shops and taverns. Many of these taverns serve traditional Cretan food, while some of the shops sell embroidery, laces and other colorful, handmade folk art.

The most important thing to keep in mind is that the village of Anoya imposes upon its people the idea that they are the authentic local Cretans through whom all the Cretan ideals are expressed. Anoya does this by virtue of its position, in the mountains of Psiloritis, and because of its beliefs, traditions and legends. The most important figures in the history of Cretan music come from the village of Anoya, such as Nikos Xylouris and one of the main protagonists in these writings, Vasilis Stavrakakis.

As a child, I remember going to Anoya with my family to listen to traditional music, attend weddings, play in the snow on Psiloritis and, most importantly, enjoy the marvelous food, such as macaroni with a n t h ó t y r o s (a special type of salty white hard cheese), o f t ó (roast), as well as wonderful deserts, including g a l a k t o b o ú r e k o (a sort of milk pastry) and s a r i k ó p i t e s (cheese pies) with honey syrup and fresh m i z í t h r a cheese.

I still go to Anoya to experience the "authentic" Cretan "traditions" still alive today. In the winters, I enjoy a cup of coffee or r a k í next to a fireplace. In the summers, when several feasts for various occasions take place, I often have some ice cream made from fresh goat milk in the main square of the village.

The people of the village are hospitable and friendly, as Xenios Zeus, "their" god, calls on them to be . On several occasions, such as small gatherings in restaurants, they do not hesitate to take down instruments that decorate the walls to play and sing. Willing to start sharing folk sayings, poetry or m a n d i n á d e s with visitors, the people of Anoya definitely make you feel both astonished by a "live" tradition and yet very much at home.

> The sea is a huge loom where Crete sits down and weaves;
> Lucky those eyes who've seen her shuttling on the waves.
> If you're sick, you sprout wings, if sluggish, you grow wild,
> And if cares crush you, your dazed mind glows like the moon,
> And you forget black pain and raise your arms on high
> And bless your happy parents who once gave you birth.
> Kazantzakis, *Odyssey*[62]

By now, you have a sense of the Cretan landscape and tradition. Agreeing with Dimou, I still need language to complete the picture. Indeed, Cretans speak (modern) Greek, of course, but they have a distinct dialect, with a variety of local elements mostly regarding pronunciation and vocabulary. I can assure you that Greek speakers can tell the difference: I definitely sound Cretan.

From this language, Cretans derive their names. In respect to the Greek tradition, Cretan names often contain symbolic meanings beyond the Greek Orthodox tradition. Cretans may thus carry the names Socrates, Simon, Erofili, Aretousa, K r í t i-Crete, D ó x a -fame, E l e f t h e r í a-freedom.

In the preface of Xanthinakis's *Monolingual & Etymological Dictionary of the Western Cretan Idiom*, we find many grammatical and structural details regarding the Cretan dialect. Here I provide you with some subtle observations that, I believe, show how the Cretan dialect differs from the modern Greek language.

Generally, the Cretan dialect carries a rich, distinct vocabulary. For instance, the word k o u z o u l ó s, namely "crazy," is found only in the Cretan dialect and not in the Greek language.

A sacred call
to meditation,
a stoic look
on life

In addition, the Cretan vocabulary contains remarkable lingual differences. These variations cannot be strictly isolated by geographical borders. For example, the local dialect of the Mylopotamos prefecture, to which the village of Anoya belongs to, shares resemblances with the eastern Cretan lingual idiom. At the same time, because the people of Anoya live rather isolated atop Psiloritis, they believe they have preserved their language and distinctive "heavy" Cretan dialect.

The Cretan dialect uses the same letters as the Greek language but involves different sounds. For instance, Cretan speech contains thicker consonants, such as the letter "k," which in Crete is pronounced "ch." In addition, the Cretan accent includes lots of "b," "d," and "g" sounds, whereas mainland Greek correspondingly uses the "v," "th" (as in the definite article "the"), and "y" (as in the word "yes") sounds.

Particularly, in the village of Anoya, the retroflex "l" and the use of t s i (instead of the "standard" t o u s and t i s respectively for the masculine and the feminine accusative plural pronouns and the definitive article) are stereotypically regarded as two of the diagnostic features of Cretan speech, as Herzeld attests. Moreover, the final "n" of the plural genitive is omitted. Oftentimes, when they talk, Cretans develop additional vowels and consonants, or even syllables, to achieve euphony.

The Cretan dialect still makes use of several ancient Greek — specifically Dorian — types of words. Michael Herzfeld maintains that the most perfectly organized language medieval and modern Hellenism has heard is the one spoken in Rethymnon and its villages, such as the village of Anoya. Georgios Sbokos, an ex-major and native of Anoya, writes in his book Anóya: I istoría mésa apó ta tragoúdia tous (Anoya: Its History Through its Songs) that "their" language relates more to ancient Greek and the particularly characteristic Dorian pronunciation.

The intonation of the Cretan dialect covers a wide and intense range of timbres and dynamics. This way, when Cretans talk, they have distinct, almost musical endings to questions and expressions of awe or wonder. Sometimes Cretan words are pronounced together as one word. Other times, one Cretan word may carry even two accents at the same time, or two different accents depending on who is talking, when and why. Lastly, an exception to the Greek grammatical rule that places the accent only in one of the three last syllables of a word is the fact that Cretans may place it even on the fourth before the last syllable.

For all these nuances, and according to a group of linguists, "though previously considered to be nothing more than a dialect of Greek, K r i t i k á (Cretan) has been recently acknowledged as a living language, in its own right, with roots stretching further into antiquity than even Ancient Greek," (http://www.helleniccomserve.com/ cretan_language.html).

Cretan history is found in a variety of literary forms, ranging from chronicles to novels and drama (for example, the scene of Ida in Vitsentzos Kornaros's E r o t ó k r i t o s). At the same time, music in Crete manages to establish a unique link between tradition and history.

For Greeks, fighting for something better under every circumstance is attributed to the mentality of the Cretans.

Because of its geographical position, its human power, its productive ability and its historic cultural base, Crete acts as an example of a living organism in continuous motion, inspiring and encouraging, designating a deep meaning regarding the idea of country and homeland.

In November 2001, to celebrate the inauguration of a monument (designed by the Cretan sculptor Manolis Tzobanakis) commemorating the "Battle of Crete," Cretan dances were performed in Athens outside the War Museum. According to the Cretan newspaper *Patrís*, this was one of the most important and significant events of the year: "a dream of all the Cretans and their friends came true." This reflects the importance and the meaning of the historical "Battle of Crete," the contribution of Crete and Cretans to the nation's "journey."

Because of its geographical position, Crete may be destined to become the educational and research center of the region, as well as the intermediate station between Europe, Africa and the Middle East; a central bridge of communication and cooperation in artistic, cultural, and other fields. As the best ambassador and, at the same time, as a modern peaceful conqueror,[63] I envision Crete playing that role.

Mythologies

Dancers
The moon appeared in all her fullness
As virgins took their place around an altar.

In old days Cretan women danced
In perfect rhythm around a love altar,
Crushing the soft flowering grass.
Sappho poems[64]

Greece is known as the birthplace of music (m o u s i k í: art of the nine Muses). Greeks always extol Cretans as exceptional artists and acknowledge them as masters of dance: They believe that the best Greek dancers come from Crete.[65] Today, among Cretans, the dominant belief is that the art of dancing originated in Crete. Here, I provide you with a bit of information that refers to "a" past (thus, history). Basically, I am giving mythologies that may help you understand the mysterious spirit surrounding contemporary Cretan music and dance. In other words, in order to respect what is going on in Crete today musically, to understand what Cretans believe they are when they perform music or when they dance, we must look back.

Historical testimonies prove that music had a significant place in the everyday life of Minoan Crete. Cretan people used music to educate youths and particularly to shape their ethos and character. The roots of the Cretan dances are very deep. According to scholar Georgios Hatzidakis, tradition credits Rea as the one who taught dance to the ancient inhabitants of Crete, who considered it a special gift, proper for their religious ceremonies.

Greek mythology sets the birth of music and dance in Crete. A legend says that the Kourites, the ancient inhabitants of Crete, danced and played instruments loudly so that the crying of young Zeus could not be heard and his father Kronos could not find him. Moreover, Theseus, on his return from Crete, performed a dance with his companions that resembled the turns and the curves of a labyrinth. Even the famous shield of Achilles was, according to Homer, decorated with a scene from a feast at the palace of Knossos.

Over the years, there has been much speculation on the connection and relationship between the various Greek folk musical idioms found today and those of the past. I agree with Ross Daly when he says in *Welcome Crete* magazine:

> My own personal opinion is that it would seem to me to be very unlikely that everything from ancient music has been lost. It would seem to me to be equally unlikely, however, that ancient music has come down to us intact, unaltered; the truth would seem to be somewhere in between. Some things have been lost, some things have been preserved at least in spirit if not in form, and many new elements are continually being introduced to a musical tradition that is anything but a fossilized relic from older times. We must never forget that Cretan music is a very dynamic tradition, continually developing and adapting to the reality of the times, while simultaneously struggling not to lose its relationship with its probably very ancient roots.
>
> In addition, Greek and Cretan music accept elements, such as instruments or aspects of musical "languages" and "dialects," coming from "foreign" musical traditions, mainly from those of the eastern Mediterranean area, the Balkans and North Africa. Ross Daly recalls his first experience of Cretan music, which surprised, confused, and certainly amazed him because he "could clearly hear very distinct influences from a wide range of eastern Mediterranean and North African sources."

We are inspired from the past, we borrow from our neighbors, we create. Yet, we are unique: Regional music is everywhere, in Greece, in Crete, even within Crete. As the music of an island, Cretan music through the ages has expressed the influences of all its "colonizers-inhabitants." It may be erotic when speaking in the romantic tongue of the Venetian literary forms of the fifteenth to the seventeenth century. It may also be full of sorrow and pain, when recalling memories of the Ottoman rule.

Scholarly work talks about the elements that 465 years of Venetian occupation have left on the musical culture of Crete. Do the Cretan m a n d i n á d e s , these improvised couples of fifteen syllable lines, come from the Italian *mattinate*? What about the violin, which is mostly used in western Cretan music? Did the Venetians bring it with them as well? And what is the case with the l a o ú t o ? Did they also introduce it to Cretan music, or did its predecessor, the Arabic o ú t i (oud), reach Crete with the Andalusians? And what about the m a n d o l í n o (mandolin), the instrument that Vasilis Stavrakakis plays today?

Other works talk about the rebellions that took place during the Ottoman rule. For example, they look at the Cretan r i z í t i k a (songs of the foothills), as one way of examining that specific historical period of time. The same holds for Turkish dances and songs, repertories (such as the t a b a c h a n i ó t i k a), which merge Greek and Turkish elements developed during and after this period. Scholars also attempt to see how Cretan music intermingles with Turkish elements as well. And they ask: How "oriental" is this adaptation?

Cretan music is a rich and complex entity, encompassing a variety of genres and types. My purpose here is neither to analyze nor to describe them.

So far, I offered you all you need to know before going to the second step of this dance. More mythologies are to follow. First step: past step.

step 2

Into the labyrinth

STEP 2: INTO THE LABYRINTH

*H*yacinth and Zeus are one of the most favored, adorable, and worshipped pairs of our Odyssey. Predecessors of many Minotaurs to follow, they have playfully shaped living cultures that still make music for and dance to them. At a later point in time, more medieval, but at the same place, in Crete, two young people, a man and a woman, Erotokritos and Aretousa, speak profoundly and sing their passion, their love. Gods and humans teach us this second step. Here, I write what I see on the colorful fresco wall paintings of the Minoan palace of Knossos.

Iakinthia 2001[66]
Moon, you have been entrusted with so many secrets,
How come I never heard you revealing one?
Mandináda

Full moon: Anoya, July 6, 2001. We are in Kouradovrisi, a plain field high up on the mountain of Psiloritis, where shepherds take their flocks to pasture. Brown soil, dusty clouds and a wild landscape with sharp rocks, thorny bushes and trees; the air smells of thyme (t h y m á r i) and d í k t a m o (é r o n d a s; dictamnus). A rectangular stone stage faces us. On one side, high up to the left, I can see a curved, sculpted bronze head: It is Zeus![67]

Blessed (Zeus), hide your heavy anger in the waves of the sea and in the peaks of the mountains. We all know your power; as long as you enjoy the libations, give to the mind all the rightful things: An extremely happy life and also eternal health, and goddess Peace — the one that brings up children and moves brightly — and an always blossoming life in joyful manners.
Zeus's Hymn[68]

We are here to honor Saint Hyacinth. We celebrate the martyr of love in a m i t á t o (shepherd's shack), located a couple of miles away. Saint Hyacinth, "imprisoned," fasted himself to death for his love of Christ. He represents ecstatic love. His view is different than that of the Apollonian serenity of the O r t h ó s   L ó g o s (Right Thought; Logic) and suggests risking everything, even life itself, for the sake of love.

Love makes me a young child and urges me so often
To leave this life without having grown up.
Mandináda

Loudovikos of Anoya welcomes us to the feast. I meet with Vasilis, Laodikis, the members of the Cultural Club of the village, other musicians, relatives and friends. I find a chair and set up my equipment: video camera, notebook, mini-disc — all ready to go.

> We welcome you, spring swallows,
> In a thousands-of-years-old civilization.
> Mandináda

The brochures and the newspapers advertise this event as a celebration of the shepherds. "Take a jacket with you and be ready to sit on the ground, on the soil," they forewarn. It is 8 p.m. and the moon is not visible: darkness is all around and there are few lights on the stage. Miracle! The moon appears. Jealous of the sun, it attempts to outdo its brightness. The night becomes day and the feast begins:

> Leaping dancers Kourites, you walking in rhythm holding guns, clapping, hitting, striking on your legs, spinning, coming from the mountains, shouting in Bacchic voices, playing the líra harmonically, stepping lighthy, swinging guns, guards, leaders, of a bright fame, mates of the mountainous earth, wild celebrators, proceed flattered by the praising words, closer to the Shepherd, always in joyful spirit.
> Kourites' Hymn[69]

For the first time in 2,500 years, the timpáni sound on the peaks of Psiloritis. Yiannis Fertis recites the hymn to Kourites and old men dance to the rhythm of a pyrrhíchios war dance (Anoyanós pidihtós [leaping]), a most artlessly elegant feat: Three small steps back, three big steps to the front, defense and attack, and pound on the ground to hear the thump. Five members of the Cultural Club of the village (Kalomoiris, Skoulas, Manouras, Sbokos[70] and Pasparakis) dance in Cretan traditional costumes [black shirts, saríki, stivánia (boots), and beige pants] to the accompaniment of big timpani. The emptiness of the landscape contributes to an incredible echo. A young boy, dressed in black, comes to dance. He is Zeus and his friends, the Kourites, saved him once more today with their loud dancing steps.

> Zeus, you should only forgive the Kourites,
> Because they covered your crying by hitting the timpani.
>
> Zeus had very few chances to live,
> But, he was saved by the shields of the Kourites.
> Mandinádes

Here come our "cousins" from Chania. They represent the western Cretan musical tradition, where the violin and the laoúto prevail. The men in white shirts and beige vests sing a rizítiko. Dancers from the village of Lousakes, "original and real people," first the women and then the men, dance "unknown" dances.

> I hear birds flying tonight among us,
> It must be Zeus's soul that is around us.
>
> From three peaks the timpani sound in Psiloritis,
> They are doing a big favor to you, Zeus born in Crete.
> Mandinádes

The evening's host announces: "Zeus and Kourites, Cretans and guests, it is time to listen to the main Cretan traditional instruments: the mandolíno, the líra, the askomadoúra (bagpipe), the laoúto."

From Kouradovrisi I will shout tonight,
That I'm in love and I feel unable to change my attitude.
Mandináda

Two actors interpret the "Dialogues of the Gods," a brief theatrical sketch that talks of Aphrodite and her favorite child, Eros (Cupid).

I have stopped falling in love — this is, I think, a problem.
Because one who doesn't love, has nothing to hope for.
Mandináda

Vasilis Stavrakakis, "maybe the most lyrical presence, with a voice that cuts time into two, with one foot in the past and the other in the future," follows. Laodikis plays the t o u b e l é k i (daraboúka).[71]

(...) To be quiet so that the news will be heard,
Those having their roots deeply underneath the soil,
In ruined graves and broken bones, watered with various colors of blood,
So that the voice that struggles all these times and years will eventually come out,
The voice that drags behind its clans and innumerable predecessors,
To say with male pride all over the world, this land is not scared,
It won't get erased, it won't die.
Rizítiko song

There is no other pain that hurts, a pain that kills,
Such as the secret love that remains unknown.
Mandináda

Michalis Kallergis, "a mature representative of the Cretan sound in l í r a and voice, coming out of the Nikos Xylouris school, an epic singer of passion and rhythm," comes next.[72]

Without drinking I got drunk by your love:
I behave like crazy when next to you.
Mandináda

Kourites, performers in tonight's event, members of the audience and villagers join in dancing. Meanwhile, the women of the village treat us to hot mountain tea mixed with r a k í and p a x i m á d i (rusk), to warm us up.

On my knees, Christ, I worship your passions,
Because, for a strong love, I myself,
Have been going through them for years.
Mandináda

The highlight of the event is next. Everyone is here to listen to the m a n d i n á d e s composed for and devoted to love. Men from Anoya, members of the Cultural Club as well as others (Gialaftis, for example), come up to the stage and improvise, "fighting," competing with lyrics devoted to the gods of love, Zeus and Hyacinth.

> Kronos got fooled for many days and nights,
> Zeus grew up because of the Kourites.
>
> Zeus, father of Gods, I'm recalling you tonight,
> You were born in Crete; we never forget that.
> > Mandinádes

Everything moves in a circle: The event closes as it started, with the Kourites dancing, one more time, "their" p i d i h t ó s dance.

> To be able to walk on the clouds you must deserve it,
> That is why it is difficult to topple those up high.
>
> Love is, at the same time, a god and a child.
> Spoiled. Every time it sees something, it wants it.
> > Mandinádes

After the event on the mountain, we all go to the Mitato of Kouroupis, a restaurant in Anoya, where we dine on ancient Cretan cuisine.[73] On that evening's program notes we read: "Zeus, father of gods and people, I offer you dinner tonight at the Iakinthia. I thank you because, for thousands of years after you grew up, I am able — in the same way as the Kourites — to sacrifice and make a libation to your name."

> Even though Zeus is mythical, I think of him
> As the real god, and even higher.
> > Mandináda

Zeus lives in history and myth. He is the Zeus of ancient Greeks and Cretans, but of contemporary Christians as well. With music and feasts, Cretans celebrate their love for him. All the "stars" come down to the earth to join us once more in these celebrations: Kourites, Idaean Dactyls (demons believed to live on Mount Ida and the first metallurgists), Amalthea, Minos, Radamanthis, Epimenides, Pythagoras, Plato, Euripides and many others. All compose the legends and the historical traditions of the village of Anoya and of Crete, with Zeus, the god that each year dies and is reborn being the protagonist.

> I will stop worshipping the saints of Christianity,
> Because I have started believing in the twelve Gods.
> > Mandináda

"Contemporary elements of the local culture, such as language, music, dance, worship, architecture, athletics,[74] as well as other traditions,[75] all lead to archetypal cultural forms that are four thousands years old." As evidenced by this phrase from the Iakinthia program notes, Cretans want to show the stable links between past and present through a chronological continuation. Their aim is the preservation of "their" tradition.

> Descendants of Kourites live in Anoya,
> After many years they honor God Zeus.
>
> The timpani of the Kourites make a big sound:
> It seems that you cried, again tonight, Zeus.
> Mandinádes

Nights never end in places that hold such rich traditions. Before leaving the village, I stop by Manouras's restaurant. A young boy, 11 years old, plays the líra for his family and friends. With his young brother, they improvise on mandinádes. Later on, driving one of my friends home from the village, I stop the car. I roll down my window and listen to a group of teenagers with a mandolíno, singing and walking under the moonlight on the streets of the village. They engage in a dialogic improvised mandináda conversation with my friend, seated in the car:

> Like the old woman's passion from Anoya your passion possesses me,
> When you go out for a walk, everything inside me turns upside-down.
> Mandináda

Yet, the question is this: Am I dreaming, or is tradition alive and well?

> The timpani of the Kourites sound after many years,
> Continuing the story where civilization was born.
> Mandináda

Minotaurs

A sample of dialogues:
   a) Between a non-Greek and a Greek:
      NG: Where are you from?
      G: Greece.
      NG: Ah! Athens, Parthenon, Acropolis, bouzoúki, syrtáki, Trojan horse, saganáki, tzatzíki, gýros, baklava, Zorba the Greek: "Teach me to dance"!
   b) Between a Greek and a Cretan:
      G: Which part of Greece are you from?

Anoya: Where the earth joins the skies

C: Crete.

G: Ah! Knossos, shots fired at weddings, stealing sheep, wild men, vendettas, l í r a music, good food, ó p a - ó p a !

c) Between a Turk and a Greek:

T: Are you from Greece?

G: Yes.

T: So, you know Karagiozis, b a k l a v á , Ayia Sofia, a m á n - a m á n …

d) Between a Cretan and a person from Anoya:

A: Do you come from the town, the plains?

C: Yes, from the prefecture of Heraklion.

A: Oh! Have you been to Psiloritis, to the cave of Zeus? Did you ever attend a wedding feast here?

"He is an ideologist, he has ideals. Don't confuse ideals with ideologies. Ideologists do not have ideals, but doctrines." In this spirit, Flaubert wrote the *Dictionary of Accepted Ideas*[76] and, a century and a half later, Nikos Dimou was inspired to compose his *Ironic Modern Greek Lexicon (E i r o n i k ó   N e o - E l l i n i k ó   L e x i k ó)* whence the preceding quote was taken.[77] Yet today, the stereotypes continue to multiply and oppress our thoughts.

Because of all the "complexities" I described in the previous step, Greece is a country that internalizes and reinforces a variety of stereotypes: European and Oriental, ethnic and national, Mediterranean and local. Stereotypes, one of the currencies of social life, portray the Greek character as fixed, simple and unambiguous. Greeks also make use of them. Even though they occasionally critically scrutinize them, stereotypes are still very much alive and well in Greece.[78]

In Crete, despite the fact that they may also be viewed negatively, stereotypes are part of the everyday life of the people on the island to such an extent that Cretans very consciously reproduce them (for the benefit of tourists, for example).[79] The island of Crete is well known and famous all over Greece for its culture and traditions: "There is another air blowing there," the tourists believe, and "Cretan people are different from the rest of Greeks." People, thus, tend to believe that Crete is one of the few places in Greece where the traditions and customs are still alive today: "God targeted Crete." As a Cretan, of course, I occasionally reinforce and support these notions.

What makes us so different? Here I try to give some answers or at least speculate on this issue. I feel this is important because who Cretans are, in a broader sense, influences us in all respects, including the way we make music and dance. And remember that we are in the labyrinth now, gently "enslaved" to King Minos. Do we really want to escape? Don't you wish to meet as many Minotaurs as possible? I certainly do!

Zorba the Greek and *Never on Sunday* are two films in which non-Greeks first encounter Greek culture. Two scenes in particular — Anthony Quinn "teaching dance"[80] on the island of Crete to the music of Mikis Theodorakis and Melina Merkouri dancing with sailors to the music of Manos Hatzidakis — are two images that portray Greeks as extremely emotional and passionate people, who have retained their spontaneity. Abandoning themselves to song and dance, Greeks are eternally romantic. At the same time, the two scenes become stereotypes for Greek and Cretan music and dance.[81]

In the end, how Greek or Cretan is Zorba? Did Kazantzakis ever imagine that his love for and vision of Greece would go through such a "being-like-the-Zorba" procedure? Would I ever think that this is how people I meet in the United States see me? Even worse, how authentic are the Greeks who want to play this role?

Blood is the basis of the Greek r á t s a (race); it is also a symbol. The Cretan Captain Michalis, in Kazantzakis's *Freedom or Death*[82], cuts his finger. So does the Turkish pasha. They exchange blood and become "brothers." From then on, their friendship is based on blood and nothing stands as a hindrance between them. Despite Kazantzakis's vision of Cretans and Turks living harmoniously, many Cretans today still consider Turkey as their bad and aggressive neighbor and talk of the barbarians, the murderers, the uncivilized Turks. How can they sing, then, "Filedem," a popular and famous Cretan song that talks of a Turkish girl in a mosque that has stolen the heart of a Cretan man?

Like other Mediterraneans, Cretans engage in vendettas for various reasons: bride abduction, dishonoring a woman, disagreement among families about the boundaries of adjoining farms and stealing sheep, for example. Vendettas were the subject of a movie[83] recently filmed in the Cretan village of Limnes (lakes). In the last scene of the film, the protagonist maintains that "when the Greeks dance, they answer very well why they exist in life".[84]

It is not accidental that Kazantzakis wrote books such as *The Greek Passion* (1954) and *Freedom or Death* (1954). He is not the only one to praise the Cretan village as a community and Crete as a distinct island. His reactions are not unnatural if we take into consideration the history of the island and the suffering it endured through the ages. Crete is alive because of the passion it inspires in its people.

One thing that characterizes Cretans is that each time an enemy threatens their freedom, they react as one, united. Since ancient times, Cretans have managed to be self-sufficient and independent. Inspired by the idea and practice that "we are all Cretans" (s i n g r i t i s m ó s; syncretism, concretism), Cretans constantly struggle to maintain their autonomy.[85] They are proud people with intense emotional power and endurance. They are brave and courageous, hospitable and honest. They are easily insulted when it comes to matters of honor and shame. They are compassionate. All these characteristics are forces that unite Cretans into one body, especially when difficult times come for their island, their village, their families and themselves.

Cretan men are often depicted as dressed in black, with mustaches, looking wild, as shepherds or animal thieves, and carrying knives and guns. It is not surprising, therefore, that the people of Anoya are particularly thrilled by the fact I always visit the village dressed in black. In villages such as Anoya, many people, mostly old men, still wear their traditional outfits. As a symbol of Cretan male identity, Cretans also favor mustaches. They often use their guns to mark celebrations. Above all, Cretans are enthusiastic and merry people, who partake in a joyful life.

The unity of the inhabitants of the Cretan community is unique. They characteristically claim they walk easier uphill than downhill. They do not get tired easily and they can endure all kinds of difficulties. They know well — history taught them — that, because of their geographical location and their special character, they can play an important role in any national struggle. Many Cretans help their birthplace even when not in Crete. For instance, the Pancretan Association in the United States shares these sentiments: "In Crete only heroes live," "All the United States learnt about the p a l i k á r i a (brave men) of Crete," and "I live in the States, but I am proud I am Cretan."[86]

The island of Crete has become famous through the ages for its independent spirit. Throughout centuries of revolution and subjugation, Cretans developed and refined the notion of the p a l i k á r i, a concept of harsh, unthinking heroism, a major facet of Crete's perception of itself, even today. The term p a l i k á r i can better be translated as "brave man." Another term that shows an attitude of gallantry and is used in Crete is the word l e v é n d i s.

An arena for the expression of individual identity and the negotiation of community boundaries in Crete is a celebration called g l é n d i. Cretans who are capable of experiencing and conveying true k é f i (high spirits) in the g l é n d i a are usually called m e r a k l í d e s, l e v é n d e s, p a l i k á r i a. Thus, m e r a k l í s, l e v é n d i s, p a l i k á r i refer to the passion and skill displayed in performance, combining aesthetics, moral and ritual elements. Observing and participating in events like wedding feasts offers a sound representation of the village of Anoya and its people.[87]

M e r a k l í s, l e v é n d i s, p a l i k á r i: That is what Cretan people want to be when in a k e f á t o (high-spirited) g l é n d i. And this is what they aim for in life, what many (if not most) of their songs talk about (for example, "A bird with m e r á k i (yearning)," "God took aim at a brave of Sfakiá," "Giving-birth-to-gallants Crete"). I wonder, however, whether they realize that the words they use are not "theirs." Where then do they originate? Turkey? Italy? The Middle East?

Cretans and the people of Anoya must focus not on "being a good man," but on "being good at being a man." The squares of their villages are public spaces, controlled mostly by males. The distinctiveness of their community, as well as that of Crete as an island, is reproduced in the e g o i s m ó s (ego; pride) of the individual performer. One who is "good at being a man" must know, for instance, how to wield a knife, how to dance the acrobatic steps of the leader of the line (b r o s t á r i s), how to eat (especially meat) and drink a lot, and how to stand up to anyone who dares insult him. Moreover, f i l ó t i m o (love of honor) is the unifying characteristic through which Cretans have been able to unite in the past against common enemies. The concept of f i l ó t i m o is complex, incorporating the importance of freedom and the importance of the individual at the same time.[88]

In addition, hospitality in Crete is certainly lavish. Village rules dictate that one who enters the coffeehouse must treat those already present. Treating (k é r a s m a) with drinks and nuts is still common in most villages in Crete, according to anthropologist Michael Herzfeld. During my research, I often had to secretly empty my glass of r a k í in order not to get drunk and, at the same time, be able to have it refilled. Moreover, when I had guests, I always advised them not to deny any food or drink people may offer them so as not to offend them.

Cretans need few excuses for social gatherings with all the merriment, music, dancing, food and drink that constitute a true g l é n d i. Cretan g l é n d i a are famous all over Greece. Herzfeld is not the only one to underscore, as he does in T*he Poetics of Manhood: Contest and Identity in a Cretan Mountain Village*, how Crete is famous for, among other things, its music and dance. Vasilis Stavrakakis also tells me how special weddings are, particularly in the village of Anoya and how many people from all over Greece come to the island to attend them.

Before coming to Greece, Ross Daly was familiar with b o u z o ú k i music. He commented that this has always been the stereotype of Greek music abroad. When he came to Crete, he was surprised that what he heard was very different. Instead of the b o u z o ú k i , Daly discovered the l í r a .

L í r a , indeed, is the trademark of Cretan music and has become a symbol of Crete. Typically, two l a o ú t a accompany it. There is also still a lively tradition of m a n d i n á d a contests to which improvisatory skills are key.

Feasts may take place in the mountains where one can see bearded vultures, the Cretan eagles or the Cretan wild goats, the kri-kris. At their houses, the people of Anoya plant v a s i l i k ó s (basil). Its leaves are curly and have an intense aroma. Usually, some basil is put behind the ears of the musicians and the people who dance. Many lyrics refer to basil and compare it to the virtues of a woman.

V a s i l i k ó s stands for beauty and dignity, just as the wedding bread is a symbol of continuity and a healthy life. At weddings in Anoya, the round bread is "embroidered" so as to look like a traditional cloth. Bread in Crete is important and as necessary for life as weddings are. Serving massive amounts of meat and food at feasts signifies health and prosperity. Villages in Crete are famous for their music and dances but also for their weaving, olive and dairy products. Villagers decorate their homes with handmade embroidery and carpets. Local Cretan food and drinks are served almost everywhere.

The uniqueness of the Cretans lies in the fact that they do not only say things, but they simultaneously act them. Like Zorba, their kinsman, they can dance them as well. Being from Crete is an art, a performance. Being Cretan is not a concept; it is a sensation. The Cretan lifestyle allows people to have something of their own and at the same time to be different from other Greeks and the rest of the world.

Hyacinth and Zeus

Culture is the way the mind is molded through interaction with the world.[89] The world relates to space, which, like time, is relative. What I mean is that "my" world may not be "your" world. "Why" depends, I believe, on our cultural knowledge, ideas and beliefs, which may be shared, common, or otherwise. In the Cretan world everything becomes local — "ours." This way, Cretans create "regional traditions" according to what the communities conceive of as being "Cretan." One way to build a notion of "local Cretanness" is through music and dance.

Music and dance construct "places" that involve notions of difference and social boundary.[90] When I listen to Cretan music, memories flood my mind. I imagine myself being on the island: I give a living dimension to what I hear.

I choose to focus on Crete and Anoya because I was inspired and moved by all the experiences I have. I allow myself to be allured by a strong nostalgia not only for my country, Greece, but also for my "special" and "particular" country, Crete. The presence of another place, the United States, contributes to my decision, reinforcing it even more. As a result, my nostalgia makes me fall in love with places I and many others consider to be ideally, authentically and traditionally Cretan.

In a sense, Cretan music colonizes me intellectually.[91] Perhaps, these lines help me decolonize myself. At the same time, the music that makes me feel comfortable at home, and when not at home, is not only my story. It may be yours, ours.

In each locality, various levels and multiple relationships coexist. In the case of this book, these conceptual threads spread among the worlds of the Greeks, the Cretans and the people of Anoya. But I also have my own worlds. Thus, I am Greek and Cretan, but not of Anoya.

Moreover, this book challenges locality and invites it to a serious game. I provoke locality by kindly requesting it to listen to the music I choose to play when not in Crete. A key question here is whether the following people can be considered locals: Ross Daly, of Irish origin, who lives in Greece and plays the Cretan l í r a ? Vasilis Stavrakakis, of Anoya, who plays the m a n d o l í n o ? And Laodikis, the percussionist from Syria? Are the answers in my mythologies?[92]

Once upon a time, as recounted by reporter and writer Nikos Psilakis in *Welcome Crete* and in *K r i t i k í M i t h o l o g í a (Cretan Mythology)*, Cretans worshipped Hyacinth, a god who is born and dies every year, like the Cretan Zeus. Apollo, the deity of music and harmony, plays his lyre and enchants immortals and mortals alike. Hyacinth often listens to his friend playing, just as he watches him holding his wonderful bow and aiming it. When he takes this instrument in his hands, a magical, divine music is heard. Graceful Hyacinth plays in the forest and throws the discus as far as he can to be better than his teacher, Apollo. At that moment, a strange whirling sound is heard in the air. The discus does not go far. The strong wind lifts it up and makes it hit a stone, sending it back. Hyacinth is hit and falls dead to the ground.

As Apollo watches the blood flow from Hyacinth's head, an idea suddenly comes to him. He cannot resurrect Hyacinth, but he can transport his breathtaking beauty somewhere else: The blood of the handsome young man is transformed into a flower, the hyacinth. Apollo inscribes the capital letter Y of the Greek alphabet, on the inner part of the flower, next to the stamen, the first letter of the Greek word for Hyacinth. Each time we see that flower, we recall the name of the most handsome young man ever born on Earth. The hyacinth sprouts, blooms, dries, but always leaves bulbs on the Earth that can re-sprout the year after. On its petals we see the god's mourning in the shape of letters: A and I! We never forget Hyacinth. We remember his death by organizing great celebrations each year that last for several days.

Always Eros catches me, no matter how fast I run,
Because he has wings, while I don't.
M a n d i n á d a

Saint Hyacinth Chapel
and its source
of inspiration: Musician
Loudovikos of Anoya

In 98 A.D., in the mountainous region of Fournoi, 12 kilometers south of Anoya, 20-year old Hyacinth became a martyr for the common faith, his love of God. Hyacinth suffered for his love for Christ. The poet, songwriter and singer from Anoya, with the nickname "Loudovikos from Anoya," took the initiative to make the history of the young martyr — who overcomes his fear with love — known to the public. Nineteen hundred years later, he decided to honor the Saint of Love. Thus, Loudovikos co-founded a non-profit company that organizes a festival: It takes place every year during the first week of July at Fournoi, near the village of Anoya and is called Iakinthia. The name day of Saint Hyacinth is officially held on July 3rd.[93]

The Archbishop of Rethymnon, Anthimos, approved Loudovikos's idea to build a church at the same place, financed the project and laid the foundation stone himself. The chapel was built in the shape of a Cretan m i t á t o , a circular building made of flat stones without mortar. The building follows the rules of the Late Minoan architecture with a dome. Its inclination starts two meters above ground and leaves a hole of 30 centimeters at the top, all planned by the architect Stavros Vidalis. The special commission of the Iakinthia wished, in the memory of the Saint of Eternal Youth Hyacinth, to make the festival the nucleus of a cultural and artistic feast for the village of Anoya, for Crete, and Greece.

The people of Anoya devoted the Iakinthia of 2001 to Hyacinth and Zeus. They still offer sacrifices to them. They owe their unique language, tradition and landscape to these two gods. Because they live rather isolated atop the mountain of Psiloritis, they believe they have preserved almost uncorrupted their manners, customs, traditions and language (a distinctive "heavy" Cretan dialect). At feasts held in the village of Anoya for various reasons (weddings, baptisms, and saints-feasts, to name some), the musical repertoire is mostly Cretan. The l í r a is preferred here. The people of Anoya are known for their talent in playing this instrument and in composing and singing m a n d i n á d e s .

Among several contemporary famous Cretan l í r a players from Anoya is Michalis Kallergis. He is also among those invited to perform the night of the Iakinthia: with his l í r a , he accompanied the m a n d i n á d e s contest. Vasilis Skoulas, another l í r a player and singer, owns and performs mainly at his restaurant, Delina, up on Psiloritis, a few miles south of Anoya.

Nikiforos Aerakis plays occasionally at weddings. He performed with Lefteris Kalomoiris (an "older" l í r a player and singer from the village of Anoya) at the wedding I attended on July 14, 2001. Finally, another "big" name who comes from that village is Psaradónis.

Nikos Xylouris, Psaronikos, was born on July 7, 1936, in Anoya. Even though he died at a young age, he is "our" Nikos forever. His first recording was the song "My Cretan woman" (alternate title: "A woman in mourning passes by"). In 1967, he opened the first Cretan club, Erotókritos, in Heraklion. He became the voice of Crete, the "archangel" of Crete, as Cretan people say. Every August, Anoya holds a feast devoted to his name in the open theater of the village that also carries his name. During this weeklong event, one evening is devoted to Cretan music, where l í r a players from Anoya, old and new, exhibit their talents.

Vasilis Stavrakakis emphasizes the particularity of Anoya as a village. He was born and raised in Armanoya, the village where many refugees from Anoya fled after the Germans burned the village. According to him, Cretan music is a strong form of art that expands and influences audiences more than any other Greek music.

I provoked him during our conversation, in August 2001, by expressing the opinion that maybe it is not nice for the people of Anoya to think of being the best. He reacted by saying that Anoya is the only place with great history and tradition that is still alive and unique. Everything is different there: the audience, the place as a landscape, as art, as a way of life — it is all different from the world at large.

Besides all the praise Vasilis and other people give to Anoya, the locals definitely have a strong sense of autonomy as well. During my research, a new gorvernment law refiguring administrative districts came into effect. However, the people of Anoya resisted electing a mayor, even though it was required by the new legislation. A group of people under the name "Cultural Club" took over for a while but ultimately a mayor was elected.

Crete is "our" land. As our ancestors fought for it, we also must protect it and keep it strong. Our songs that speak of the Cretan Zeus, the mountain of Psiloritis, Anoya show that. "Our" songs show our history and connection to our land. Such is "The Song of Nida," for example, that speaks of the ideal pastoral areas around the mountain of Psiloritis, which belong to Anoya. You may try to change the songs, but you will not succeed in changing the land.[94]

Besides Hyacinth, other saints in Crete may have a local flavor. I can see them in the iconographies, wearing traditional Cretan costumes and s t i v á n i a . Saint Manouil (Emmanuel) from Sfakia is one example.[95] His church at the village of Petrokefali was built in local style, with stones from the villages around the Messara. From the church, I can see the whole village, Phaistos, the Libyan Sea (its mother), and Psiloritis (its father).

Landscapes untouched by time remind us of past values which strongly influence and shape our present and future. Cretans consider Messara the crossroads of many civilizations. It is in Gortyna, for instance, that Zeus slept with Europe. The name Europe was first used there, where the Minoan civilization blossomed[96] and where one can see the double nature of Crete, the face that opens its arms to Africa and to the rest of the world.

Even music in Crete relates to land. Cretans identify different musical idioms in western and eastern Crete. Songs originate in the mountains or in the plains. Musical pieces may be from the provinces of Chania (Chaniotis dance, 'C h a - niótiko mou yiasemí'), Rethymnon (R e t h e m n i ó t i k i soústa, Amaríotika pendozália, Anoy-anés kondiliés, Rethemniótika syrtá), Heraklion (H e r a k l i ó t i k e s kondiliés, Messarítikes ko-ndiliés, Kastrinós horós) or Lassithi (Sitiakés kondiliés, Lassithiótika pendozália, Ierape-trítikos). Even within a province, there are differences. In Heraklion, for example, there are M e s s a r í t i k e s besi-des the H e r a k l i ó t i k e s kondiliés and in Rethymnon, the A m a r i ó t i k a pendozália.

Hercules, the older Kouritis, moved to Olympia, where the first Olympic Games took place.[97] The Idaean Dactyl decided to hold running races against his four brothers, the winner to be crowned with a branch of wild olive.[98] Domenicus Theotokopoulos, the great painter who was born in the Cretan village of Fodele and is commonly known as El Greco, signs his works as *The Cretan*. E r o f í l i , inspired by the Italian tragedy *Orbecche*, by Giambattista Giraldi, was written in 1543. *Erotókritos*, mainly influenced, as believed, by the French novel *Paris at Vienne* (written in 1432 by Pierre de la Cypede), becomes songs that Vasilis sings, Ross Daly orchestrates and Cretan people, wherever they live in the world, refer to as the "Cretan poem." In the past, they were "ours." In the present, they are still "ours."

Restaurants blossom everywhere in Crete carrying traditional names such as Anaktoro, Embolo, Erganos, Lykastos, Logari, Raeti. Vasilis Stavrakakis performs in ΄Embolo, owned by one of his Stavrakakis relatives. Recently, his wife informed me that there is a new place called Xatheri, a bar more or less, where Stavrakakis also performs. There, as in Embolo, he plays "our" music, Cretan music.

My role here is not to agree or disagree with the "local" views expressed throughout this essay. I understand why the people of Anoya do not regard Ross Daly as one of "their own." And Daly admits it was never his goal to become a Cretan líra player. Thus, nobody should judge him in this spirit. In the same sense, I can see why Cretans may not treat Laodikis, of Syrian origin, as one of "us." Laodikis does feel like a Cretan, not only because after so many years on the island he has adopted behaviors and manners, but also because he sees profound similarities between his culture and "ours."

In addition, I feel that people in Crete, in Anoya, even elsewhere, localize their cultural identity for their own sake in order to construct a sense of distinctiveness, in other words, or in "our own" words, a sense of Cretanness.[99] We already saw how people and their ideas may often become stereotypes. Here I deal only with stereotypes and ideas as they have been created on a local level. Gender stereotypes and other ideas follow. Finally, in the last step of this dance, I move from the local to the global, also examining their relationship.

Landscape, tradition and language: These three concepts, as proposed by Dimou in *Apology of an Anti-Hellene*, define who and what the Cretans are. I used scenes from the Iakinthia to begin this step. Yet, there are far more histories and stories to be told:

> The tradition of Saint George the Methistís (Inebriant) revives in Venerato. At the sounds of the music of Psaradonis, the inhabitants of this very beautiful and historical village, as well as of the whole surrounding area, pour their wine in honor of Saint George the Methistís, each November 2, 2001. Women from the village offer wonderful Cretan cuisine and specialists talk about wine and its history, that has its roots in Venerato, as it is proven by Venetian documents as well as from the wine patitíria (presses) found in the village.
>
> *Patrís* newspaper[100]

Erotokritos and Aretousa

At this point, I feel the need to discuss issues regarding gender. I am inspired to talk about these topics and illustrate them with specific examples by my experience with Cretan music and dance. Social and cultural values, gender notions in particular, are expressed in feasts where the community celebrates a particular event. Music and dance function as non-verbal languages to "construct" male or female identities.

Gender issues eventually came up in my research because most, if not all, musical scenes in Crete are dominated by men.[101] Herzfeld specifically talks about manhood in Crete in *The Poetics of Manhood* and how the l í r a is a symbol of Cretan male identity. Additionally, ethnomusicologist Jane Sugarman notes in *Engendering Song* that music performance is often the principal means by which appropriate gender behavior is taught. Music, and more particularly dance, provide an arena for pushing back boundaries, exploring the border zones that separate male from female, as pointed out by anthropologist and ethnomusicologist Jane Cowan. In *Dance and the Body Politics in Northern Greece* she asserts that, while dance is a vital means of gender socialization and an enactment of masculinity and femininity during ritual events such as weddings, it is also an arena in which gender categories can be contested.

"The idea that men and women in Crete are somehow different from people elsewhere is ludicrous. It is also insulting. People I know of in Crete dislike this kind of garbage," Dr. Chris Williams told me and I agree. As long as people act according to what they believe, I accept "their" realities. Here, I present some, as my eyes see them, as Cretans want me to see them, and as they present them.

Cretan instrument players are most often (but not always) males, in contrast to the audience of such performances, which is mixed. Moreover, through the lyrics of most Cretan songs, it is almost always the man who addresses the woman. The main Cretan music instrument, the l í r a , is a Greek word of female gender. I do not wish to do a gender study on Cretan music. I only expect to give the right of speech to both Erotokritos and Aretousa and illustrate their roles. My main wish, moreover, is to show that it is the actors, both male and female, of a specific place, through time, that shape their roles through music and dance in a dialogue with their social and communal beliefs.

Erotokritos is often depicted as a shepherd. He competes in animal-theft, in which the strongest of the shepherds are engaged. Moreover, he constructs narrations of his male identity and represents his deeds in them.[102] He usually carries a knife and may also own a gun. He avoids quarreling, but he will do so if someone insults his Aretousa. He may draw his gun and shoot in the air to mark a celebration. Aretousa, on the other hand, does not get involved in such behavior. Patiently, she waits for her Erotokritos who, one day, will attempt to "steal" her and make her his bride.

In order for Erotokritos to be a man, he must have a mustache. He favors dark, preferably black, clothes. He wears a black s a r í k i on a daily basis, but switches it to a white one when he celebrates a wedding or a baptism. Usually, his father and his friends wear plain dark shirts, v r á k a (breeches) and s t i v á n i a . His uncle maintains this regional dress as an important part of his Anoya heritage. He is proud of his family and respects his clan. He is ready to stand up to anyone who dares insult him.

Erotokritos focuses on "being good at being a man." In Anoya, he gets involved in improvising and knowing many m a n d i n á d e s , such as the ones he and his friends devoted to Zeus over the Iakinthia of 2001. He dances well and performs the acrobatic steps of the leader of the line (b r o s t á r i s) . He is ready and feels comfortable in responding with elegant answers to friendly challenges. His dancing is agile. Without disrupting the basic steps of the other dancers, he embellishes the dance with intricate steps (f i g o ú r e s). While watching him, I focus not on *what* he does, but on *how* he does it.

While dancing, Erotokritos's goal is to give the impression of a crane, like the ones in the mountains of Psiloritis. Flying symbolizes his desire for independence. His elder relatives and friends move with slower movements. Oftentimes while dancing, he and his younger friends perform many leaps, trying to show off their manhood.

Aretousa joins in the dance later in the evening. Her dancing steps are conspicuously chaste, avoiding the acrobatics of the young males. Her mother walks sedately up and down, minding children or chatting in small groups. Her friends, mostly young women, line the wall on the "female" side, watching the general activity, but avoiding direct personal contact with individual young men.

Aretousa's posture, when dancing, reminds me of the ancient Minoan goddesses of fertility, holding snakes and with an exposed chest. She assumes this posture when she comes in the middle of the circle to perform turns and other dancing maneuvers. She hardly moves her torso while she keeps her arms in an open position in contrast to Erotokritos, who keeps his hands behind his back, especially when dancing as a couple with her. Generally, Aretousa is expected to dance demurely, but with a proud posture. Her torso must remain stable and upright, while nothing moves from her waist to her head.

When Aretousa is present at a wedding, she knows well that the bride is the central and most symbolically elaborate figure in the entire wedding ritual, since in a wedding the act of taking a woman out into the world is legitimized in ritual. Aretousa dreams of her wedding, when she will dance with Erotokritos in public, in an open circle with all their relatives, in order for their marriage to be established.

Even though both Erotokritos and Aretousa dance, singing and instrument playing are almost always "male matters." As far as we know, Aspasia Papadaki was the first woman in the history of Cretan music to play the l í r a . Her mother (after her father died) wanted to stop her playing the l í r a : "Only men play the l í r a . It isn't suitable for a young girl to play the l í r a , " her mother would say to her, in a quote taken from the liner notes of *Cretan Musical Traditions: The Masters, 1920-1955*, a compact disc produced by Stelios Aerakis.

I recall one of the main protagonists of these writings, Vasilis Stavrakakis, performing with female singers. At the Iakinthia, Maria Fasoulaki accompanied Vasilis for both summers that I followed their group (in 2000 and 2001). She occasionally played some percussion as well, but her main contribution to Vasilis's music group was to sing solo or accompany Vasilis and the rest of the group. She owes her "percussion" knowledge to Laodikis, the main percussion instrument player in Vasilis's group, another of the protagonists in these writings. Laodikis, in turn, had other students who wanted to learn how to play the t o u b e l é k i or the bendír. They were all female. When I asked him to comment on this issue, however, his opinion was that the percussion is a man's job because it needs strength and power that women do not possess.

Ross Daly, our third "hero," has many students. He teaches them the l í r a and other instruments. For him, gender has nothing to do with the instrument his students choose to play. In the summer of 2001, on the island of Rhodes, Kelly Thomas, one of his female students, played the l í r a next to him. I have seen them playing together since the summer of 2001, as part of one of their concerts in the village of Astritsi in Crete.

Cretans, in general, see the l í r a as the embodiment of the female presence. L í r a is a male matter because "she," "herself," is female. Writing in www.cretaphone.gr, Anna Stergiou talks about the Cretan l í r a as though she is a female body. She describes her full-of-fire eyes, her apocryphal spots, and her melodic honey-voice. Thanasis Skordalos, one of the most famous Cretan l í r a players, believed that the "l í r a is like a woman; and if you don't love her, if you don't take care of her, you will lose her". Moreover, the "l í r a is the woman that needs k a n á k i (pampering) and h á i d e m a (caress). She wants you to wash and comb her hair, to love her, the same way you love your eyes as well as yourself," Spyros Sifoyiorgakis, another l í r a player, comments, in the same Stergiou article.

When the l í r a , therefore, is a female matter, it naturally sings for a woman. In all cases, however, gender in Cretan music and dance is always powerfully, expressively and passionately manifested. Erotokritos takes his l a o ú t o and composes songs and melodies for Aretousa: "All night long he sings; she likes him so much that she feels unable to sleep. She grasps his songs; she often repeats them. Even in a distance, the desire functions as a bow, and without knowing Erotokritos, because of these songs, Aretousa gets perplexed into love and longing".[103]

The second step is now complete. Through it, we may feel better and understand the locals, male and female. You have more, if not all, of the clues now. There is no way you will get lost in the labyrinths. You have officially entered them and … surprise! You are about to meet Ariadne and Theseus, listen to their music and watch them dance. Second step: past and present step.

step 3

Ariadne

STEP 3: ARIADNE

After wandering in time and space, this third step brings us in touch with specific people and their actions. According to ancient Greek mythology, Ariadne sweetly hands the thread to Theseus so he won't get lost in the labyrinths and eaten by the Minotaur. Dancing in step three, we admire the relationship of Theseus and Ariadne. The mythologies go on: Theseus comes out of the labyrinth safely. He marries Ariadne. We are about to attend their wedding feast, in this central step of our dance.

Anoyanós gámos (Anoya wedding feast)

July 14, 2001. With my sister and her friend, I drive to the village of Anoya. We are here to attend a wedding celebration.[104] I am excited, as are my companions: They have heard of my adventures for years; they are looking forward to tasting the culture of this village. From the windows of the car, we see the proud mountain of Psiloritis bathed in sunset colors. We are almost there: A strong afternoon wind wafts the melodies of the l í r a to our ears.

We park and walk to the lower part of the village (Kato Horio or Perahori): The sound of the music and the smells of the grilled meat lead us on. Our destination is the groom's house. There, with his male friends, after the church ceremony, he drinks r a k í and treats all his guests to big pieces of meat and watermelon. He wears a white s a r í k i with his suit. I congratulate him from a distance.

Happy faces, smiles and loud voices greet us at the wedding feast: On a wooden stage, the musicians perform. Around it, people dance continuously. Few are sitting. My friends treat us. They bring huge pieces of meat and they cut smaller pieces for us: In one hand we hold the meat and in the other a glass of red wine. They honor us with a white handmade handkerchief. Later, they bring us a whole watermelon. We "slaughter" it with the knife they hand us.

Old and young men in traditional attire "own" the first dances. The dance floor is theirs. As I find out, it is the groom's close male relatives, excited and full of joy for the wedding event, who are among the first to dance. The older men perform dragging steps. When improvising or making solo moves, they keep their arms extended, ready to fly with the eagles of Crete. Younger men and women join the dance later.

Meanwhile, the musicians accept requests — if you give them some money. Men gathered in front of them ask for particular songs. If there is enough k é f i, the money is plastered upon the sweating brow of the musicians. The time comes for every request to "be played" and the dance goes on. "How slowly do moments pass when waiting, but how fast sweet moments go by," the l í r a player sings. The men who know this m a n d i n á d a shake their hands, swing their heads and clap while dancing. It is almost midnight and the whole village is still awake.

Groups of people who do not dance sing along with the melodies or comment on the dancing of others. In the beginning of the event there was just one dancing circle. Now, more and more circles of dancers are added, and they often mingle into the labyrinth of King Minos, as Cretans envision it.

Men and women, children too, excited and full of joy, give themselves to dancing. Everybody who dances shares r a k í from the same bottle. "My basil with your curly leaves stand where you are, so that your lovely smells can be spread all over the world," is a m a n d i n á d a a young man requests. While dancing to it, he also sings and performs acrobatic dancing movements and agile leaps.

Lefteris Kalomoiris and Nikiforos Aerakis perform dancing melodies on the l í r a . The l a o ú t o players keep the rhythm. A solo melodic invitation by the l í r a players invites the dancers to the dance floor, the narrow street where the bride lives. It is the l í r a players who also indicate which group's turn it is to dance.

The bride and the groom join the dancing after midnight. In a circle with their close friends and relatives they "conquer" the dance floor. Men who carry guns shoot in the air every once in a while to celebrate the wedding event. Y i a s o u ! (to your health!), n a z i s' i K r í t i ! (may Crete live forever!). Hearts are united, the village is united and more people are dancing. Our friends request a dance and we join them. We hold hands with people we do not know. Life is beautiful.

Good food and drink, live music and dance, nice company and people: These are memories of home, memories of my country. We have music and dance. It represents a culture and it confirms community bonds. The night goes on, the bodies continue moving. 4.30 a.m. and Nikiforos performs "Stop Living with Dreams": Dance is never-ending and life goes on.

Labyrinths

While in the labyrinths, Cretans perform music. They look forward to hearing the instrumentalists and the lyrics of old, new and improvised songs. Full of energy, they are ready to dance. Their performances may be life cycle events, rituals or of secular context. Performers and the audience participate in each of these events, depending on their functions. In all cases, however, they "speak" through these events about who the Cretans are.

As a Cretan, but also a researcher, after having observed and participated in various Cretan music and dance performances over time, I present to you some of the things these events may express. To do so, I look into the structure and the components of the Cretan musical ensembles, as well as their roles and position within Cretan culture and society. In other words, I call upon the music events and performances I have attended. I observe the instruments used, the lyrics composed, the expressions and vocal timbres in use and the musicians themselves.

Ideas about social exchange are of great significance to my work at this point. In *The Social Construction of Reality*, Peter Berger and Thomas Luckman support that reality is socially constructed, whereas Ruth Stone's work (1978 and 1982) shows how music events are arenas where identity is produced and negotiated.[105] At these events, there is a dynamic interaction and communication established through music. All these ideas apply to Cretan music and dance events, which are socially constructed; they become arenas where the above notions come to the fore.

I draw on Stone's ideas in *Let the Inside Be Sweet* to talk about music and dance events on the island of Crete. Moreover, I draw from her theoretical foundation, inspired by symbolic interaction and phenomenology. At the same time, I also look at *The Voice of Egypt* by ethnomusicologist Virginia Danielson, who addresses the issue of the agency in a society, particularly the role of the exceptional individual in expressive culture. Danielson rests on the rather large literature that has become known as practice theory, as well as the literature associated with cultural studies. I use her ideas when talking about specific individuals, musicians on the island of Crete and their relationship to society and culture.

In *May It Fill Your Soul: Experiencing Bulgarian Music*, Timothy Rice, also an ethnomusicologist, presents his study object and makes two individuals the center of his study. He follows the history of their interaction with the world into which they are thrown, hoping to show ideas that support his thesis statement. Rice works with social units, villages where music at social functions is performed. In my case too, Cretan music is a social phenomenon more than anything else, and this I wish to highlight.

In the same sense, anthropologist Anna Caraveli writing for the *Journal of American Folklore* deals with the symbolic village community born in performance, the notions of g l é n d i and k é f i . Ethnomusicologist Steven Feld shows transitions from sound to community in *Sound and Sentiment*. Finally John Blacking, another ethnomusicologist, depicts how musical processes are based on patterns of interaction and cultural forms in *Music, Culture and Experience*. All the aforementioned deal with specific musical identities and aesthetics that are shaped and negotiated in particular communities.

All the above, explore cases where high spirits, ecstasy, repetition and other forms of expression appear through music. These cases are indeed related because of the common expression of k é f i and ecstasy that can be traced between the Cretan and other cultures. For example, k é f i , the Greek word for high spirits, is the same for both Turks and Arabs (keyf). When investigating these notions, I left the ground open for local reactions and interpretations of instances that might have not been investigated before.

Traditionally, Cretans perform folk music in rural settings, such as the village of Anoya. These rituals may be collective celebrations that commemorate important moments in individual lives. In my trips into the labyrinths, these moments are mainly weddings (life-cycle events) and baptisms. Often, especially over the summer, the Minoan calendar is marked by events of religious nature, such as the feasts in favor of the community's patron saint, the p a n i y í r i a (big celebrations). The most famous and well known among those is the one for the Dormition of the Virgin Mary on August 15.

In the summer of 2001, the preparation and promotion of traditional Cretan food is a particularly distinct and popular theme, and a good reason for music and dance events to take place in the palace of Knossos. Another event of similar character and nature — which I pursued and very gladly witnessed several times in different Cretan villages in May 2001 — is the k o u r é s (sheep's shearing). There, after the animals' wool had been shorn and removed and after an early morning religious ceremony in a church or the outdoors, a festive atmosphere with traditional Cretan music and dance follows.

Dancing at these festive events is a highly structured social practice with rules that vary from one locality to another. According to Cowan, in addition to striving for exuberant k é f i, locals in these events "perform" gender, class, political and regional identities, negotiate power relations, express solidarity or rivalry with kin, neighbors and friends.

In the Cretan labyrinths, music and dance events may also take place in schools, theaters,[106] concert halls, restaurants, clubs, houses, the squares of towns or villages, and even in the streets. The occasions of these events vary. Cretans have lots of feasts and celebrate many national events and holidays, as well as personal anniversaries. They enjoy giving concerts for commemorative[107] and other reasons; they often hold m a n d i n á d a contests. Cretan musicians and traditional dancers also travel around the island to exhibit their talents.

We may see Cretans on the streets of the labyrinths singing for the ones they love or as the preparation for weddings. We may observe Cretans listening to live music under the full moon. Vasilis Stavrakakis, on September 5, 2001, played the m a n d o l í n o on the top of Ida, on the plains of Psiloritis. That day, the locals sang for the moon and for Saint Mamas, the protector of animals.

More importantly, however, we experience Cretans performing music and occasionally dance in their own palaces, formally or informally. Name-days, birthdays, graduations, professional achievements, family events, engagements, reunions, are all good reasons for Cretan feasts to take place. Instruments hanging on the walls, music playing on a radio, tickle Cretans' appetite for merry music-making and dancing feet.[108]

For example, on July 6, 2001, at Manouras's taverna in Anoya, Anna, my American cousin, and I witness two young brothers who sing m a n d i n á d e s. At the same time, their families and friends, gathered around a table rich in food and drink, participate in the event by repeating the couplets.

Yet, musicians and dancers also travel outside the labyrinths of Crete. On May 21, 2001, Vasilis Stavrakakis and his group — including Laodikis — were part of the celebration in Thessaloniki, held to celebrate the "Battle of Crete." In August 2001, Ross Daly organized a multi-ethnic festival that brought together on the island of Rhodes string instruments similar to the Cretan l í r a. In the contemporary Minoan era, social gatherings of regional immigrant associations use folk music and dance performance to speak of their identity, whereas Cretan music feels comfortable enough to stand next to its immediate or distant musical cousins.

Of course, nowadays, Minoans record and produce music for commercial purposes as well.[109] Their "traditional" ensembles mix established instruments with new ones. Cretans may admire or complain about the "exotic" attire their music takes on. In addition, more young people entertain themselves in clubs where Cretan music recordings are played next to popular Greek songs. Lastly, in places like Xatheri, people can listen to Cretan music performed live while having a drink, like in a bar, standing.

Wedding events are unique in the labyrinths. Cretan weddings are "traditional" attractions not only for locals, but for non-locals and even tourists, because they reflect the Cretan culture.[110] Because dance is the central activity in them, I call them dance events.[111]

Identity is shaped through those events. Dance functions as a symbol, a way of constructing identity; in other words, dance is a socially constructed movement system and, in that sense, dance performance is a way to construct identity. I am using the ideas of anthropologist Rena Loutzaki on locality and repertory to show how identity is shaped. Dance anthropologists Judith Lynne Hanna, Adrienne Kaeppler and Sally Ann Ness also talk about dance as a movement system, and they view performance as a way to construct identity.

Such events include not only dancing, but also drinking, singing, eating, talking and, more generally, people in k é f i, who are willing to celebrate the wedding event and share these moments with people in their community, their relatives, friends and other guests. Through these dances, the people of Crete show their community spirit and represent their Cretan identity. When people dance at weddings, they express themselves, they communicate with each other, they indicate what it means to be Cretan, and, in particular what it means to be a man or a woman from Anoya.

Specifically, in *The Poetics of Manhood*, Michael Herzfeld comments on the distinctiveness of Cretan weddings and the Cretan tradition of bride theft. Other scholars, such as Kevin Dawe, came to Crete to study its music.[112] Locals informed him that, to have an understanding of a real Cretan wedding, he had to attend one in the village of Anoya. Vasilis underscores the importance of these events and Anoya as the place where weddings are major entertainment venues as well as rich musical and dancing occasions.

Nikos Kazantzakis and his disciple, Pandelis Prevelakis, spend numerous pages talking about wedding events and other celebrations in their novels.[113] Magazines advertise representations of Cretan weddings mostly for tourist purposes. My family looks forward to attending such events. We even arranged the wedding of my Greek-American cousin in this spirit. And I anticipate the day my "traditional" wedding will take place in my homeland.

In contrast to traditional weddings, where music and dance performances take place in mostly rural and traditional settings, today concert halls also welcome Cretan music. In his July 2001 interview to me, Ross Daly said that he was the first to hold music concerts in Crete, which was not hard for him because of his exposure to traditional music concerts in other parts of the world. Initially, he explained, because Cretans were unfamiliar with the traditional music concert idea, they thought he was trying to provide a substitute for their traditional feasts. They raised objections. However, Daly's first concert in collaboration with the University of Crete was a great success.

Ross Daly also commented on how concert programs differ from traditional feasts. In a program of two hours, for example, coherence in presentation is the toughest job. His l í r a teacher, Kostas Moundakis, Daly argues, knew how to make good programs for concert halls and theaters. When in London, for example, Moundakis, without corrupting the Cretan musical tradition, would modify his presentation so that it could appeal to an audience unfamiliar with Cretan music. In any case, Daly maintains that it is impossible for a two-hour concert to give a taste of a Cretan feast.

Here, I attempt to give you a taste of Cretan music and dance performances. Toward the end of this third step,

Ross Daly, coaxing "sympathetic" sounds from his líra, harmonically
blending the East with the West

keeping these words in mind, we find "instant photographs" of the children of these performances. Their poses "speak," revealing much about the structure and the components of the Cretan musical ensembles, their roles and position within Cretan culture and society, the instruments they play, the lyrics of their songs, the musicians and performers, the expressions and aesthetics in use, and much more.

Ross Daly — quoted by Manolis Alexakis in *Ostria* magazine — has this to say about musical performances: "The musician is gifted by nature and works in service for all the people. He or she is a professional that knows well how to do his or her job. To deify…, idolize musicians is…tragic."

Such are the main heroes, the musicians.

Next! Three. Still. In black and white.

Theseus

According to Thucydides, phenomena repeat in different historical periods of time. In this spirit, the story of Ariadne and Theseus takes place many times over in history. Here, I give you the life histories of my three Theseus's. The first one is that of Ross Daly, a musician of Irish origin, who among others, also plays the instrument of the island of Crete, the l í r a . The second musician, Vasilis Stavrakakis, from Anoya, is a singer and a m a n d o l í n o player. Finally, the third musician, Laodikis, is a Syrian percussionist who moved to Crete several years ago and who, during my research, performed traditional music on the island to make a living.

I agree with ethnomusicologist Tulia Magrini who maintains that focusing on case studies of musicians points out the role played by individual men and women in the process of transmission and transformation of oral repertories and musical style. This way, we are becoming more aware that what we, as ethnomusicologists, study as a "genre" or "repertory," is the cumulative outcome of interacting accomplishments, framed in personal life histories and with specific social and historical backgrounds.

Ross Daly, Vasilis Stavrakakis and Laodikis become, in this sense, historians. They live in a specific time, experiencing and sharing the main musical practices. As musicologist Amnon Shiloah shows in his study of Jewish and Muslim musicians, the latter are extremely important in determining the character and dimension of all musical production. My choice of these three musicians is not accidental. The diversity among them, but — at the same time — their common engagement with Cretan music supports my main thread; in other words, it helps us see how identities are constructed on a local base.

Apart from these three interesting identities, I must underscore the relationships among them. Daly and Stavrakakis collaborated in the past and still do. For example, in the summer of 2001, they collaborated on the compact disc *S t i d í n i t o n a n é m o* . They are friends who occasionally perform and record together. Laodikis is part of Vasilis's group. In a concert in Astritsi in the summer of 2001, all three musicians came together. In the first part of the concert, Vasilis Stavrakakis and his group, including Laodikis, performed, and in the second part, Daly performed with Vasilis and his group.

But I shall stop talking and let them speak: Listen…

Ross Daly

Eh… traveler thought[114]

Ah! I wish it was possible before I lie and die
To accomplish half of what my black thought has in mind

I don't hunt partridges anymore and I don't grow violets
I am watering slowly, fast, the tree of my loneliness

My loneliness becomes a tree and I am watering it:
Every day I am sitting under its wide, thick shadow

Eh… traveler thought with the rebellious body
Don't let a single, small street all over the world unsought

Eh… traveler thought, my winged horse,
Take me for a ride to meet my baby

Since it is written for me one day to die
Let me, poor soul, to live as I wish.

Tall and thin, with long salt and pepper hair and a thick mustache, a sincere smile, plenty of honest words in a Cretan accent, armed with a good heart and kindness, Ross Daly invites me on several journeys of sound and silence in the realm of music. Curious about the so-called and so-believed Irishman, I interview him in July 2001 and I discover an artist of no nation, an eternal traveler.

Sound

During his childhood, Daly studied the cello and classical guitar; in other words, he had what he calls a "normal classical education on that stuff." However, he thought he was "not particularly talented in the cello," that he was "not in a great mood for it," so he abandoned it. "With the guitar, so to say, I became more tight." But neither the classical guitar nor the cello ever fully expressed him; this tradition was very "suffocating" for him, "especially the way it used to be taught then".

As a child in the 1960s, he found himself in San Francisco, "where many interesting sounds of contemporary music exist." Daly listened to these sounds and liked them: "I myself was playing them on the guitar, starting with blues." Still though, something in all that did not "fit." He remembers: "the first time I listened to Ravi Shankar playing the sitar…and, then I had the chance to attend live, Indian music, and I am very impressed, I like it immediately, so I see a music that has all the structure, and all the discipline that one can see in classical music, but at the same time has all the freedom that you see in other kinds."

That very first contact for Ross Daly with Indian music sparked his interest in non-European musical traditions and specifically Eastern ones. "I was trying to do with my guitar several things from what I listened to from the sitar and from other eastern instruments. I was collecting records and I was listening to them, Persian, Turkish, Greek, Arabic, whatever you want," Daly said. Soon, however, he realized that, if he wanted to get seriously engaged with these traditions, he should occupy himself with the instruments they employ, because the guitar is not the proper one.

Daly finished school in England where he was born (September 29, 1952) and was partly raised,[115] and took his first classes of Indian music at a music college. He concentrated on the sitar and went to India for sitar lessons. Around that time, at age 18, he still remembers very clearly his first experience with Cretan music:

> [It is] a hot summer evening in August of 1970 when, during the course of a brief stay in Crete, I am taken to a neighboring village to a p a n i y í r i (feast) — somewhere in Messara — to listen for the first time in my life to Cretan traditional folk music. I have no idea what I am going to hear; all I know is that it is not going to resemble the urban b o u z o ú k i tradition, which is all that I knew of Greek music… I had almost no knowledge of rural Greek folk music to prepare me for the surprise that I was going to experience.
>
> Daly, quoted in *Welcome Crete*

> The whole sound of the music during my first encounter with Cretan music is something quite unique in my musical experience. I had never heard something similar, and I remember that I was very much impressed by this, because I immediately liked it very much.
>
> Daly, July 2001 interview

> I never make qualitative comparisons between different musical traditions because I believe them to be so subjective as to be without any real meaning, but I would go as far as to say that my first experience with Cretan music is definitely an experience which surprised, confused, and certainly amazed me. I could clearly hear very distinct influences from a wide range of eastern Mediterranean and North African sources, but it had a character all of its own, which distinguished it from all of these other idioms.
>
> Daly, quoted in *Welcome Crete*

Ross Daly continued his classical music studies in England with deep thoughts of abandoning them. He stopped in Crete again in 1972 and also traveled to Turkey, Persia and Afghanistan, thirsty for learning their music. Around 1973, he felt capable of playing the Indian sitar and the Afghan r a b á b (string instrument belonging to the lute family), but — out of money — he returned to England in 1974 and worked as a street musician. In 1975, he told me, his plan was to travel to India, but he remembered the l í r a he heard in Crete. Tired from the whole experience in India, where he had stayed for a year, he changed his plans: "I will pass by Crete: There things are more resting, relieving… I will stay for some time to engage myself with the l í r a, to see where things will lead me."

Daly went to Crete again in 1975 to spend some time, but also to make some money working so that he could go to India again. In Chania (a major city in western Crete), he opened a coffee shop with some friends. In the summer, he worked as a fisherman, catching mainly swordfish. At the same time, he also started his musical wanderings with the l í r a , entering its world. Since then, his "chair" transferred to Crete and Greece, where he stayed permanently. He never returned to India, as initially planned.

In our talk, Ross Daly recognizes his Cretan teacher, Kostas Moundakis, as a "very positive and very important person in his development". While in Crete, he constantly seized opportunities to listen to l í r a music being performed live. He started performing with other musicians, at weddings, feasts and so on, gaining experience, but not making it his profession. As he pointed out in our talk, he did not intend to become a Cretan l í r a player; his goal was to learn to play the l í r a well, and those are two different things for him.

Sometime in 1980-1981, Daly went to Heraklion, the capital of Crete, to perform. "Young" and "inexperienced", as he admitted to me, he formed his first group, Lavirinthos (Labyrinth), more or less a kind of a music workshop. He started giving concerts. In 1982, he made a record with Vasilis and Mitsos Stavrakakis, the *O n e í r o u   t ó p o i* (*Dreamlands*), which reflected his concert experience. In 1984, they recorded a second record, under the title *L a v í r i n t h o s*.

Daly went to Athens and returned to Chania, working and teaching at a private music school, but at the same time practicing and playing with other musicians. In 1986, he made a record in which he included music other than Cretan, such as Ottoman classical pieces as well as some of his own compositions. Welcomed in Athens, in 1987-1988, he was offered many jobs and he moved there to collaborate with artists and to work with some elements outside the borders of Cretan music. He continues to teach, record music, perform in concerts, learn and travel.

Silence

Ross Daly has studied the rich and varied "classical" and folk traditions with master musicians from many parts of the world. For example, he studied classical guitar with Brent Knowland and Patrick Benham, sitar with Jachindranath Saha, rabáb with Mohammad Omar, Cretan l í r a with Kostas Moundakis and kementzé (a type of l í r a played especially in the Black Sea region of Turkey) with Ohsan Oezgen. He is known as a composer and multi-instrumentalist, a respected master in his own right and an acclaimed virtuoso on a wide range of instruments, including the Greek l a o ú t o , the Turkish saz, the Arab oud (short-necked lute), the Persian tar, and the Indian sarángi (North Indian instrument) among others.

Daly loves many traditions. During our talk, he wonders: "[It is] good, all this engagement, all this work I have been doing for all these years, but, where does it lead me?" .

An eternal traveler, a man of no nation, identity, and tradition, by definition, Ross Daly combines in his compositions and in his performances the musical life and living experiences he has gained through his travels and education around the world. He thinks of "not belonging to anywhere" as an advantage. In addition, he does not ignore his whole education and experience in classical music.

Daly initiates: a movement at the village of Houdetsi, 20 kilometers south of Iraklio, in the summer of 2003: He brings global attention to Cretan music and fulfills his quest for constant learning. Moreover, he is able to live in a much more pleasant environment. The village of Houdetsi itself also benefits because Daly renovates one of its old manors, which he bought and which hosts a permanent exhibition of rare musical instruments from all over the world.

Daly organizes: "seminars with musicians invited from all over the world, from various traditions, where the teacher as well as the students are from different places, so that more or less I can share with a whole world, a personal acquisition of this place, so that other people can benefit from this. A contribution of my own could be to make such a thing that could gather here, all these sounds and those very special people from several places of the world that they do something, and to give a chance to everyone to listen to that, and of course that could keep my own interest as well, because I would also learn many things , I would receive…".[116] A creator of a unique musical universe that welcomes us all, Ross Daly invites us with his sounds, but also the silence of his music:

> Perhaps we do not really know anything about the source of music, but if ever we hear it, even for a fraction of a second, we want only to go there. To achieve that, we become instruments of this music. We have to resign from our positions as artists, creators, indeed as individuals, giving way to a re-defining and a re-discovery of ourselves as silent, still, and even given to the movement and sound of the music. This silence dissolves any false perceptions of the music belonging to the one or the other.
>
> Daly, quoted in the Oriente Musik website

Vasilis Stavrakakis

> And when the cool, fresh night rests every man
> And every animal looks for a place to sleep,
> He was taking his l a o ú t o , walking softly,
> (And he was) striking its strings sweetly-sweetly across the palace.
> His hand was sugar; he had a nightingale's voice;
> Every heart — that listens to him — cries and weeps in tears.
> He spoke of and remembered the passions of love
> And how he got perplexed into love, and languished, and withered.
> Every heart took fire, even if made of ice,
> As it was getting closer to such a sweet voice;
> It was taming everything wild; it was smoothing everything hard,
> Whatever he was with sorrow saying to the man's mind;
> He spoke of complaints that slaughtered hearts,
> Broke marbles, warmed up ice.
>
> *E r o t ó k r i t o s* [117]

Vasilis Stavrakakis speaking to our hearts with a nightingale's voice

Song

"Ross is a big chapter for Crete, very big... Namely I feel, I swear, proud that I happened to collaborate with Ross. I'm telling you, I owe him so much gratitude." We are listening to the compact disc *Sti díni ton anémo*, a collaboration of Vasilis Stavrakakis and Ross Daly, while talking with Vasilis on his home's balcony on a hot August night in 2001.

Vasilis Stavrakakis comes from an artistic and musical family. We trace his origins to the village of Anoya. Vasilis collaborates and still works with members of his family. At the same time, he also works with his own music group.

One of his family members, for example, is Michalos, known as the Nidiotis,[118] who composed the song "I'm Worshipping Your Beauty, My People." Vasilis honored him in the summer of 2000 (July 20) with a concert in the Oasis Garden-Theater "Nikos Kazantzakis" in Heraklion.[119] Other family members are Vasilis's brother, Nikiforos, a l í r a player, who occasionally performs with Vasilis; Mitsos, Vasilis's first cousin, who writes most of the lyrics Vasilis sings; Michalis, also Vasilis's first cousin, a m a n d o l í n o player; and, finally, Yiorgis, the son of Michalos, a l a o ú t o player who occasionally performs with Vasilis as well.

In our talk, Stavrakakis remembers that he began playing the mandolin at the age of 20 "for himself, for his part". His big passion, however, has always been to sing. "I prefer much more to sing than to play. Namely, when I was among friends, I felt I was the richest person in the world. Whatever else I was going to do, it didn't move me that much, as it would to sing m a n d i n á d e s to a group of people that I would like. My big passion was singing... the song itself. I don't know what other job I could do in my life to satisfy me that much as singing".

The first memories that Stavrakakis has are when he was a kid, 5 to 8 years old: "... very often, very regularly, let's say that there would happen to be two people in a house somewhere and they would be having a m e z é s (appetizer) and they would be drinking wine [and] as soon as a third or a fourth person would join them, immediately a [music] company would be established... because people at that time needed that. They were playing instruments as well in my village in the past — [there were] l í r a players and l a o ú t o players — so it was not once a month or once every two months, it was much more often organized."

It is in such an environment, therefore, that Stavrakakis grew up. This helped him to bring forth what was inside him, the m e r a k l í k i. Till he was 10 to 15 years old, he did not do anything else except listen to Cretan music. From the age of 15 onward, he wanted to create a musical company, to take the m a n d o l í n o and to sing.

As a grown man, he went to the village of Anoya, where they held the "Musical Feasts" event with Manos Hatzidakis.[120] Part of it was a singing competition. Stavrakakis participated with a known t a b a c h a n i ó t i k o song performed by Nikos Xylouris, "I'm weeping with complaint." He received a prize and that was the chance for him to formally and finally engage professionally in music and singing.

Throughout the 1970s, Stavrakakis performed mainly in Erofili, a k é n d r o (club) in the Heraklion area, which he partially owned. At the time, he felt like "the sailor of Cretan music": Cretan music was very popular then. Vasilis's performances were very successful: "... namely the people were coming in at 10 p.m., at 11 p.m., and I was tired of staying up, till the sun came out... yes, I swear to God, it was a summer k é n d r o of course, and the sun was coming out to hit us on the forehead, and we were playing, still, till sunrise..."

Vasilis Stavrakakis met Ross Daly, and in 1982, they made their first record (*Dreamlands*), which was very successful. Unfortunately, after a couple of years, because of some problems with the record company, the distribution of that recording stopped.[121] Daly and Stavrakakis also made the *Labyrinth* in 1984. Besides recordings, they gave concerts together all over Crete. Stavrakakis recalls they were seen as innovators: "you know, 5 to 6 people playing traditional Cretan [music] and many other instruments, the s f i r o h á b i o l o (fife), the a s k o m a d o ú r a ... The established [stereotype] — one l í r a and two l a o ú t a — wasn't this way. People liked it a lot, I remember. As an attempt, it was dangerous".

Passion

Without song and music, Vasilis does not exist.

> ...Whatever anyone does, any type of job anyone does, in our case, in music, the thing is to do it with your own will, to do it because you believe it, you feel it, not do it for the spectacle, to show off. Namely, to feel this thing one does, this thing one says, to bring [it] out, from your inside. For example, I myself sing. I do not do it to kill time, nor do I do it only for the money. You give yourself, with your soul, and I believe that you gain from the people, you don't lose. I believe this is also the greatest respect. What matters is how you give it to the other, whether you express it with your soul and your heart.

Stavrakakis still records and performs with a deep devotion to the music of the island of Crete, "our music".

> It blossoms now, it started again and keeps growing and growing. Cretan music, our music, is very good... I myself like it more because since I was 5 years old, I've been involved in it. Cretan music has very deep meaning, and it is not accidental that Ross [loves it]. You know, Ross, before ending up here he had been to India, Afghanistan, Turkey, Persia, America...

Vasilis Stavrakakis is always anxious about his audience's reaction and comments. Until he sees that the audience a r p á (is catching fire), he feels as if he is sitting on a n a m é n a k á r v o u n a (live coals; implying impatience, worry). When he feels a response, he then gives himself to the performance and participates even more. Even if only two people are watching him, he will musically be there for them.

The last performance of Stavrakakis I attended before leaving for the United States was in August of 2001. His beautiful wife Viki and his two children, Yiorgos and Katerina, were present as well. A wonderful farewell to my sister (who departed the next morning for England) and to me was Vasilis's beautiful, passionate voice:

Absence
Your absence is rain that falls little by little:
The world around me becomes a sea and drowns me.[122]
Stavrakakis, Sti díni ton anémo

Laodikis

Everybody asks me why do I cry and if I cry, who do I bother,
I was born in this world to test hearts.
I'm searching-seeking-wandering around-questioning-asking-looking
Where will I find the medicine that cures sighs?
Halepianós manés "Everybody asks me why I cry"

Outsider

Laodikia is the older name for Latakia, a major city of Syria. Laodikis was born there on December 17, 1960, where he also grew up. He has been in Heraklion, Crete, since 1988. His voice has a Cretan accent and his warm, expressive eyes and brown mustache look familiar to Cretans.

While in Crete, for several years he performed with a local group called Hainides under several nicknames because, at that time, he did not have a permit to live in Greece. A musician from that group suggested that he should be called Laodikis and he has used the name since then with no intention of changing it: "Even if I'll eventually get the green card [nationality]," he tells me in our July 2001 interview, "I won't change my name, I can't change Laodikis, I like it so much, because I'm from there".

Laodikis has loved music since he was a young boy. It is something in his blood: "Since 6 to 7 years old, I started playing, alone, not on an instrument, [but] on the tables, on my feet, everywhere. I never went to music school, to a teacher, everything I have learned, I learned by myself". When home in Syria, he played every day "for the company's entertainment, for food and drink." He never made money from that and he never imagined that some day he would "eat bread" from this instrument. He forgot all about the t o u b e l é k i when he went to Greece in 1988.

Insider

When in Crete, Laodikis was asked to play t o u b e l é k i. He accepted, but "with doubts, with fear." He never expected to make a living only from music; he had several other jobs while on the island of Crete.

I met Laodikis performing Cretan music with Vasilis Stavrakakis and his "team." He has been with them since 1997 or 1998. He hopes to join a group that performs l a i k á (popular music) or r e b é t i k a songs (urban Greek music), but he cannot find any currently in Crete. On the other hand, moving to Athens, where he could possibly find work, would require some acquaintances in that professional field. He tells me he compromises with "the role of being a stranger" and does not easily "accept to play with just anyone".

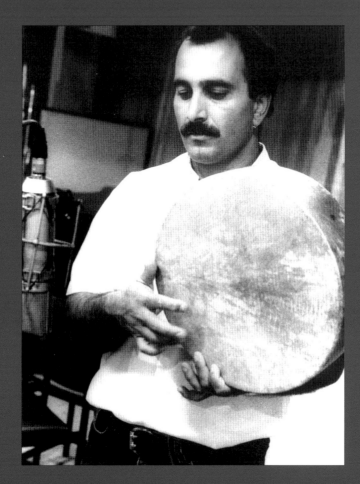

Talking fingers: Laodikis

Laodikis speaks of his instrument with sweetness. He became very sad when, during a summer boat trip, his "about eight years old child" broke. According to him, percussion fits with everything, because it adds to the rhythm, the base. People that think of it negatively are wrong; t o u b e l é k i is a beautiful instrument, which indeed nowadays has become very popular in the Greek musical culture.

Laodikis grasps his instrument to indicate to me the way he practices when at home. As a warm up, he starts with a tape playing some Syrian-Andalusian pieces, heavy pieces. He continues with some t s i f t e t é l i a. Fast music and complicated rhythms prevail.

Young people in Crete are interested in taking private classes with Laodikis. Interestingly, he remarks, for the past few years, he had only female students. With few exceptions in the past, his students want to learn this instrument because of their personal interest in Middle Eastern cultures or for their own entertainment. In the past, Laodikis taught young gypsies as part of an education program of the University of Crete. He remembers the gypsies as his best students: "The rhythm, the beat, was inside them".

When I spoke with him on the phone from the United States sometime in November 2001, after he had returned from a trip to his home in Syria, Laodikis told me that music will not be his major profession any longer. Without a green card, he must find other ways of making money and surviving.[123] His house, facing the port, the sounds of the waves and the blue Cretan ocean, will always invite his eyes to sadness. Laodikia: "Justice for the people."

Ariadne

Pictures at an exhibition

In ancient Greece, the nine Muses were the goddesses-embodiments of the arts, including music. M o u s i k í (music) was an "in-harmony" way of life inspired and surrounded by all the arts (and sciences). In all my pictures, I clearly see Ariadne. She is not merely the wife of Theseus, but also the companion of every Cretan. Under her auspices, people on the island of Crete perform music and dance in the labyrinths.

Frames

In *The Potter's Art*, folklorist Henry Glassie looks at pottery as something that comes from the earth, in which the potters live. In the same spirit, I view music and dance events as artistic expressions of the people who participate in them. I can tell stories of a community by looking at its material culture, but at the same time, I may also choose to talk about it by looking closely at the way it expresses itself on occasions when music and dance are performed. These artistic behaviors occur in many places all over the world in various ways. In all cases, one way of understanding a specific community, society, or culture is by looking at the way its people express themselves through singing and dancing.

In Crete and all over Greece, music, dance and song coexist in unity. These are the basic elements of the Cretan g l é n d i . Cretan music, itself, is a rich and complex entity, encompassing a variety of elements (for instance, western musical idiom versus eastern musical idiom) and genres (for instance, church music, different song categories, dance music). In all cases, Cretan music "behaves" socially. To exist, it needs the Cretans. Without them, it cannot breathe. I cannot hear it without imagining all kinds of interaction among the participants: dancing-singing, eating-drinking, chatting-remaining silent. In addition, Cretan music is mostly vocal. I cannot think of it existing in isolation from the traditional Cretan proverb poetry.

Instant pictures
I do not accept Crete without l í r a , g l é n d i , without dance…Crete is m a n d i n á d a , companies and p a r é e s (groups of people) merry-making, k o u z o u l o ú s (crazy) people.

Yper-X magazine

T r a g o ú d i *(Song)*
Keep in mind, O groom, there never was a woman like her.

Sappho poem[124]

It is naturally Cretan to know how to perform proverbial couplets, m a n d i n á d e s . Cretans improvise mainly on these lyrics, occasionally on their melodies as well. For Cretans, even nowadays, m a n d i n á d e s are an integral part of their musical tradition. More important, they are the blood of their culture. They shape their identity powerfully and symbolically. To be considered a Cretan, one must know m a n d i n á d e s .

In the summer of 2001, while meeting and dining with members of the local Cultural Club at a taverna in Anoya, after an invitation, or rather after a challenge, I participated in composing a m a n d i n á d a as a response to flirting. Shy, as the only woman among men, I recalled and recited a very popular, well-known, and beloved couplet. It was appreciated. I, as the researcher, gained respect and became a capable part of the p a r é a : I am a worthy Cretan.

I compose m a n d i n á d e s based on conventional thematic, musical, and linguistic patterns. As a result, my poetry rhymes in distichs. It is a couplet that consists of two 15-syllable lines, often imbued with "gnomic" force. To be good, my m a n d i n á d e s must be rhythmically and metrically correct and possess poetic excellence and coherent meaning. To echo Anna Caraveli, their meaning, if sung, may be judged for its performing and social appropriateness. M a n d i n á d e s are not judged by themselves, but in relation to the entire g l é n d i , as well as to the larger social and historical context of the community.

M a n d i n á d e s are the lyrics that accompany most of the songs and dances performed at feasts in Crete. They may consist of praises and congratulations to the married couple and their parents and relatives, discussions about the feelings of joy and sorrow the situation created as well as broader philosophical discussions about the merits of a good life, of Cretan traditions, of honor. Sometimes, they may also address individual participants.

Thus, as Herzfeld noted in the 1993 m a n d i n á d a symposium in Anoya, as Cretan music in general is the product of social relationships, so is the Cretan m a n d i n á d a . The use of the Cretan dialect in it and its context, which represents the everyday Cretan life, give this art social dimension. The residents of Anoya, by performing m a n d i n á d e s in music and dance events, manage to transform these experiences into the living memories of their community. Thus, the purpose of m a n d i n á d e s performed at Cretan wedding feasts may be seen from both a communal and a performing aspect.

Whatever the case, m a n d i n á d e s emphasize our unique identity. Our language, our dialect, with its local variations, is distinct, different from town to town, from village to village. We recall our oral poetic traditions. Our couplets can be witty, bawdy, erotic, nostalgic, or insulting, and their exchange is often amiably competitive, a verbal duel. Throughout our m a n d i n á d e s , we depict the inevitable consequences of the joy, drama and traumas of love seen through time. Definitely our m a n d i n á d e s , as it often happens with all verbal and performing arts, constitute sources of historical knowledge.

For instance, the m a n d i n á d a "if with a needle you dig the Cretan soil, you'll find in it blood and bones of brave men (p a l i k á r i a) " contains the notion of p a l i k á r i , in other words, the human hero who always stands ready to defy death in order to obtain liberty. The people of Anoya strongly maintain this belief, and wedding feasts are one of the occasions where we can see it being vividly represented: good dancers are p a l i k á r i a as well. Thus, this ideal notion reaches its completion by being both sung and danced.

Sometimes, a male friend recites a couplet and then, after a musical intermission by the instrumentalists, a second person offers another couplet that echoes, elaborates on, answers or challenges the first one. In the village of Anoya, there is a lively tradition of m a n d i n á d a contests to which improvisatory skills are key. They call them k o n t a r o m a h í e s , which translates to "fights with poles." It is easy to compose the first line. The complementary, the rhyming one, the second, requires the best skills: It is those compositional strategies that are important devices the performers use to gain authority and recognition.

As in folklorist-ethnomusicologist Yildiray Erdener's case, Cretan m a n d i n á d a contests derive from the social interaction of everyday life. Erdener examines song and poetry in the process of creation and attempts to understand how the meaning of the song duel emerges from the social interaction between the performers and the audience.[125] His main question seems to be: "How do the competing minstrels establish, maintain, and rearrange meanings in the process of interaction?"[126]

For both Erdener and myself, some of the poetic meanings are directly expressed or implied in the song texts, whereas others are communicated indirectly through actions.[127] In a song dueling context, the people in the audience and the performers interact with each other on the basis of the meanings that words, music, and social behavior have for them.

In Crete, the process of learning how to recite poetry is identical to acquiring one's own native tongue. Like Erdener's minstrels, Cretans lay the foundation for composing poetry spontaneously after hearing thousands of poems in their childhood and their early years of adulthood from those around them. "By hearing, memorizing, and imitating the poems of others, a young minstrel absorbs the rhythm of singing and the rhythm of rhyming and constructs the basic rules of composing poetry."[128]

The m a n d i n á d a verses reveal shared images, ideas, concepts, and symbols. They are a culturally determined symbolic behavior and a form of artistic communication in which competing Cretans have the opportunity to demonstrate their creative competence in an artificially constructed game atmosphere. However, as in Erdener's case, during a song duel the performers do not mechanically reproduce the verses they have learnt by heart. "Because of the anticipation of people in the audience, a competing minstrel must incorporate an unexpected situation, topic or the presence of an unexpected individual into his poetry."[129]

Such a contest takes place on July 6, 2001, at the Iakinthia. There, several locals from Anoya get on the stage to improvise on lyrics devoted to the god that is born and raised in their mountains, Zeus. The audience approves, applauds, gossips and speaks with good or bad comments on the various m a n d i n á d e s. Some of the m a n d i n á d e s they remember and repeat; some they forget. Apart from this pre-arranged contest, many are also the occasions and the times they informally compose m a n d i n á d e s. Once in the central square (p l a t í a) of the village, men compete with m a n d i n á d e s for love. The news spread: the "Black Eagle"[130] "hits" with his "pole."

Crete was under Ottoman rule for almost 250 years. Many rebellions took place on the island during that period. The Cretans fought defiantly against their enemies. To express their resistance, they sang. Besides the m a n d i n á d e s, they performed r i z í t i k a to express their resistance. This repertory became a strong symbol of identity for all the people of Crete. Folk songs performed mostly by the inhabitants of the foothills (r í z e s means roots) of the villages in the province of Chania, especially those in the White Mountains (Lefka Ori or Madares), which are traditionally lands of the shepherds, the r i z í t i k a are mainly vocal and male. A soloist usually leads the performance and introduces each stanza. An informal choir repeats them. Moreover, r i z í t i k a are performed as responsories.

The r i z í t i k a have diverse lyrical functions and contexts. For example, they may refer both to death and the underworld, speak of friendship and love, evoke the preparation for political rebellion, or belong to the heroic song genre. The night of the Iakinthia, men from Chania perform r i z í t i k a. Later that same night, Vasilis Stavrakakis and Michalis Kallergis perform r i z í t i k a as well. At a wedding feast I attended in the summer of 1998 in the village of Anoya, I witnessed Chaniotes singing r i z í t i k a of the t á v l a (table). The relatives of the groom were from that region and they had to represent their musical traditions. In all cases, r i z í t i k a are an important part of the Cretan repertoire.

Cretans and Turks lived together and moved back and forth between Crete and the western coasts of Turkey (Asia Minor) for many years. Their dances and songs became intertwined. They gave birth to children that peacefully intermingled Greek and Turkish musical elements. Their songs speak of love and life, sweet and bitter, with all its games and fortunes. Tulia Magrini engaged in the thorough study of such a song genre, the t a b a c h a n i ó t i k a, an urban type of Cretan music played in years past mostly in coffee shops and restaurants in the harbor districts of Chania and Rethymnon.

The singing that accompanies this music is definitely of an oriental nature, with a specific and deliberate use of a certain nasal quality, and highly embellished. A m á n - a m á n is an exclamatory expression Cretan singers oftentimes use to denote, among other things, sorrow, pain, misfortune. Wonderful melodic improvisations (a m a n é d e s) can be based on the word a m á n. In synchronization with the singers, dancers may translate them into movement as well.

Vasilis Stavrakakis officially began his singing career by participating in a singing contest in the village of Anoya with a t a b a c h a n i ó t i k o song, where he won a prize. A capable Erotokritos, he fulfills all Cretan singing expectations. His melodies are sweet as honey, his tongue a nightingale. Aretousa desires to listen to his songs without even having met him. His melodies comfort us and his voice is our doctor. The strings of his m a n d o l í n o are singing birds; his songs contain power that can even cure the sick.[131]

Cretan song is full of passion and k a i m ó s (sorrow). Erotokritos suffers. He sings of the pain he is going through. But he stops getting burnt: the songs become water drops to put out his fire. Vasilis Stavrakakis sings for everything, white and black, life and death, and all the in-between. His audience f o u n d ó n e i (fires up) and a r p á : Cretan singers surrender to the performance.

M o u s i k í (Music)

Besides the r i z í t i k a that he sings solo, Stavrakakis also makes use of instruments in his performances. Ross Daly performs a wide range of string instruments and in general is in favor of mostly instrumental music. Laodikis feels more comfortable with percussion sounds. Here, we come closer to instruments other than the human voice. I merely unfold the structure and the components of the Cretan musical ensembles as I experience them in time and place. I look at the pictures of these events.

In all events I attended, when Cretan music was performed, men were almost exclusively the singers and the instrument players. Maria Fasoulaki, a friend and musician, is an exception. She has performed with Stavrakakis in summer and winter concerts and events. With his group, she sings and occasionally plays the d é f i (tambourine) and the bendír. That knowledge she owes to Laodikis, who usually sits next to her on stage.

Many women, most of them Ross Daly's students, perform all types of instruments with him and his group Labyrinth. The last compact disc he made with Stavrakakis featured a female singer (Spyridoula Toutoudaki) and a female f l o g é r a (fife) player (Rachael Cogan). In the concert Daly gave on the island of Rhodes, one of his young female students was on the Cretan l í r a (Kelly Thomas) and another (Angelina Tkatcheva) played the s a n t o ú r i (a type of dulcimer). In another concert Daly gave with Stavrakakis at the village of Houdetsi, the percussion players were two of Ross's female students on the bendírs.

Stavrakakis plays the m a n d o l í n o. At the performances I attended, his group also included the l í r a , the l a o ú t o, the t z o u r á s (long-necked lute), the bendír, and the t o u b e l é k i. When he performs with his group, the l í r a does not always have the first word. Stavrakakis is not against this instrument. He strongly emphasized that to me throughout our conversations. However, what he wants is through his music to give voice to other Cretan instruments

Artful "fire eaters"
at holy places;
Yiannis Markopoulos
at St. Minas Cathedral,
in Heraklion (above)
and Psaradonis
at St. Mamas

besides the l í r a . According to him, Cretan music has a very rich tradition. Many of its instruments have started disappearing because of the monotonous and continuous use of the l í r a .

Laodikis plays the t o u b e l é k i and the bendír when performing with Stavrakakis. That percussion element is not associated with the stereotypical Cretan musical ensembles, of the two l a o ú t a and the one l í r a , where the singer and the l í r a player are usually one and the same person. I heard mostly l a o ú t a and l í r e s at the weddings I attended in the village of Anoya and elsewhere. At the same time, at the Iakinthia, I saw Laodikis playing with Michalis Kallergis.

The present Cretan lute is the l a o ú t o , a larger, deeper-sounding version of the l a o ú t o found elsewhere in Greece. However, until quite recently, the most widespread Cretan l a o ú t o appears to have been the b o u l g a r í , a long-necked lute with a flat soundboard and a hole in the body, essentially very similar to, if not the same instrument as, the saz. Dr. Chris Williams points out[132] that, under the influence of the Greek l a o ú t o , the b o u l g a r í eventually died out. Stelios Foustalierakis played the instrument and we have many fine recordings of his playing style, which seems to owe more to the b o u z o ú k i than to the Turkish saz. Again, though well known through recordings, the b o u l g a r í is not encountered often as part of the traditional Cretan musical ensembles.

I admire Ross Daly's playing on the saz and I have heard him playing it often. In general, Daly experiments, performs and composes Cretan music, moving constantly among a great variety of instruments. Because of his rich training in western classical music, but also his many travels and educational experiences in other countries, Daly knows how to paint his performances with many sounds and musical contours.

The organizers of the Iakinthia chose to emphasize four traditional Cretan instruments. They invited four players onto the stage to perform short, solo, mostly instrumental pieces. Under the full moon, we listened to the m a n d o l í n o , the l í r a , the a s k o m a d o ú r a and the l a o ú t o . Following these four instruments, music associated with the region of Chania was performed on the violin with the accompaniment of the l a o ú t o .

Then we heard the Cretan bagpipe and the violin. Up to that time, I had never encountered the former live and as part of Cretan music and dance events. I recalled, however, my family's visit to the village of Voriza, where the same performer at the Iakinthia, Manolis Farangoulitakis, constructed a bagpipe that we currently own.[133] There, for the first time, I saw him performing it for us. In general, I usually find recorded music of bagpipes in stores and I see decorative instruments of that type hanging on the walls of restaurants that serve traditional Cretan food.[134] Regarding this, I recall Dr. Chris Williams's words, who hears instruments such as the bagpipes being imitated at the heart of Cretan music, particularly in certain l í r a techniques.

As for my fieldwork experience with the violin, I attended a daily seminar in the city of Chania in the summer of 2001. The closing event was a concert of Cretan violin music. The prevailing idea and message, in a sense, was that there is a live violin tradition on the island of Crete, a tradition that is associated more with its western part. Besides this information and due to my musical education and experiences, I am also aware of the presence of the violin on eastern parts of the island as well (for example, in the province of Sitia).

Today, what is established as the trademark of music on the island of Crete is the l í r a . The name itself, as a Greek noun, is female. The relationship between the l í r a player and this instrument is an erotic one. Vasilis Skoulas, the famous l í r a player from the village of Anoya, traces his music progress on his love relationship with this instrument. Psaradonis, another famous l í r a player from the same village, sees reflected on the l í r a the heart of all the people. Many Cretans talk about the l í r a as their greatest love, the instrument which, as Erotokritos's l a o ú t o , speaks to their souls and comforts their sorrows, the voice of Crete. "L í r a is my life," the l í r a player believes; "l í r a music is my life," the Cretan agrees. Lastly, for Cretans, Crete and l í r a are one and the same.

The sound coming out of l í r a — quite a little instrument — is unique, even though the music being played on it can be clearly recognizable as eastern Mediterranean with an obvious resemblance to other traditions belonging to the same geographical area. Upon closer observation, we notice a rather interesting detail concerning its playing.

The fingering technique of the left hand is rather different from that of the vast majority of string instruments. Instead of pressing the string with the tips of the fingers to produce different notes, the strings are touched lightly by the back of the nails, thus producing a very strong, sharp tone and facilitating a wide range of embellishments which considerably enrich the melodies being played.

In this respect, a resemblance to the Bulgarian g a d o ú l k a and the Turkish kementzé become more concrete, given that both of these instruments make use of the same technique. The only other region in the world where such a technique is used, according to my knowledge, is north India, especially Rajasthan, where instruments such as the saràngi are found.

Next to the l í r a player are usually two other men who play large lutes called l a o ú t a . These instruments — like most of the large-bodied lutes found in the eastern Mediterranean — are clearly related to the very old Arabian lute known as oud. Even the name l a o ú t o is quite obviously a derivative of the Arabic word al'oud, namely, "the wood." The l a o ú t a have four double strings, a very low tuning and are played with long plectrums, which, as I am told, are originally made from feathers from a type of buzzard commonly found in Crete. They also have moveable frets, indicating that non-tempered intervals must have been in use at some time, even though most contemporary renditions of Cretan music tend to limit themselves to the use of the western tempered scale.

Cretan music employs a modal structure. The concept of absolute pitch does not exist and a pitch designation does not indicate an absolute pitch, but rather an approximate pitch. A musician may tune her/his instrument higher or lower so that the range of the instrument more closely matches the range of her/his voice.

As Dr. Chris Williams maintains, improvisation in the Cretan context is firmly anchored to the social function of the music. The l í r a player or violinist must vary the melodies to maintain interest. A l í r a player who cannot improvise is simply *not* a musician. At the same time, the performer must conform to the very strict rules of the music so that the dance can be maintained in time and in step with the performer's playing.

I do not wish to examine l í r a players as entrepreneurs. I am interested in showing how Cretan music is a social phenomenon. Playing Cretan music is being part of a group. And when I say "group," I mean not only the instrumental and vocal ensemble, but the whole society and community that participates in the event. Viewed in this way, Cretan music brings forth a social idea and, by extension, a social ideal, in contrast to the western classical tradition where the performer's ego is usually at the center.[135]

The Cretan band itself is a flexible unit with a central figure. Vasilis Stavrakakis and Ross Daly are both leaders; they both act as the unifying centers of their groups. Occasionally, they even bring their groups together in concerts or recordings. Music talent is prevalent in Vasilis's family. Through oral traditional rules, Stavrakakis learned how to sing and play the m a n d o l í n o . Laodikis started tapping on a table and later became more serious about instrument playing. Until he came to Crete, music was not a profession for him. Stavrakakis and Laodikis did not attend music schools. For Vasilis, however, music is a profession. Laodikis, on the other hand, also looks for other ways to make a living.

Ross Daly first encountered the music of the West. He then decided to abandon this tradition and use the knowledge he gained to engage himself more seriously with sounds from other parts of the world and other musical traditions. He acknowledges his teachers, and learns through continuous traveling.

The internal conflict created by the desire, on the one hand, to follow his own personal creative inspiration while, on the other, not to betray the often rigid and uncompromising traditions to which he has dedicated his life, project Ross Daly into a totally new dimension of creative reality, where a quite different set of rules determine the nature of things.[136] It is in this spirit then that Daly adds sympathetic strings to the bow of his l í r a to achieve the lengthy, underlining drones that characterize mostly eastern music rather than Cretan.

Besides being a musician by profession, Ross Daly is a teacher as well. A great instrument player himself, he encourages young people to engage themselves seriously in the study of musical sound itself and to meet with instruments that know no borders and are able to communicate in languages considered foreign.

> Music is based on two things, initiation and inspiration. It is life, not a game. You are judged well, but you do not judge. I know well my work, and now I see what work my students also do.
>
> (...)
>
> My course is nothing more than being careful for having an open and clear line toward whatever is called inspiration, in other words, the voice of your heart. I am trying to function based on some ideas. I do not theorize, and I do not create "tights" to my stimuli. When the artist starts to think if she/he will create or not, then she/he is not an artist.
>
> Daly, quoted by M. Alexakis in *Ostria*

In the village of Anoya, I encountered situations where people, not musicians necessarily, grab instruments to play music. Young kids pick up the l í r a dreaming of reaching fame as have some of their local musicians. Teenagers, playing the m a n d o l í n o, perform k a n t á d e s (serenades) on the narrow streets of the village of Anoya. My grandfather, my family's Erotokritos, though not a musician, told me stories about the times he used to play the m a n d o l í n o to sing to the girls of his neighborhood.

Feasts connected to the life cycle, such as weddings, are a very demanding task for musicians. In the village of Anoya, for example, weddings are arenas where the musicians have to demonstrate their abilities by playing for several successive hours. In the wedding feasts I have participated, I listened to many comments referring to the power and the endurance of the musicians. For instance, many were proud of their musicians because they can "make" many weddings in a row by performing for consecutive hours and days, and in different villages.

C h o r ó s (Dance)

I speak about songs. I spend time with the musicians and the instruments they play. Time has come for the dancing to start:

> According to Euripides, the whole earth moves to an eternal dance. The source of the dance is the rhythmical movement of the human bodies that later on gets enriched with purposeful beats, so Euripides must have been right. The beauty of a dance is when it is danced well, demurely as well as rhythmically. A dance needs talent, harmonic movements, modesty, beat, fantasy and most importantly seriousness. The dancer cannot be good without a good l í r a player.
>
> *Yper-X* magazine[137]

Today, dances in Crete are of two categories, dragging (s y r t ó s) and leaping (p i d i h t ó s). Some dances may contain elements of both. The most popular form of these dances is the open circle with the regular handhold position. In this position and when facing the chain of dancers, we hold our arms in a shape that resembles the letter W. We may also have our arms outstretched, placed on the shoulders of the adjoining dancers. In all cases, like most Greek dances, the movement is counter-clockwise. We mainly perform five distinct types of dances. Other dances of local significance exist on our island as well. For instance, such are the "old, unknown" dances performed at the Iakinthia by both the women and the men from the province of Chania.[138]

One dance we often perform is the C h a n i ó t i s or C h a n i ó t i k o, a circular dance that is occasionally called s y r t ó s. Its name C h a n i ó t i k o s s y r t ó s indicates that it is a "shuffling" line dance originating from the city of Chania. When my brother is the leader of this dance, he performs various hand-slaps on thighs and heels and does numerous leaps, turns, and acrobatic maneuvers, while we move smoothly and evenly in line. According to the feeling of the music, we may move vigorously with sharp, quick steps or very smoothly, almost daintily. As a circle, we move slightly forward and then backward.

K a s t r i n ó s, H e r a k l i ó t i k o s K a s t r i n ó s, K a s t r i n ó s p i d i h t ó s,[139] M a l e v i z i ó t i s,[140] A n o y a-n ó s p i d i h t ó s[141]: All are names of quite similar leaping dances that offer the dancers the opportunity to execute difficult movements and various dancing maneuvers. Listening to or performing these dances excites me; they are my favorite ones. Usually, no lyrics accompany them, because the emphasis is on the dance itself. Sometimes, I perform them slowly and lazily (for instance, the K a s t r i n é s k o n d i l i é s) or more quickly and lively. Then my cousin, leading, does various leaping steps. He enjoys exhibiting his dancing abilities through acrobatic movements.

P e n d o z á l i s (meaning "five-stepped dance," "five dizzying steps," or "giddy five-step rhythm") is the dance associated with the island of Crete. According to the Cretan tradition, the p e n d o z á l i s was first performed in 1770 in Sfakia, during the Daskaloyiannis revolt against the Turks. The name of the dance derives from the fact that this revolt was the fifth during the period of the Turkish domination of Crete (1669-1898). I consciously chose to compare my present writings to this dance, which is springy and energetic. They both work up to a great speed. We dance the p e n d o z á l i s in a line in which the participants grasp one another's shoulders and perform leaping steps. Moving with increasing speed, we perform intricate steps on the spot. Frequently the dance breaks up into smaller groups, with dancers bouncing with vitality while in line, and the leader elaborating on the basic steps and leaping in the air.

S i g a n ó s (slow dance) is another dragging dance, usually followed by the leaping p e n d o z á l i s. Characterized by the singing of m a n d i n á d e s, especially at weddings, it is the first dance that the bride and the groom dance. The singers praise the newly married couple (the bride in particular) by singing m a n d i n á d e s composed for the wedding feast. Among various m a n d i n á d e s is the following: "Today a wedding is taking place at a nice garden, today the mother is being separated from her daughter."

Finally, we also dance the s o ú s t a (spring), a pair dance with a man and woman facing each other. This type of dance has a love motif. The dancers perform a number of variations to the basic steps, sometimes facing each other, sometimes revolving around one another. In some of the events I attended, instead of the s o ú s t a, we danced the b á l o s (Greek folk dance, mainly performed on the islands by couples). It does not have a springy character, but it definitely shares the same meaning as the s o ú s t a does.

When we refer to the feasting experience of dance events, we talk about the aforementioned dances as "our" dances. When dancing, both women and men must be careful how they move and what they say. Everyone must know what her/his position in the dance is; at the same time, everyone must eat, drink and dance. In other words, everyone must participate in the dance event as a whole. As I intentionally and constantly emphasize throughout my writings, in Crete, dance is not only the steps, it is not only the dancer that matters; it is the music and the musicians, the song and the singer, everybody who dances or does not dance, the history of the whole place, its past, its culture and its traditions.

For most of the dances we perform at feasts, especially when they take place in villages such as the village of Anoya, we respect and, thus, follow the traditional ritual-protocol with the open circle and the order of participation according to gender and age ranking within the family and the community: elderly men, younger men, elderly women, younger women, and then children. The dances that do not follow the traditional ritual-protocol take

Two performers,
three Cretan
folk instruments:
Yiannis Romboyiannakis
on the askomadoúra (above)
and the daoúli (right),
and Psaroyiorgis on the laoúto

place later at night or in "bigger" cities. In Anoya, for instance, older persons enter the dance first, and then younger ones, men first and then women: the intermingling of genders and ages establishes and fulfills the concept of "community."

While sitting outside the circle of dancers, I observe, drink, and talk with other people. We all are an integral part of the dance event: We watch and judge who is a good dancer. Sometimes, we applaud the good dancing figures and give the impression that the important thing celebrated is not the specific event, but the dance itself. Men next to me enthusiastically may shout: "nice, opa-opa I'm saying!" ("o r é o s, ó p a - ó p a l é o !"), or whistle.

My friends from Anoya may comment negatively on the people coming from the town, Heraklion, who, according to them, prefer "foreign" dances instead of the Cretan ones. They recognize Cretan dances as a living history of their place refusing to "pollute" their dancing repertoire with "modern dancing." According to them, women should not shake their chests and hips while dancing because these are "immoral" movements. Even men should keep a balance while performing acrobatic dancing figures, otherwise they become "clowns" and K a r a g i ó z i d e s.

However, in Crete, we all consider good dancers those who are careful enough to keep their bodies dignified and upright. Because most of our dances are done in a circular chain formation, arm gestures are practically excluded. When we lead, then we may leave the chain and dance individually. It is then that my brother will extend his arms, whereas my sister with place them around, hugging, almost squeezing her waist.

While dancing, our facial expression is important. We try to be happy and serious at the same time. Happy because we are dancing, we are enjoying rhythmical, group moving, we are celebrating a wedding event, or another occasion, but also serious because there are so many people out there watching us, because we know well we are going to be judged by the whole community for our performances, and because, in the end, it is our dancing tradition that we must represent in the best way.

Most of our dancing consists of open, single curved lines or serpentines. Progressive step movements move directly over the advancing foot. Overall, the quality of our movements is clipped and nervous with a smoothness primarily attributable to the fact that our feet are kept close to the ground. There is variation between slow and quick steps, with an emphasis on a gradual increase in speed. The great diversity of rhythms and their combinations may result in many types of steps and maneuvers, as outlined by Mary Ellen Makreas in *Cretan Dance: The Meaning of Kéfi and Figoúres*.

When I am the lead dancer, I can execute complicated steps consisting of whirls, turns and lively jumps. My movement is toward the right: I am leading all dancers around a ground pattern best described as half-moon-like. When my male cousin leads, he is particularly encouraged and expected, as the head of the line, to indulge in various hand slaps, slaps on thighs and heels, in addition to numerous leaps, turns and acrobatic movements. As it is usually the case in many Cretan villages, it is the first dancer who pays for the dance. They "order the dance" and the song they prefer. Thus, they also have to start the dance. Their relatives and friends are among the first to participate.

People who join the dance later should not become leaders: This is considered rude. When the leading position has been offered, my friends are obligated to assume the position at the head of the line, even briefly, and even if they cannot execute f i g o ú r e s (acrobatic embellishing steps). After this, they retire to the rear of the line. Sometimes, they pass their position to the person immediately to their left: As the lead dancers, they step in front of the person dancing on their left. They take the left hand of this person while moving to the left and thereby maintain their presence at the front of the line. This is especially the case when my brother and male cousin serve as the catalyst for each other's acrobatic maneuvers.

Because most Cretan dances at wedding feasts in Anoya are danced in an open circle, usually it is the first dancer who takes the initiative. In most of the dance events I attended, the first dancer was a man who chose and ordered the song which was going to be danced, who controlled the movement of the circle, and who was free to do whatever he wanted while dancing. In a way, he owned the dance, he kept the honorable position in it and everybody was looking at him.

The people of Anoya believe that the improvisation and generally the behavior of the first dancer show his personality, which is being critiqued by the whole village. Consequently, while the Cretan circle dance may look like a group dance, it is mostly a dance performed by the first dancer. The first dancer expresses his individuality in dancing, while the rest of the dancers convey the communal spirit. Both the first dancer and the rest of the dancers "talk" through dancing about social embodiment. The dancer has to dance throughout the whole dance, because his abilities may also be judged in relation to the length of time.

Good dancers can also improvise. In Anoya, the position at the head of the line of dancers is considered the most important, because the person (usually male) who orders the song has the privilege of dancing first. The first dancer leads not only literally, by drawing the other dancers with his body; it is also the first dancer's prerogative to set the tempo and the steps and to execute improvisations. The first dancer is, thus, set apart from the other dancers for the watching public, "she/he" is the object of attention and of commentary.[142]

Cretan dance, the actual steps of the dancers, is traditionally a largely improvised art, with the ability to vary and invent steps being prized. In the words of Dr. Chris Williams: "With dancers and musicians both striving for expression within a closely defined form, a very interesting process takes place and its historical evolution can still be delineated in the present form of some older dances."

In the wedding feasts, the bride and the groom must dance in public and in an open circle with all their relatives in order for the event of their marriage to be established. The bride and the groom usually dance in the first positions in order to honor everybody for coming to their wedding. The dance of the bride and the groom has a symbolic meaning; it establishes the unification of a woman and a man, it is the dance for the bride and the groom, the male and the female entity.

Girls and women in Anoya regard a dance event as a valued break in their daily routine, as a chance to get out of the house and to socialize with friends. A woman in Anoya is also expected to please the spectators by dancing in a particular manner. The square, where most of the dance events I attended took place, is a public space, and as such is controlled by male-defined conventions. Thus, when women join the dances that take place at the conclusion of a wedding ceremony, they do so with conspicuously chaste steps, avoiding the acrobatics of the young males.

Women in the village of Anoya join the dances late in the evening. Their dance is differentiated from that of men. It is best described as being both simple and dignified. They should control their movements and also follow the men's steps and dancing f i g o ú r e s, especially in dances performed in pairs. In general, women, while dancing, typify a much smoother movement with very little elevation, even in hopping steps which are performed with a slide. The female torso tends to be held relatively still with most movement occurring from the hips and downwards. This hip action should be slight and not emphasized.

Women of all ages can and do get to dance, although with varying degrees of skill and grace. Young girls tend to add more swerves and bounces than do young adult women. The foot movements of older women are differentiated from those of younger generations as far as style is concerned. Young women tend to take larger steps than older women do. Married women may also join in on fast-tempo dances and perform with verve and liveliness, but generally, as these women get older, their style of dancing is expected to become more serious and less playful. Older women tend to use walking, rather than springing steps, when they dance.

The male dancers, as Herzfeld observes[143], try to self-consciously symbolize the old devil-may-care Crete of the wars against the Ottomans. They usually dance in the first position, a fact that gives them the freedom to perform improvisational movements whenever the dance allows them to do so. Older men move with slower movements, that seem to be simple but are, in fact, very thoughtful and wise.

In lively dances, men give themselves to dancing. They jump in the air, they perform agile leaps, trying to show their l e v e n d i á (gallantry) and pride and that they do not fear anything and anybody who threatens them and their village. They improvise and change positions. They feel independent and free because they can dance. The wildness their dance might exhibit is a sweet one: self-protection against any misfortune.

Male Cretan dancing in Anoya is sometimes executed with new embellishments that do not, however, disrupt the basic steps of the other dancers. While dancing, men hold hands with each other. People who watch the male dances, instead of noticing what men do, focus their attention on *how* they perform. In Anoya, the agile male dancing also implies aggressive masculinity.[144]

Basically, the technique that attracts attention in Cretan male dancing in Anoya is the utilization of acrobatics. This is the demonstration of strength and agility. The virtuosity is reflected in their steps, jumps, springs, turns and the improvisation of complicated steps, which are performed within the confines of the melody. The remaining dancers perform steps until their turn comes to take the lead.

Men in Anoya usually wear black or dark clothes. Moreover, they still nowadays wear the traditional Cretan boots (s t i v á n i a) and the typical Cretan scarf (s a r í k i), which is put around their necks and not upon their heads (as is normally done), and which at wedding events is not black, but white. Most of them carry knives in their pockets or on their waists.

The male
independence
"flight" (top)
and the dancing
circle of life

The whole attire of the male is still worn by older and younger men in present-day Anoya and is another means of speaking through dancing at wedding feasts. That is usually a plain dark shirt and a v r á k a . The pants of the v r á k a are exaggerated breeches with a fullness of fabric that somewhat resembles a tail. Stuffing the shirt in the v r á k a adds weight and makes for a nice swing while dancing. In general, this regional dress comes into play while the dancers are performing.

The father of the bride maintains the first position in dancing for a long period. His steps are, because of his age, heavy. He may wave a handkerchief with his right hand. His arms are in an extended position. The emphasis is on his steps. He dances full of joy and pride for the marriage of his child. He invites others to come and join the dance, sharing this way in his joy.

Cretans may dance for hours. Often their dances take the form of a competition for stamina and bravery. These thoughts and observations are also related to the notion of tradition and preservation of the heroic past that has made Crete and its civilization known all over the world. And this past comes into life through Cretan dancing.

Usually, before each dance takes place in Cretan feasts, the person who expects to lead it "throws" money to the musicians. One of the musicians, the leader of the group, the player of the l í r a , picks up this money. This practice is not considered payment. It is called "gifting money" for "ordering a dance." Usually only men are culturally allowed to do that. And every man has to do it in order to honor his name, his family, his clan.

On September 1, 2001, at a friend's wedding in the village of Anoya, I ordered a C h a n i ó t i s and a M a l e v i z i ó t i s for my p a r é a . The l í r a player, Vasilis Skoulas, accepted my dollar bills. The feast took place inside his club, Delina, after a wedding ceremony at Saint Hyacinth's church. Vasilis knew that, in a few days, I would depart for the United States. Touched by my request, he immediately executed it, although many other orders preceded it. At the wedding of Theseus and Ariadne, on July 14, 2001, male members of the Cultural Club of Anoya requested specific dances to honor my sister, her friend and me.

In the above examples, a relationship of dialogue and communication exists between the dancers and the musicians. Men "order" favorite songs they want to dance to and whose lyrics are meaningful to them. This way, they try to give to their emotions an expression through not only dancing, but also singing. While dancing, they move their heads to the tunes and rhythms. They sing along with the musicians; they feel the music and pay attention to the lyrics of the songs.

I thus agree with the folk song scholar Samuel Baud-Bovy, who states that the researcher of the Greek dance should not only observe the dance per se, but also the lyrics of the songs that accompany the dancing melodies. This way, the ethnographer of dance may draw conclusions about the dances themselves. As a result, dance is not separated from music and song in the Greek folk tradition. Rather, it should be studied as part of a triad, which is music, song, and dance.

Wallet pictures

In July 2001, I picked up Ross Daly from his home at Houdetsi. We drove to Katalagari, a village nearby. We sat at a table at the edge of the balcony of a new restaurant called Logari. The view was wonderful: Under the moonlight in the dark blue sky, villages seemed to light up like stars. In the winter, the owner of this restaurant uses its basement as a boiler room to make r a k í . We tasted excellent food: grape leaves and feta cheese p í t a (pie), rooster and handmade macaroni cooked with red sauce and onions (s t i f á d o), chickpeas with garlic and tomato in the oven, to name a few. With a glass of delicious fresh red wine, I listened to Daly play and improvise on his l í r a . His performance was part of a night devoted to the promotion and advertising of this local restaurant.

Musicians with their groups perform at restaurants all over Crete. Such places serve traditional Cretan cuisine. The prerecorded background music is always Cretan. Day by day, more restaurants of this type appear in villages and areas outside the cities. One is Anaktoro, for example, in the village of Panayia (Virgin Mary), 45 kilometers south of Heraklion.

Erofili is the name of the club Stavrakakis opened in Heraklion. There, he performed Cretan music. He sang parts from *E r o t ó k r i t o s* , some under Ross Daly's instrumentation. He is not the only one. Almost all Cretan singers include 'E r o t ó k r i t o s ' in their repertories. Cretans often recite pieces from this masterpiece. We hear it from our grandmothers too.

Slide show

Song, music and dance: People in k é f i interact with each other — musicians, singers, dancers, audience, a whole community.

Why "music?" Ross Daly recalls a Persian legend that speaks of music as something that can lead our soul somewhere. Etymologically from the Greek language, music á g e i t i n p s i c h í ; in English translation, music "leads the soul"; thus, the Greek word p s i c h a g o g í a usually, though not accurately, is translated into English as "entertainment." Quoted in an article by Manolis Alexakis in *Ostria*, Daly illustrates further: "My music has no message. If somebody wants to collect, gather a message from it, she/he is free. What I, myself, am trying to do with my music is to exceed my personal world and self. I expect to enter into another dimension where the borders for myself and the audience have fallen and have become much less clarified".

Music and dance in Crete may lead to ecstasy. In addition, Cretan music is usually played loud: intensive sounds, loud speakers, microphones, technical support, tension. Vasilis performed with his brother Nikiforos at the village of Pyrgos over the summer of 2000. Across the restaurant from us, another l í r a player (Vangelis Zervakis) performed that same night, at the same time. Michael Herzfeld would call it a "competition."[145]

Negatives

1. "We think that there is one that gives something (musician) and others that accept (audience). Everyone deposits her/his energy in this action and the fact is the music, not the musician. Further, the musician is a human being, a man (ánthropos) that grasps, takes all this energy, and transforms it into music."

2. "As Heraclitus said, everything exists on its course toward its opposite, meaning that we will always have a peak, a decline, and this is a natural, unavoidable, inescapable cycle. Decline means that human beings miss their true, real goals. If a musician works for music because of a need to serve human beings that will correctly guide her/him. Thus, it is very important for the human being to speculate with great attention and concentration (I am not saying with lots of thought). If you reach that space, then things come out front by themselves"

Daly, quoted by M. Alexakis in *Ostria*

End of the show

The schoolmaster grasped the bow, bent over the lyre, and became one with it. The bow danced over the three strings, the little bells tinkled, the dark yard filled with bright laughter, as if it were a schoolyard in which the children were playing and chasing one another during recess. Or as if birds in a leafy poplar were awaking at dawn and rejoicing in the sunlight.

The fiddle bow leaped, laughed, danced, and the hearts of the old captains became children, birds, gurgling springs. The grandchildren and daughters-in-law moved nearer, the men and maids sat down on the ground together. And in spite of the falling rain, they listened.

(…)

But slowly the voice of the lyre altered. It became wild and furious. The bells on the bow rattled like those on the neck of a trained hawk as it shoots upward in search of prey. Those were men's voices that rang out from the strings. The captains thought of their youth, of war, of the groaning men who lay dying, of the women mourning, of the horses whinnying and standing on the field, bloodstained and riderless. "Give me back my youth or be still, schoolmaster!" Captain Mandakas almost cried aloud. But already the lyre had again changed its tune; it was soft and lulling and the old men listened with happy smiles.

The sound, through the moist air, was like a distant humming of bees, or the murmur of a deep stream. The sound was like a woman's love dirge far beyond the mountains, on the shore of the foaming sea. Or was it the sea itself, lapping at the shore and moaning? Or was it yet more mysterious, more magical voice from beyond life, from the other bank, sweetly and sadly and lovingly feeling souls from the flesh? Was it perhaps God Himself, hidden in the moist darkness of the night, Who was calling and raising up to Him with gentle allurement His eternal beloved, the soul of man?

The schoolmaster played as one possessed, so that the fiddle bow seemed to strike sparks. Deeper and deeper he was lost in the darkness. It was as if the lyre, alone and erect under the lemon tree, were intoning a funeral hymn. But its wailing was also a seductive call.

A deep, broad smile overspread the old grandfather's lips. His flying, light body rose in one sweep from the lemon tree further into the air, and now lay like a cloud above the house. Soon it would, by a soft transformation, become a cloud, falling as rain to the ground, to nourish the young shoots.

That is death, the grandfather felt deep down in himself, that is Paradise. I am going to Paradise. I am there, already. Greetings, Oh my God!

Kazantzakis, *Freedom or Death*

"Esthitikí (aesthetics)? Where did you find this word?" my friend and musician Dimitris Kontoyiannis asked me when, in the summer of 2001, I met with him, after many years, at a concert he gave in the village of Anoya.[146] "It is nothing complex," I replied. "What I look at is specific principles of beauty, maybe of local character, that guide the creation and assessment of music and dance performances on the island of Crete. It is simple; I just take pictures of Cretan music and dance events and later frame them." What I missed teaching him was the fourth step, the strenuous task in-between: the development of the film.

You have observed and participated in Theseus and Ariadne's wedding. By now, the labyrinths sound very familiar to you. But we are not done yet. We have more mythologies and mysteries to unfold. Third step: present step.

step 4

Unraveling

STEP 4: UNRAVELING

*O*n the mountain of Psiloritis, Zorba the Greek flirts with a young woman, Erofili. In a dialogue on relativism, they speak about identity, local and non-local, traditional, national and ethnic. They agree that the identity of the labyrinths is shaped by socio-cultural ideas. But who are they? Where do they come from? Let's start spinning!

Sea Songs 2001

We are in the medieval castle of Rhodes. Next to us, on the Mediterranean, across southwest Turkey, is the port of Rhodes. Near one of its towers, we sit on amphitheatric seat-steps. On the back of the stage, facing us, a real boat sails in place: several groups perform sea songs, among them, Ross Daly and his group. On August 6 and 7, I attend two consecutive nights of concerts, part of a second multinational music festival.

The first night fills up with sounds from Sweden, Tunisia, and Bulgaria. For the first time, I encounter sounds of instruments that belong to the Swedish Nyckelharpa Orchestra. I am familiar with the qanún (a kind of psaltery), the violin, and the o ú t i (oud). With the group Ambar, Lamia Bedioui performs Arabic tunes and melodies that are familiar to my ears. The Bulgarian sounds of the gadoúlka (Bulgarian l í r a), the gáida (bagpipes), the accordion and the d a o ú l i (cylindrical, double-headed drum) speak to the audience in "broken" Greek.

The next day, Ross Daly and his group Labyrinth represent Greece. We hear Cretan l í r a s , saz, rabá b , bendír, flute and s a n t o ú r i (type of dulcimer). The pieces performed are Ottoman classical, Armenian, Cretan-based and inspired. A band called Toud 'Sames from France follows with songs, wooden flutes, bombard, fretless bass and percussions. The closing is miraculous: under Daly's magical guidance, the musical traditions of Tunisia, Bulgaria, France, Greece and its neighboring cultures come into one interplay.

Ross Daly is a capable captain. With music, he takes us to our homes and to foreign lands. Waves of sounds reach our ears and become one — a sea song.

Psiloritis

The words you read are ethnographic: honest, true, authentic. The words are mine. Actions here resemble Psiloritis, a mountainous area surrounded by mythologies, ancient and contemporary. In the past, these mythologies functioned as ideas, ideals, sources of inspiration, which gave birth to music and dance performances. They also become capable vehicles for the rebirth of these performances. Naturally, Hyacinth and Zeus are their relatives. Because we are still dancing in the labyrinths, these mythologies socialize with the Minotaurs as well. Erofili is their first cousin: All together they travel with Odysseus.

What the people of Crete are — or want to be — cannot be "inauthentic." We find the power that shapes Cretan music and dance performances among Cretans themselves. We immediately sense how great and persuasive this power is. To feel Cretan music, to perform it with its rules, we become friends with Zeus and Hyacinth. To communicate with them, we learn the languages they speak. Finally, we accept to dance in their labyrinths, where, among others, we attest to the wedding of Theseus and Ariadne, past and present, mythological and real.[147]

At this point, significant is Martin Stokes's book *Ethnicity, Identity and Music: The Musical Construction of Place*. Stokes starts his writings with an emphasis on the relationship between music and anthropology, as do I. For Stokes, music is not just a thing that happens "in" society. A society, Stokes argues, might also be usefully conceived as something that happens "in music." His writings make a powerful argument, which, among other things, breaches the theoretical divide between the study of music and the study of society.[148]

An idea prevalent in Stokes's book is that music informs our sense of place. That is also the case with music performed on the island of Crete. Here I emphasize this relationship between music and place when I talk more specifically about the concept of locality in relation, always, to music. Music is social because it provides a means by which people recognize identities and places, as well as the boundaries that separate them. In this sense, Cretan music becomes "our" music. The word "ours," however, has a different meaning for Cretans that come from different parts of the island.

The roots of songs are found in mountainous soil, in the r i z í t i k a . Songs nurtured in the region of Chania are the t a b a c h a n i ó t i k a . M a n d i n á d e s are born in the same place with Zeus — Psiloritis. Contemporary Kourites, the people of Anoya, cherish their performers. Lyrics that speak of life in Crete, in all times, are improvised, genuine and true. Cretan songs are the voice of Crete.

The l í r a speaks the truest Cretan language ever. "Our" instrument, the Cretan l í r a , is a symbol of "our" musical folklore. The l í r a stands for Crete, and brings back memories of the glorious, classical ancient Greek past. The l í r a music *is* Cretan music.

The dance of the Kourites to cover Zeus's crying and Sappho's dancers is reborn in the p i d i h t ó s dance of Anoya and the wedding bridal dance. Labyrinthine movements are leaping steps, improvised movements. Cretan dances are circular, symbolizing the circle of life, or, as expressed in a m a n d i n á d a : "As long as Crete is singing songs and the dancing is never-ending, fearlessly flying like the eagle, it will be forever living."

Songs, music and dance in Crete are authentic evidence of the continuity of Crete's popular tradition and rhythm. In villages such as Anoya, I observe "authentic" life. I can "taste" real Cretan music and dances in lands where Minotaurs-l í r a players come from. Cretan people are honest in their performances.

"Not ours" is "foreign," and therefore not authentic to our performances. We Cretans defend and preserve our music and dance culture in order to excel. We decide what is "ours" and what is not. If you want to participate in our music and dance, you have to understand us. We ask you to think relatively and accept what we believe, that is, what we know to be "our" truth. We are islanders and we have suffered much throughout history. We cultivate our uniqueness and resist intruders daily.

Is anything "authentic?" I try to respect everything. In my writings, I apply "measure" as much as possible, the ancient Greek value:[149] I balance the love for my country, my culture, so that my passion does not harm anyone else. Am I a dreamer?

Authenticity in Cretan performances relates to and is closely interlinked with notions of tradition and identity. Here, we learn a step of a dance that Cretans call "theirs." Next, we are about to meet Erofili, a lead dancer, whom we particularly favor.

"We have to protect the background and be strong because our ancestors fought for their rights. Through words and feelings in our performances, we show our history. We claim land through song. You can change the song, but not the land."[150]

Erofili

> Man needs to have strong shoulders to hold
> Everything the older with pain have left behind.
> Mandináda

Crete is a geographical part of Greece that still supports and embellishes its traditional identity.[151] Since antiquity, our people managed to leave their own traces in Greece, architecturally as well as educationally.[152]

Erofili learned how to dance by holding hands with her grandmother at Cretan wedding feasts. When she went to school, she practiced Cretan dances, at school feasts and national holiday events. Outside school, she also joined folkloric dancing groups. In all cases, her steps were not a mere matter of mimicry or the product of past inspiration.

Erofili thinks of herself as a bearer of tradition: she connects the past with the present through her dancing. Consciously or not, she becomes living proof of Cretan traditions. Through music and dance, all her feelings (joy, sorrow and love), historical references and particular way of life find their expression.

Once upon a time, I showed Erofili's picture to someone who disagreed with the way my photographic lens captured her dancing. I dared to claim continuation: I see tradition as a common thread between past, present and future time. The roots of the word help me: tradition, from the Latin verb *tradire* (to deliver).

I do not accept that Erofili is dead. She is a living, breathing, existing part of the picture. She is still on the spot. "The gunfire of Laden, my girl, you have and made my heart Manhattan."[153] She goes on in history; her repertory gets enriched; she transforms emotions to eternal remembrances. She, a picture herself, becomes an experienced photographer. Her pictures talk, in all colors, in black and white.

Rebel, boisterous Psiloritis

With my sister and our four female first cousins from my father's side, on a hot night in August 2001, we dine at a fish restaurant by the Heraklion port. We are all in good spirits and enjoy our reunion. I start reciting a m a n d i n á d a that I make up to fit the occasion. My cousins compete to complete it in the best, most proper way. On white paper napkins, with a black pen, I write our poetry. I carry with me to the United States dozens of m a n d i n á d e s : "We are like the gorge's opposing sides: They never become one, but they always face each other."

Erofili grows up by drinking milk — like Zeus — from Amalthea. She caresses Ariadne as if she were her mother. As we can see on the wall paintings at the palace of Knossos and as part of her school training, Erofili dances on the back of Amalthea to please queen Ariadne. In November 2001, in Venerato, she attends the music and dance revival of Saint George the M e t h i s t í s .

Cretans always remember and honor Erofili. Next to *E r o t ó k r i t o s* , she becomes a "classical" work of the Cretan literary school. Cretan girls take her name or that of Aretousa, *E r o t ó k r i t o s* 's heroine. Erofili also gives her name to Stavrakakis's club in Heraklion. Other clubs and restaurants seem to prefer her as well. In the name of Erofili, Cretans baptize them Anaktoro, Embolo, Erganos, Lykastos, Logari, Raeti, Xatheri. They all serve Cretan food and play Cretan music.

Stavrakakis is not the only one to include parts of Erofili's cousin, *E r o t o k r i t o s* , in his singing repertory. Cretans memorize and recite his extensive deeds. Ross Daly and Dr. Chris Williams are amazed when, on the western coast of Turkey, they encounter people who moved there from Crete in the 1920s, after the exchange of populations. These Turkish-Cretans still remember parts of *E r o t ó k r i t o s* and weep when singing.[154]

> Usually tradition is a term that refers to the past; "faithful to tradition" refers to someone that reproduces and copies things from the past. Unfortunately, we do not emphasize the creative aspect of tradition. Tradition is nothing else than a way of life where each act has such a balanced relationship with the past, the present and the future, so that it goes over the determinations of time and even place. This way we forget the sterile notions of folklore and we reach closer to an essence of a suggestion to life that substantially unites people into creation.[155]

With these words, Ross Daly describes his own, unique relationship with Erofili. For him, all music is traditional because it "walks" through time and has a past, present and future. "All music is traditional because it is creative, it lives," he tells me. Though Daly cannot by definition say that he has "a" tradition, he performs on a very traditional instrument, the Cretan l í r a . For him, music traditions are similar in the way they perceive the relationship between tradition and originality.

In my interview with Vasilis Stavrakakis, he talks about the preservation of music instruments that we rarely find in today's Cretan music. He believes that Cretan traditional music blossoms again, especially today, and expands to other parts of the world, in and out of Greece. More often, Cretan artists play Cretan music as part of a game that aims to save "a world that is getting lost."

I see Cretans treat Erofili as a queen. In her, they see a great communicative force and a power that helps them bridge space across time. With her help, their histories connect. Cretans speak in their music and dance performances in chosen, traditional languages.[156] Erofili nourishes their identity[157] and identifies with their notions of authenticity. One day, the eternally young woman decides to climb up to the mountain of Psiloritis. There she meets with Zorba the Greek.

Zorba the Greek

Erofili meets Zorba somewhere on Psiloritis, near the cave where Zeus was born. It is sunny and there are no clouds in the sky. Zorba looks like a demigod to her. She seems to like Zorba, but hesitates. First, she wants to learn more about him, his cultural background, his family, his beliefs. She interrogates him, seeking answers to her questions.

Zorba leaves his abrupt manners aside. With a soft, philosophically relativistic tone in his voice, he encourages Erofili and advises her not to be so worried, but to learn to accept people as they are. He reminds her of the labyrinths and how identity is shaped by socio-cultural ideas. Expounding on Henry Glassie's idea, Zorba goes on to say that for him, there is hardly any ethnic tradition; instead, over the years, this has been replaced by regional traditions that invariably contain influences from other regions as well.

Zorba continues: "I was born a long time ago. My identity is time oriented. It grows up like a child. It is nurtured with memories and habits of the past, approaches and performs in the present by socially and culturally selected behaviors. Simultaneously, it also builds a future by making use of both past and present idioms. To give you a concrete example, an illustration, our conversation takes place now, at a specific point in time. This is what people who will read one of its many possible transcriptions and translations should keep in mind. At the same time, what we say now is not merely what was in our hearts and minds when we were born or grew up." Erofili is even more confused now. At the same time, she is more in love with Zorba. Why do complicated and hard tasks always attract her? Why can't she take the easy road? She yearns to listen to him more. She sits on a stone, on the plains of Psiloritis, prepares mountain tea on a small wood fire and serves Zorba and herself a cup; she is all ears.

"I do not wish to perceive myself as part of the so-called Greek classical heritage that folklorists adopt and use as a path to European identity. Viewed from many aspects, my national identity is ambiguous."

"Although I definitely feel Greek, I cannot identify myself with all the characteristics that Greece shares with the so-called West as part of a European geographical and political entity. For example, I guess my ability to dance with another man in a spirit of uninhibited camaraderie — throwing pain and care into a passionate dance — is something lost to Europeans. Through dancing, I express ecstasy, sure of my manhood.[158] My father nurtured me based not on the western dream of organizing and governing a renewed Byzantine Empire. Instead, he urged me to favor and listen mostly to my heart, rejecting the mind."

"I have many brothers and sisters. One of them is Buddha.[159] With his own words, he investigates two forms of human dignity — the oriental and the western — as everyone and everything in his life is overwhelmed by an inexorably destructive fate. He questions much: What is Greekness? How can we be patient? How can Greece have a nationalism rooted both in her ancient heritage and in her contemporary reality? How, at a time when the entire world seems to have lost its humanity, can we act humanely? What does being human mean? I listen to my brother's ideas and decide to act in a way that is self-validating and therefore unaffected by fate's destructiveness. This is my secret; this is, I believe, what has glorified Greece and enabled her to survive."[160]

Erofili takes her time to meditate on Zorba's words. Now, it is her turn to talk. She is a bit overwhelmed. She takes a deep breath, looks Zorba in the eyes and starts her monologue.

"Dear Zorba, I do not wish to put borders between the East and the West. For me, names are only external, related to prejudices and other ideas. What I see is that, deep inside, we are all humans."[161]

"As you may already know, long ago, through a theatrical play, my father gave birth to me.[162] Having a strong Cretan personality himself, through me, he wished to remind the Cretan and Greek people who they are. With the very first words he wrote, he made me resemble the prominent Cretan school of painting of sacred icons (a y i o g r a f í a). Simultaneously, he also praised Crete through a hymn, with references to Crete's Minoan past. In addition, he often asked me to recall the glorious ancient Greek past, from which he believed we originate."

"In a sense, my father partially shaped what he thought the Cretan identity is or should be. Giving to his work my name and letting my voice sound throughout his drama, he empowered the female presence. His main ideas I also share and identify with. After all, he was my father. As he used to say, 'Fame is vain, and the good fortune doesn't last for long, because of fate's games'.[163] Freedom is our greatest virtue, and tyranny our worst enemy. More than anything, we should feel and be free to love what we want."

"Interestingly, however, looking into diaries and other accounts from my father's life, I can see that the main source of inspiration that gave birth to me is the Italian tragedy *Orbecche*, by Giambattista Giraldi, in 1543,[164] whereas my father himself seemed to be of Asia Minor descent.[165] Thus, my father's identity and, by extension, my identity — though we both definitely feel strongly Cretan — are shaped by various other idioms than the Cretan one."

"My father managed to form a lingual instrument of the Cretan literature by denying the use of the mixed language form of the middle- and later-Byzantine tradition of the early Cretan production.[166] Thus, the language he taught me to speak is the everyday Cretan dialect, the language my father himself spoke, a mixture of western and eastern elements on the island of Crete."

"You may be wondering why I keep talking about my father. Well, as a faithful Cretan daughter, I respect and love him. At the same time, I view his whole life as perfectly fitting with the central dilemma and question of our current

"Ah! If only I were an eagle, to admire the whole of Crete from an airy height!" — Nikos Kazantzakis's wistful cry

conversation. In other words, I rely on my father's personality in my attempt to understand how someone who has a 'complex' identity comes to defend the identity the region where he lives nurtures him with. Also, because of his powerful words, my father imposed this identity on others, locals and non-locals."

"Now I feel more than anything else the need to talk about my cousin, Erotokritos. My uncle[167] wants him to live in an ideal environment. As a result, he composes a mythical world in the Greek space, a world shaped by the elements that are purposefully and consciously chosen from different historical eras: antiquity, the Byzantium, medieval Peloponese. Scholars notice how "Homeric" the nature of Erotokritos is. For and through him, time confirms an identity based on a glorious past, but also in the present, to give life to a bright future."

"Erotokritos defends his renaissance qualities and spreads a message of freedom in order to reach personal happiness. This is mainly the demand of the young woman he is in love with, Aretousa, who — through psychological and real collisions and through bright images — gives the final solution. In their love relationship, we see — in all its greatness — the triple ideal and eternal passion of bravery, beauty and wisdom. Erotokritos expresses these ideals from the nature of the Greek and the Cretan identity. For example, when Erotokritos fights, Cretans see in his face the symbol of their own battles and freedom."

"My uncle himself, born in Sitia, Crete, in the beginning of the 17th century, comes from a Venetian-Cretan royal family. There is no doubt that the official language of the "Nobili Veneti" is Greek and, more specifically, the Cretan dialect. By choosing to speak that language and teach it to Erotokritos, my uncle again emphasizes his Cretan identity. Thus, though he was born in Venice in 1793, my cousin speaks a language that is a mix of the eastern and western Cretan dialects. In addition, the way my uncle raised Erotokritos was inspired by the French novel *Paris at Vienne*. So I have come to see my cousin as a mixture of Italian, French, Greek, and Cretan elements and qualities."

"Moreover, you know well that I give my name to young women and to places all over Greece. So does Erotokritos. People memorize his words and recite them with the accompaniment of a plain, repetitive melody, not only in Crete, but also elsewhere."

Zorba foresees a very passionate relationship with Erofili. He is surprised with all the similarities their lives share. He imposed a monologue on her and she replied with another monologue, with even more arguments. The challenge is to see them acting in dialogue. They read and share aloud excerpts of notes from their diaries:

Zorba: "Music itself is a potent symbol of identity; like language, it is one of those aspects of culture that can, when they need to assert 'ethnic identity,' most readily serve this purpose. Its effectiveness may be twofold; not only does it act as a ready means for the identification of different ethnic or social groups, but it has potent emotional connotations and can be used to assert and negotiate identity in a particularly powerful manner."[168]

Erofili: "Tango is the only place in which I feel comfortable, restless, but at home, especially when not at home. Such is the story of the tango. Such is my story. Tango hurts me and comforts me. Tango is my changing, resourceful source of identity. Tango is my strategic language, a way of talking about, understanding, exercising decolonization."[169]

Zorba: "In a sense, our past has been written in the folk and popular songs. Through these songs — when they are authentic — and through their history, we discover ourselves as well as our ethnic identity. The context of folklore is ethnic: We need a metaphysical analysis and view so that we don't look for a scientific explanation." [170]

Erofili: "Our songs are us[171] — our music is us — and we are what we dance."

Zorba: "Speaking of music and identity, Dr. Chris Williams agrees with me that Cretan music has both a local and an oriental aspect that coexists in the same repertoire, yet the two are not fully reconciled." [172]

Erofili: "Yes, Zorba. And my friend Jane Cowan[173] remarks that, 'classifying Greek music as a branch of Near Eastern and Middle Eastern music makes musical and historical sense.' For her, ecclesiastical and secular Greek music have become imbued with tonalities that sound 'oriental' to western ears, though they may also bear witness to more archaic systems, which predate the separation of East and West. The contemporary array of distinctive folk, classical, popular, and ecclesiastical music reveals the position of Greece in the geographical and ideological crossroads between Europe and Asia."

Zorba: "To support his aforementioned idea, my friend talks about the rehabilitation of the demotic song in Greece, which has found its parallel in Turkey. He cites the example of Yiannis Markopoulos, a contemporary Greek composer of Cretan origin. He specifically refers to his 1972, 'Ithageneia' ("Citizenship"; "Nationality"), with the Cretan singer Nikos Xylouris. Dr. Williams observes that the songs in this recording are suffused with Cretan styles and the whole work arguably anticipates later attempts to combine Cretan and oriental styles, containing, for instance, some interesting use of the saz." [174]

Erofili: "Your friend is right; I agree with him. Yet, that reminds me of the Turkish composer Livaneli, who moves with the same steps, in very similar paths. Now that we are talking about all this, I think Dr. Williams also e-mailed me the other day. I assume you gave him my address. Among other things, he reminded me that Markopoulos has written a concert for Cretan l í r a and orchestra."[175]

Zorba: "I recently found on the Internet the Cretan musician Yiorgis Koutsourelis's web page.[176] It says there that Mikis Theodorakis used the musical piece 'A r m e n o c h o r i a n ó s S y r t ó s' — which Koutsourelis composed between 1949-1950 for solo l a o ú t o and vocal — to compose 'Zorba the Greek'."

Erofili: "Whatever the case Zorba, your music sounds Cretan after all, even performed on the b o u z o ú k i, and to me, that's all that matters."

Zorba: "Good point, Erofili, but that confuses me even more. Did you ever think of all these terms that Cretans use? I end up being treated like one of them… I have no idea where exactly I come from… It seems like I am in the age where all the identity and questioning of our origin come into play, up front, suddenly…"

Erofili: "What words do you mean? I don't understand you."

Zorba: "For example, k é f i, g l é n d i, m a n d i n á d a… and many more… I hear people saying that they have Arabic, Turkish or Italian origins…Who is right? Where are the answers?"

Erofili: "Zorba, clear-cut definitions do not always exist in this life. In the end, we believe what we want to believe, and that is what we know based on our socio-cultural ideas. Come on! It's getting late for such theoretical discussions. The sun is about to set and we have no electricity. I think it's time to get going."

Zorba: "Okay. What about staying in Anoya tonight? We can have a couple of r a k í shots and continue our discussion there."

Erofili: "That's a great idea! Under one condition, though — will you teach me how to dance?"

Zorba: "Look, Erofili. This is Nikos Xylouris's theater. In case you don't know, every August, they hold feasts here for a week to honor him. Let's have dinner across the theater at the Skalomata. Till the food comes, we'll have some time to talk. What do you think?"

Erofili: "Fine, Zorba. Tell me, have you heard of Ross Daly? Do you know him?"

Zorba: "Yes, of course. While in the boat coming to Crete, I picked up the magazine *Welcome Crete*. There, I read Ross Daly's article on Cretan music.[177] Ah! Here, I saved that paper. Take a look, if you wish…"

Erofili: "Excellent! His words bring to my mind some notes in his record *Ross Daly & Labyrinth: Mitos*. There, in addition to what you just said, Daly supports that Cretan music belongs to 'these great modal systems that are not confined by political and religious boundaries, yet they seem to be linked by a common origin, which might be based quite literally on a single note.'"

Zorba: " A m á n - a m á n ! Woe is me! What a mess! We are all a mixture, but yet distinct!"

Erofili: "Don't act like an idiot! Let's try to unravel the thread… Let's talk with facts…"

Zorba: "I'll pretend I didn't hear what you just said. Cretans imported the violin from Italy during Venetian rule."[178]

Erofili: "Are you jealous? Anyway, let's calm down… Cretans emphasize l í r a music more. It became the symbol of their culture, their representation throughout the whole world. Its name even evokes ancient, classical Greece. Musicologist Foivos Anoyiannakis believes that the Cretan l í r a has Byzantine-eastern origins and that it identifies or relates to other similar instruments that exist even nowadays in the East. In Crete, as it seems, it came after the Ottoman conquest, in the 17th or 18th century." [179]

Zorba: "Ross Daly, however, plays on the l í r a the modal music of Greece, the Balkans, Turkey, the Middle East, North Africa and North India. He believes that, despite the difference in terminology, there are distinctive similarities in the way virtually all these cultures approach improvisation and rhythm and in the way they perceive the relationship between tradition and originality." [180]

Erofili: "Yes, and he further argues that Western music has an expressive character. In the West, there is a definite cerebral dimension. In the East, people are concerned mainly with exceeding themselves through music. Often we say 'Eastern music,' but Daly prefers the term 'modal music'."[181]

Zorba: "In relation to what you just said, Erofili, let me again refer to my friend Dr. Williams. According to him, and I agree, Cretan techniques entail a subtle ornamentation that is not dissimilar to certain virtuoso guitar techniques. It resembles, and is fundamentally similar to, the p o l í t i k i l í r a (type of l í r a mainly performed in the Istanbul region), which is associated with high levels of performance in Greek music of Asia Minor, as well as Turkish classical music."[182]

Erofili: "Certainly, Zorba, the l í r a , the l a o ú t o , and the b u l g a r í provide to Cretan musicians easier access to 'oriental' instruments like the p o l í t i k i l í r a , the saz, the b a g l a m á s , the o ú t i , and so on."[183]

Zorba: "Ah! You just said l a o ú t o ! Of course, you know that the Venetians introduced it. Also, it became the most popular instrument in Crete at that time. Even your cousin, Erotokritos, performs exceptionally well and sings with it. Contemporary Cretan musical ensembles also use it."

Erofili: "Today Cretan ensembles use the t o u b e l é k i as well — you know, that Eastern instrument my other "dear" friend, Laodikis, plays..."

Zorba: "What's wrong, Erofili? Why are you like that?"

Erofili: "I'm teasing you, Zorba... Anyway, we are here, next to Nikos Xylouris's theater, having dinner at his birthplace. Do you know that with his l í r a , he introduced Cretans to the so-called 'European' pieces, such as waltzes? Do you know that he also composed his own songs, which did not always belong to the traditional Cretan repertory?"

Zorba: "I don't see anything wrong in that. Whatever the case, our songs always express our sorrow, our fights and the agonies of our people. And this is true not only for Cretans, but for all Greeks, and for all our neighbors as well."[184]

Erofili: "You are right... I'm thinking of the r i z í t i k a songs that, especially in the 20th century, became a strong symbol of identity for all Cretans."

Zorba: "Yes, but we should also remember that Cretans, at that time, co-existed with the Turks. Thus, their singing and dancing repertories merged Greek and Turkish elements. In the past, this was very conscious. It is mostly recognizable in Rethymnon in the 1920s and 1930s, and especially to three musicians: Andreas Rodinos, Harilaos Piperakis, and Stelios Foustalieris."[185]

Erofili: "I would imagine that what you are talking about is also the case with the t a b a c h a n i ó t i k a , that urban type of Cretan music played at that time in coffee shops and restaurants in the harbor districts of Chania and Rethymnon. Dr. Williams told me that many of the t a b a c h a n i ó t i k a can be traced to Foustalieris and, more generally, to the post-Lausanne period. Interestingly though, some of these tunes are termed as 'P a l a i o í s k o p o í t i s K r í t i s ,' or 'Old tunes of Crete.' In general, the whole process of adaptation and adoption of 'oriental' features into Cretan music is very interesting."[186]

Zorba: "Indeed! In one case, Foustalieris did adapt the Turkish song 'Ada sahillerinde bekliyorum' ('I Am Waiting at the Coast of the Island'),[187] usually performed at the Pringiponisa near Constantinople, to the Cretan song 'Everybody Asks Me Why I Cry'.[188] I asked my Turkish friend to sing it for me, and I could not believe my ears. I was shocked by the similarities in their melodies!"

Erofili: "What a coincidence! Ross Daly e-mailed me recently about this song. In Crete, the musical piece you just mentioned is also called 'H a l e p i a n ó s   A m a n é s.' He has found two more songs that share the same melody with this musical piece. One is an old song of Adonis Diamandidis performed by Dalgas called "My Eyes," and the other is a Syrian song called 'Qadduka 'al-mayyas' ('Your flirtatiously swaying figure').[189] Daly also informed me that, in general, even the Turkish musicologists agree that this musical piece originates somewhere in the Arab world."[190]

Zorba: "Aha! I begin to get it… That song has various elements that make it sound not exactly like a typical Turkish song. Now I understand that this is due to its Arabic roots."

Erofili: "Yes! Moreover, Daly explains[191] that this Arabic song belongs to a group of songs called muwashshahat. These are regarded as the oldest Arabic songs, and today they are preserved mainly in the Syrian city of Halab — Halepi in Greek, Aleppo in English. Obviously, Cretans, by naming their version 'H a l e p i a n ó s   A m a n é s' refer to the Halepa, a region in Chania. However, it is really an interesting and intriguing coincidence that this piece comes from Aleppo of Syria and not from Chania."

Zorba: "Now I add Dr. Williams's point about the t a x í m i , which appears in a varied form in Crete at this time. Previously, Cretan musicians learned fixed introductions to tunes. Now, a freer introduction is played. However, it is not quite like the t a x í m i , being less an exploration of the mode than a kind of stage setting for the tune to come. It is often theatrical in spirit and would rarely involve modulation".[192]

Erofili: "Our whole discussion reminds me also of the song 'Black Sea,' that Ross Daly composed. You may find it in *Dreamlands* (1982), but also in many of his other recordings. In a meeting we had a few days ago, Daly told me that, for this composition, he used 'the melody of Ali,' traced somewhere in the prefecture of Lassithi. Cretans say that Ali was a Turkish violin performer. Daly, however, believes that he was not a Turk, but a local Cretan who had converted to Islam".[193]

Zorba: "'Black Sea' in Asia Minor… Doesn't your friend, Maria Fasoulaki, the one who performs with Vasilis, sing that Asia Minor song called 'T i s   t r i a n d a f i l i á s   t a   f í l a' ('The Rose Bush Leaves')?"

Erofili: "You are right…"

Zorba: "Going back to Ross Daly and his recordings, you have made me realize that he likes 'playing' with these sounds. He often performs, for instance, Ottoman compositions along with the Cretan ones, am I wrong?"

Erofili: "No, not at all. But let me ask you something else, not irrelevant to our conversation topic: What exactly do you know of the Cretan song 'F i l e d é m'?"

Zorba: "Well, I think I have some stories about it: The Cretans gave to Patrick Leigh Fermor — the British agent in Crete during the German occupation — the nickname Filedém, because of his love of this song. An American movie, *Meeting over Midnight*, about the kidnapping of the German general Kreipe by Fermor — has as its soundtrack the music of 'F i l e d é m'.[194]

Erofili: "So, dear Zorba, you are not the only one to become famous through a soundtrack…"

A natural embrace, a philosophical invitation

Zorba: "That's not funny at all, okay? Anyway, to share with you more of what I know on this particular musical piece, Stelios Foustalieris noted that he learned that song himself from the Turkish crew of a ship that was in the port of Rethymnon. The song refers to a Turk whose name was Edem and was invoked as 'fíle Edem' ('friend Edem'). Foustalieris gave other lyrics to the song — which he considered to be very serious — while later, Skordalos made a recording of it, and still later, Xylouris, recorded it with the well-known verses."[195]

Erofili: "Filedém, filedém, filedém, filedém, filedém, oh! Amán-amán! I'm in love with a Turkish girl in the mosque. . . and so on. . ."

Zorba: "Exactly!"

Erofili: "By the way, Zorba, do you remember the Turkish-Cretans we met at the Alatsatianoi[196] Cultural Club in the summer of 2000?"

Zorba: "Of course I do..."

Erofili: "Do you know that their dances and songs are Greek and Cretan?[197] Do you know that they use the líra, the laoúto, and the boulgarí, and that they dance the same dances we Cretans perform as well? Also, their songs are very similar to our melodies, and many among them are distinguished dancers and famous líra and laoúto players."[198]

Zorba: "That's amazing! But let's go back to these 465 years of Venetian occupation, which precedes the Turkish one. The word mandinádes, our improvised couplets of fifteen syllable lines, comes from the Italian *mattinate*. At the same time, isn't it strange, that to be considered a worthy Cretan, you have to know mandinádes?"

Erofili: "Not to mention that many of these mandinádes used to have an Islamic context in the past. Now, instead, Cretans have 'purified' them, using words such as, 'my Christian,' and so on."[199]

Zorba: "Of course, and this denotes not only Greek, but local Cretan identity as well. Ah! Here comes the food... Wonderful!"

Erofili: "Good, because 'a hungry bear doesn't dance'..."[200] Speaking of dance, teach me to dance, "Come on my boy!"[201]

Zorba: "Erofili, let me digest the food... Stop this game!"

Erofili: "Why? Dance is part of our identity. Cretans believe that we are a geographical part of Greece that still profoundly supports and embellishes its traditional identity, especially in regard to our music and dance. Our people, since antiquity, have managed to leave their own traces, everywhere."

Zorba: "Hey! Hey! What a chauvinist! Especially in places such as this village of Anoya, the repertoire of music and dances is strictly and mostly — with few exceptions — Cretan, in opposition to other Cretan or Greek regions, where the variety of music and dances performed may include many other categories as well, such as Greek folk dances, popular Greek music, and so on."

Erofili: "Yes! In Anoya, moreover, there are several dancing idioms, for example, the local leaping dance called

A n o y a n ó s   p i d i h t ó s . Through their dancing, the people of Anoya, show that their performances on Crete continue and will continue as a viable means of social interaction as long as the essence of being Cretan is conveyed: For them, dancing is being Cretan. In this context, social processes, those based on a dialectic relationship between individual and society, form their identity: For the people of Anoya, dancing is an illustration of 'Cretanness.' It also expresses group continuity, linking past, present, and future generations. Through their dancing, they experience their cultural identity as members of a traditional society: theirs."

Zorba: "Hey! Erofili... Do you have a degree in Cretan dances?"

Erofili: "Let me continue; don't interrupt. Dance is important to Cretans, because to dance is to be Cretan. Dance, for Cretans, takes high priority in terms of our successful adaptation to our culture as a whole. Through dancing, Cretan people show what we are."

Zorba: "Excellent! Are you ready for a shot of r a k í ? "

Erofili: "Yes, but before that, let me answer your last question... I am working on an ethnomusicological study on Cretan music and dance..."

Zorba: "Ethnomusicological? What's that?"

Erofili: "It's all Greek to me. Come on, Zorba! 'E t h n o s for nation, people, and music+(o)logy for the 'conscious' study of music... which brings us back to the beginning of our discussion on music and identity... As you can see, all this moves in a circle... as a dance... Go ahead, you may treat me now! Y i á   m a s ! (To our health!)"

Psiloritis stands tall no matter what we do. Erofili and Zorba will always be a very interesting couple. Up to now, we have been moving mostly in Crete, in Greece and in neighboring areas. It's time to dance all over the world. Fourth step: present and future step.

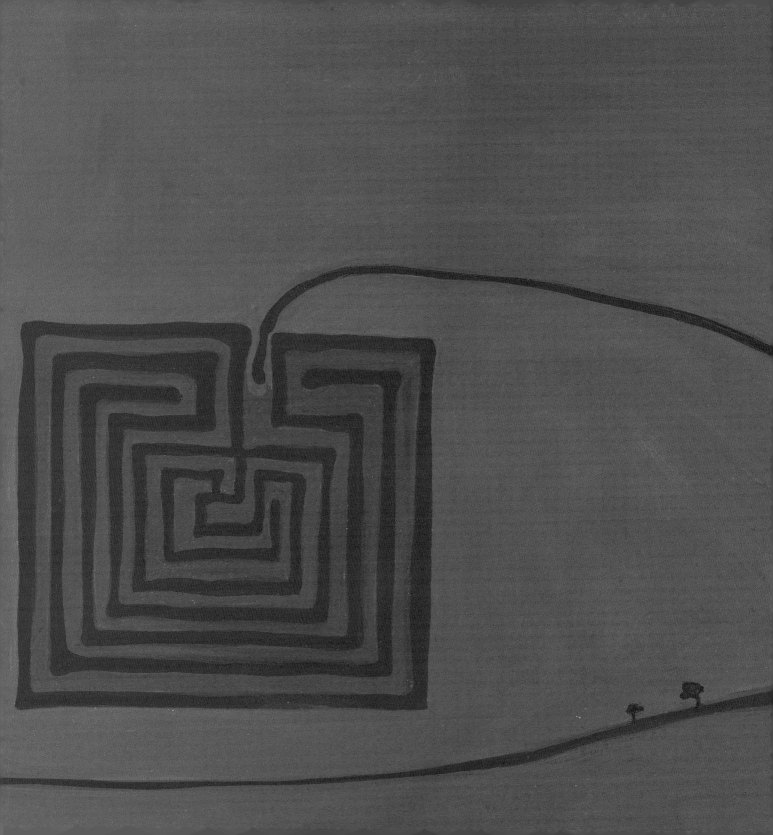

step 5

Amazing mazes

STEP 5: AMAZING MAZES

*H*ermes spreads to the world the rumors and the mythologies about the palace of Knossos. Many guests and visitors arrive. Atlas continues dynamically to carry the globe. My Odyssey is about to reach its Ithaca and to start all over again.

> Life is always the farewell and the most uncomfortable presence.
> G. Seferis, *Tetrádio gymnasmáton B (Exercise Book B)* [202]

Bravo is a new entertainment spot in Heraklion — in the region of Ammoudara — owned by Spithouris of Anoya.[203] We go there on August of 2000 to celebrate before my sister departs to complete her degree in England. On that night, Vasilis and his group perform. The local radio and television stations have been advertising this event for weeks. Excerpts of the songs from Vasilis Stavrakakis's new compact disc can be heard all over Crete.

In the promotional poster for the event we see Vasilis's picture, painted by sunset brushes in romantic yellow and orange contours,[204] on the walls around and in the city of Heraklion. On the white bottom border, handwritten, the place, the time, and the names of the musicians in his group.

I am with my family, our friends, and our summer guests from Tibet and France. At Bravo, I meet with many Cretan people I know. Tourists from the Arab countries and from Canada join the crowd. Laodikis reserves a table for us next to his p a r é a of friends. We are facing the musicians. Next to the swimming pool, around the bar, people of all ages enjoy their drinks. DJ music prevails till it is time for the live music.

My French and Tibetan friends enjoy the music. I translate the lyrics of the songs for them. In particular, they like the l a o ú t o player and singer Psaroyiorgis, the son of Psaradonis. I introduce him to them during the break. He speaks the Cretan dialect; they only understand French and English. My sister and her friends fall in love with Vasilis's voice. They observe carefully the meaning of specific Cretan words, and they admire the richness of our dialect, the genuine truth some of its phrases hold. My mom writes down some of the m a n d i n á d e s Stavrakakis and Psaroyiorgis sing. She wants to be able to recall these treasures. She may also use their proverbial character to make a wish or to illustrate her feelings on a proper occasion.

Young people repeat the lyrics. They applaud or move their heads to the music beat. The Arabs engage in a conversation with Laodikis during the break. They are curious, interested in his case. They feel at "home": He is performing during their holiday, "out of place." I invite my relatives and friends to a circle dance. Friends and others join us immediately. Our guests, shy in the beginning, finally decide to get up and hold hands at the end of the circle.

It is almost three o'clock in the morning and we must leave for the airport. The concert is over. We congratulate the musicians and share our admiration. Stavrakakis asks, as always, my opinion about the specific event. I have good words to say and lots of unforgettable memories to share.

The plane takes off. I follow the old coastal highway to Kokkinis, our summer country house, parallel to the line that the airplane's wings sculpt in the sky. The sunrise is beautiful. In a week, I will be flying back to the United States. I decide that, outside its proper world, Cretan music will also be heard through the words you now read.

Knossos

I invite you to be my guest in Crete. We arrive on my island. We make plans for our holidays. We pay a visit to the office of the Organization of Greek Tourism (EOT), located downtown, across from the Archaeological Museum in Heraklion, famous for its unique Minoan exhibits. We pick up free brochures that highlight points of interest for tourists and include a geographical and political map of Crete. On the very first page, we read:

> Crete: Of Daedalus and Icarus, of the Minoan jars and the famous wall paintings. Sparkling, in the starlight, with the black and hanging portion of breeches and the handkerchief with the fringes. Erotic Crete: With the sea, the rocks, and the amazing plateaus. Crete: Of the cooked (seasoned) wine, and the raisin, and the grappa. Crete: You stay up all night. Crete: Of the many days eating and drinking under the countless stars. Crete: of the fennel and the fresh basil. Crete: You make us dizzy. Crete: Of the p y r r h í c h i o s war-dance. Crete: Of the Diyenis and Crete warm as kiss. Crete: Of El Greco, Kornaros, Kazantzakis, and Prevelakis. Crete: You always have your door open to both West and East. Crete: You never end. Crete: The dream, where one can fly. Crete: The "Island of Miracles."

We are not the only visitors on the island of Crete. Many tourists come here especially during the summer months. Cretans feel the need to creatively reinforce "Cretanness" for outside consumption. In a world that comes closer day by day, they struggle to maintain and exhibit their uniqueness. For them, tourists are not passive listeners. They are welcomed to participate in their dances. Indeed, Cretans rely on your ears: They know you have the power to spread the word about their music and dance all over the world.[205]

Zorba the Greek takes place in Crete, but on the island today they do not listen to its music much. Though bouzoúki music is often the stereotype of Greek music for non-Greeks, this is not the case here. Cretans, for tourist purposes, consciously reproduce their own Minotaurs. In the labyrinths, they shape their performances through world musical lenses to attract the interest of their guests: They expect their audience to be a universal one.

After we pick up the brochures, we walk around the museum area. In shops, we find Cretan knives — symbols of pride — of all sizes, for a reasonable price. I buy lots of them as gifts for my male non-Cretan friends. I give one to you as well. You ask me to translate the engraving on the blade. "It is a m a n d i n á d a, a traditional Cretan rhyming distich," I reply. It says, "I am a Cretan knife, a gift of honor and bravery, but also a souvenir of eternal friendship."

On our way to the Venetian Fountain of Morozini — commonly known as The Lions' Square — we stop by my classmate's shop to buy postcards. I point out to you the ones that come with a compact disc of Cretan music.

Their contents you can read; they are in English. They are all the same, but their covers vary. Some show Cretan landscapes. One, in particular, shows a l í r a craftsman in his workshop. Another features the l í r a, among other instruments of the Cretan musical tradition, on a traditional Cretan woven tablecloth. *Sounds and pictures of Crete: Cretan Traditional Instruments; Instrumental Songs (Various Artists)* is a unique postcard series of exceptional quality, each illustrating the most popular sights of Crete. Each envelope contains one compact disc. This compact disc includes instrumental music performed by popular Cretan folk artists using the traditional musical instruments of Crete.[206]

In showcases, we see small plastic l í r a s. In magazines and newspapers and on the walls of shops, we find advertisements of "Cretan music live super shows" or even of "representations of traditional Cretan weddings." Tired of walking, I suggest that we drive to Arolithos,[207] a fairly new settlement a few kilometers outside the city of Heraklion. There, we find an enactment of a traditional Cretan village and life. During the day, we enjoy our coffee at the traditional coffeehouse and wander in its narrow streets near the workshops and the traditional houses decorated in distinctly local style. At night, on restaurant stages, Cretan dancers in traditional costumes perform with the accompaniment of the Cretan l í r a and other traditional instruments.

I recall the time when, in high school, I joined a folk dance troupe in my hometown. I learned many embellishments on Cretan dancing steps. My parents came to watch me perform at theaters, squares and events that took place both in Crete and outside the island. I show you pictures of me in a traditional costume. The first Christmas I was in Bloomington, Indiana, my mother ordered such a costume for me. Maybe you have seen it already: I wore it at presentations of Cretan traditional dances at schools and universities in the United States.

If you visit me in the spring, I will take you to the Easter celebrations and to the k o u r é s (sheep's shearing). In late summer, we will join my relatives for the vine harvest (t r ý g o s). We will attend lots of feasts and weddings. In autumn, we will make the wine and the r a k í. As we step on the grapes, squeezing them under our feet, we will dance to live or recorded Cretan music. In the k a z á n i (boiler) of the r a k í, we will get drunk from the alcohol in the air. In winter, we will gather around fires, make music and dance.

I invite you to join us.

"Teach me to dance!" the British man implores Zorba. You hold hands with me and slowly learn the steps. You start feeling the music and you seem to enjoy it; most of my guests do. I want you to leave my island with the best memories. You may visit other places in Greece as well. What, in particular, I would like you to recall vividly from Crete is its mountain villages and beaches, its food, its music and dance, its people.

I teach Greek to children and adults. In one of the books I have used[208], I see two pictures — one of a music performance and the other of a dance performance. My students see a smile on my face. "Greek music and dance" is the subtitle of the pictures. "Yes, not only Greek, but also Cretan," I add. Is this selection also a mere coincidence?

Back in Crete, we wander the streets. We get hungry. We recall documentaries we have watched on CNN: "Among

Basil for the smell, bread
for the taste,
wool for the touch:
Cretan traditions
for the senses

all nations, Greeks hold the longest life span records. Among them, Cretans are the healthiest." My mom adds: "The Cretan diet is the best example of a Mediterranean diet, and researchers have discovered that Cretans have the lowest rate of heart disease and cancer. Olive oil plays the largest role in the Cretan diet."[209]

Before eating, Michael buys a cookbook in English from my friend's bookstore. Sam purchases a large metallic tank of olive oil. We make a stop at the bakery and taste warm, fresh, traditional Cretan bread. We particularly enjoy p a x i m á d i . I remember especially the sweet one we had at the village of Anoya with mountain tea mixed with r a k í , while the Iakinthia celebration was taking place.

Then Henry recalls the "embroidered" wedding bread we ate at the wedding the night before in Anoya; momentarily we lose him somewhere between local olivewood and clay workshops. Nikos loved the honey and walnuts they gave to all unmarried women at Cretan weddings. We cross the market street. We smell all kinds of fresh herbs and spices that are sold from open sacks.

You are curious to visit historical sights, churches, monasteries, monuments, landmarks and the villages where great Cretan artists were born, lived and created. At Gortyna, we lie under the evergreen plane where Zeus took a nap after having abducted Europe. At Psiloritis, we visit Hyacinth's church and the cave where Zeus was born. Lastly, at the palace of Knossos, where my mom guides us, it is your turn to testify to the truth of my present mythologies.

Good times pass quickly. You depart, and I stay to continue my fieldwork. Occasionally, I borrow your eyes and become a tourist in my own land. I chose the village of Anoya because it was and still is a tourist attraction to my family. Later, I take you there as well. The people of Anoya give you a white handkerchief to remember the wedding celebration we attended. In order to connect with our customs and traditions in more depth, they invite you to Nikos Xylouris's theater to attend a series of traditional performances they hold there every summer.

So, who is a tourist?

You are, because you are non-Greek. My Athenian friends are, because they are non-Cretans. I am, because I grew up in the district of Heraklion and have not yet discovered all the treasures and secrets that my island holds. In addition, for the past several years, I have lived between the United States and Greece, and have traveled back and forth, which makes me very dizzy.

I have already filled up enough pages, I think, with an imaginary visit. Imagine how many more we can write together. Next, I give you more images based on real field notes I take when you visit Crete and listen to the local radio or watch the local TV, or when you buy a Cretan recording, read a book, or even get online. Hermes, the communication era god, has already put his sandals on and is ready to fly. No more chattering. We have to catch up with him.

Hermes

The Dance of the Stone: Iakinthia; Reference to Zeus, a live recording from the events dedicated to Zeus at Saint Hyacinth in the village of Anoya, was released in the fall of 2001. Accidentally, my eye fell on its advertisement in a Greek magazine that my mother brought with her to London, where we met over Christmas break. I immediately called my friends in Greece and asked them to mail it to me. Two days before, I had stayed up for two consecutive nights to transcribe my own video and audio recordings from those festivities. Now, I have the official recording in my hands. It came with a booklet in which I can see most of the things I had struggled to capture.[210]

The light gray cover of the compact disc features the title in black and red letters, along with a picture of Zeus: It is a photograph of a portrait on copper,[211] taken at the place where the celebrations for the Iakinthia 2001 were held. Hyacinth and Zeus join Hermes in these writings. In the words of anthropologist Sara Cohen: "They help him identify with his roots and present him as a real person, who embodies artistic integrity and honesty, rather than a glitzy star representing the unreal world of glamour, commerce, and marketing strategies."[212] Hermes is happy to be part of our company. He is particularly thrilled that "Cretan music is not just a live, context-specific dance music, but more and more becomes the subject of commercial recordings. Through time, the processes of production, distribution and consumption change, and, as with any dance tradition, Cretan music takes the first steps to the concert hall. At the same time — and it is clearly no coincidence — a context-free song tradition emerges."[213]

Every day, when on the island of Crete, Hermes turns on the radio. He prefers listening to Cretan music. Kritorama (Cretan Panorama) and Knossos FM are two of his favorite stations. When he drives in the regions around Heraklion, he tunes in. They play Cretan traditional music, and they keep him updated with upcoming festivities and events; they make him aware of the latest recordings and Cretan music productions.

With Hermes, we drive to the village of Anoya. We stop by Skalomata, a local restaurant, to have lunch. There, we enjoy traditional food and background music from a local radio station. "You Cretans," Hermes comments, "are unique. Not only do you perform live music and dances well, but you also know how to distribute your musical traditions to Greece and to the rest of the world. People will think that I am Cretan, because in Crete all of my manifestations and my behaviors aim at constructing a distinct sense of Cretanness."[214]

My friends who own the restaurant come and sit with us. They treat us to fresh red wine and fresh fruits. Yiannis's cell phone rings: I recognize the tune it plays as 'H a r a v g í' ('Dawn'), a popular Cretan traditional song. I am very surprised. "Technology!" I exclaim. Later, the same phone rings again: My friend reveals that he is flirting with his girlfriend by sending her m a n d i n á d e s messages. She responds replying the same way, and the dialogue goes on. "That's one more thing to keep in mind, dear Hermes," I observe.

We leave the restaurant. In the car, I play *The Dance of the Stone: Iakinthia; Reference to Zeus* for Hermes. He likes it a lot, and he regrets he was not able to attend the actual event. He realizes he missed many things that a recording cannot include. At the same time, he is excited he can listen to the music and the words performed even if it's "out of place." Through pictures and brief essays, the compact disc's booklet helps him get a good sense of all that were negotiated at the Iakinthia of 2001. We reach our destination and climb Psiloritis. On his knees, Hermes prays to Zeus. We are "in place"; Hermes can see his father's head.[215]

On the next day, Hermes meets Ross Daly and asks his opinion about the recording he heard the day before: "When we are content with recorded music, and we do not search for live music experiences, we should not wait for something better. When, however, we ask for more live music experiences, this opens up entire new possibilities in another space. Definitely, live contact brings to the surface different things. Therefore, whoever asks for genuine emotions, let her/him take refuge in live listening."[216]

Besides listening to the local radio in Crete, Hermes watches television as well. He favors stations such as Crete TV (Kriti TV) and Creta Channel. There, he can watch documentaries related to the civilization, the traditions and the history of the island, such as the program *In the Cretan Pathways* shown every Tuesday night during the summer of 2001. On Mondays and Wednesdays of that same summer, Hermes watches *Our Crete*, an hour-long show devoted to the Cretan musical tradition: Various Cretan artists perform. During breaks, Hermes takes notes and marks his calendar with the latest recording releases as well as upcoming concerts and events.

I point out to him that a national television station, NET (Néa Ellinikí Tileórasi; New Greek Television), broadcasts daily in the late afternoon an hour-long show to promote new Greek artists. Among them, Cretan musicians travel to the Athenian studios to record for this show. During the summer of 2001, I saw Psaradonis, Hainides and Loudovikos of Anoya presenting their latest work. In addition, Vasilis told me how important it is to present his latest compact disc on NET. That same summer he discussed such possibilities with Ross Daly.

Hermes often hears me talking about local recording studios. He wants to visit one. What interests him is the fact that these studios only record and produce music that somehow relates to the island of Crete. I tell him that a couple of months ago, I attended the recording of a compact disc on Cretan Byzantine liturgical music.[217]

Hermes notices that the logos of Cretan radio or television stations make him realize again that he is in Crete. On a hot summer Sunday, after my father recorded the liturgy of an old priest at the cathedral in the town of Aghios Nikolaos, I met with him and Hermes in the city of Ierapetra. There, we listened to stories the main producer of the Eastern Crete radio station shared: "The station's ensemble is the creation of the artist Anakreontas Kanavakis; it represents a cross made of two double axes, a Minoan symbol with its edges turning into waves."

I take Hermes to Aerakis's Cretan Musical Workshop in the city of Heraklion, which "writes history in the musical tradition of our place": Stelios Aerakis, the producer and headmaster of the Cretan Musical Workshop (www.cretan-music.gr), was born in Sisarha of Anoya. The rich, "live" musical tradition of that area and his love of Cretan music urged him from childhood to get involved with traditional music instruments. As a musician, he has accompanied several famous artists, such as Nikos Xylouris. Since 1974, he has been living with his family in Heraklion. That same year, he

For the travelling eye: The village of Kamares (Arches) as an international peripatetic pathway

got involved with recording companies. He collaborated with his brother Michalis, who founded the record store Aerakis in Heraklion 25 years ago along with the company Aerakis Seistron Music (www.aerakis.net).

> Today, Stelios Aerakis's activities deal mainly with productions of Cretan music that pass the test of time. His portfolio of collaborators includes eminent folk artists and renowned composers. Mr. Aerakis has produced 60 albums. Works he believes are the landmarks of his professional contribution to Cretan music are: *The Cretan Epic, The Masters of the Cretan Musical Tradition, 1920-1955,* and the *Saints of Crete.* These memorable works pay tribute to the splendor of the Cretan culture and civilization.
>
> *Welcome Crete* [218]

Aerakis's most recent work is a collection of pieces performed by contemporary l í r a players, most of whom come from the village of Anoya, musicians such as Vasilis Skoulas and Nikiforos Aerakis who played at the weddings I attended.

I invite Hermes to my house and guide him to the music studio where my father spends his free time. With a glass of r a k í in one hand, he stares at the enormous recording collection. He realizes that many Cretan people, due to their own passion and m e r á k i, listen to, record, and collect Cretan music. My father points out that there are many Cretans all over the island who own private collections.

That same day, I decided to entrust a dear secret to both Hermes and my father: In an e-mail I received in December 2001, Ross Daly talked to me about his most recent project. He was seriously engaged with the recording of works composed by the Cretan musician Nikos Manias, who is very old in age. To achieve this, he invited musicians to perform the best of Manias's works on the instruments for which his works were originally composed.

In our studio, Hermes spends time looking at the covers of some compact discs. He is amazed by the covers, but also by the titles. Through titles such as *'A r o m a K r í t i s (Aroma of Crete)*, Michalis Kallergis's work that was released in the summer of 2001, *L e v e n d o g é n a K r í t i (Crete, Mother of Gallants)*, a 1966 recording by Moundakis, and *K r i t i k ó s í l i o s (Cretan Sun)*, by Psaroyiannis from 1984, Hermes is confident that there is no way Crete will let him escape beauty and traditions.

While in Egypt at the Khan Al-Khalili market in Cairo, Hermes met with the ethnomusicologist Ali Jihad Racy. They talked about how Egyptians use specific images for their record labels so that they can better appeal to and attract a local audience. For instance, Dr. Racy told Hermes how Egyptians changed Columbia's image of the black and white dog to that of a gazelle, the most beloved and popular animal to Egyptians. This discussion made Hermes realize why Cretan compact disc covers or, more generally, why all of this business with Cretan music, uses symbols such as the palace of or a wall painting from Knossos, the double Minoan Axes, and so on.

An interesting observation Hermes made to Dr. Racy is that many compact discs of Cretan music seem to have been made for consumption outside not only Crete, but outside Greece as well. To support his argument, Hermes mentioned a compact disc by Psaradonis titled *Psaradonis and Ensemble: Son of Psiloritis.* This compact disc, produced in collaboration with a German company, Oriente Musik, is entirely in English. "You are very right, Hermes," I admit, "I keep seeing this compact disc in big chain record stores in the United States! Psiloritis... It's genuine Cretan music."

Of course, Hermes reads *E r o t ó k r i t o s*. He is interested in any recording productions that *E r o t ó k r i t o s* has influenced. Many singers include parts of it in their albums. Other artists devote whole records to this masterpiece. His favorite album is *Erotokritos: Four approaches to the Cretan Medieval Romance,* (produced in 2000), an interesting collaboration of four artists: Loudovikos of Anoya, Nikos Xydakis, Psaradonis and Yiorgos Koumendakis. Though tremendously different in musical style, the common thread among these four composers and the performers they select to work with, Hermes thinks, is the love-life-story of Erotokritos.[219]

We walk in the narrow streets of Heraklion. We stop by my friend's bookstore. Stergios, a very clever, witty, and enjoyable man from the village of Anoya, owns Photodendro (tree of light). "Hermes," I say, "do you know that Stergios sells books which come with a compact disc as well? Local Cretans write these books in traditional folk rhyming style (in m a n d i n á d e s) and have recently started publishing them as well. They also choose lyrics and make songs to accompany these books."

E m i n e attracts Hermes's attention. In this book, Karatzis, a well-known m a n d i n á d a and Cretan lyricist, builds a love story between a Cretan hero and the daughter of a Turkish pasha. On the compact disc that accompanies the book, we can listen to the voices of Vasilis Skoulas and Spyridoula Toutoudaki singing excerpts from the "Cretan Love Song," published by Aerakis, with music by Christos Stivaktakis, a local l í r a and l a o ú t o player.

I share with Hermes my theory that if schoolbooks were made into songs that fit the musical tastes of each generation, then all students would better memorize information and especially historical details, such as dates. All at once, our eyes fall on the book *Pictures from the History of Crete* by Alexandra Papa-Androulakaki. In a folksy, artful spirit, the writer selects Cretan historical periods and describes them in familiar, traditional fifteen-syllable verses.[220]

Hermes has a couple more days to stay on earth. He chooses to spend them in Crete. We get the local newspapers, magazines, periodicals, and we make a plan. As we go over the pages, we find detailed information about upcoming music and dance events of all kinds. Walking home, we pay attention to posters and advertisements on the city's walls. There, we see the musicians' pictures and all we need to know about upcoming performances. We drive to our country house.

We stop by an Internet café. Contemporary Hermes often needs to go online. After he has checked his e-mail, we decide to search the Web. We find lots web pages on Cretan music and dances. Some of them are informational: artists' biographies, lists of their works, histories and accounts of Cretan music and dance. Other websites, such as www.cretan-music.gr, advertise Cretan artists and recordings. I ask Hermes to go to Cretaphone, namely the voice of Crete, which has for 32 years been "in the service of Cretan music and the people who love it." Its web page, in both Greek and English, includes mp3 files, so that everyone can listen to new Cretan music and songs. It particularly informs its visitors about the most recent releases. Through its links, people can post m a n d i n á d e s and "chat" over the Internet. The designers of this web page provide an excellent search engine that also takes visitors to several other very interesting websites related to Cretan music.

My parents, Hermes and I go out for dinner. Our friends, Kostas Frangakis and his wife, join us. I explain to Hermes that Mr. Frangakis is the owner of Cretaphone. Through this website, which he runs with the help of his two sons,[221] he promotes Cretan music. In his record shop in Heraklion, he sells mostly, if not exclusively, Cretan music. He also produces many Cretan music recordings.

Hermes's sharp eyes notice the logo of Cretaphone on the business card that Mr. Frangakis gives him: The logo depicts "the prince with the lilies," a famous wall painting from the palace of Knossos. Above him, in a rainbow-colored background, are the following words: "Cretan musical tradition; Crete's recording company: Cretaphone."

Before Hermes departs for mount Olympus, I get his e-mail address. Now, while writing these words in the United States, I check the Internet daily for the main Cretan newspaper of my hometown and, by extension, of the island of Crete — *Patrís* (*Homeland*). When I find information related to my work, I e-mail it to Hermes as well. In my last e-mail to him, I describe how happy I am Ross Daly has an e-mail address too. From now on, when I need to clarify something in my writings, I simply e-mail him, and I get an immediate, abundant response.[222]

Hermes must go. While packing his luggage, dusting off his wings, and polishing his sandals, he meets up with Atlas, who tells him stories about the globe he is forced to carry as a lifetime punishment, and how this globe shakes every time those Cretans dance. How can Hermes forget Cretan music and dance performances? He decides to stay in Crete and learn the rest of our dances. He also volunteers to help Atlas by carrying the load of Cretan music on his own shoulders.

Atlas

Globalization: To be against it — even if you don't understand what it means. It is a chewing gum word — which has substituted imperialism.[223]
Dimou, *Ironic Modern Greek Lexicon*

Music, as a medium and a tool of ecumenical expression, allows us to have much in common: to unite with others and the environment, and to share the esoteric wealth of being. There are many kinds of musical expression, not just one. Each one deserves our respect, under the proposition that it is based on real cultural roots. All these presuppose that one should quit "showing off" and "possessing," which are merely decorative and ridiculous behaviors. To be involved with music is not merely learning to perform, but learning to listen to others as well. Music is a way of facing reality, humanity; a way of posing our thoughts for our era.
Article in *K a t h i m e r i n í* newspaper[224]

Atlas, while carrying the globe on his shoulders, accidentally overhears what people around the world say. Today, Greece reaches his ears. There, everybody talks about globalization. As 2002 begins, almost all European countries, Greece included, officially start to use a common currency, the "euro." Some Greeks complain. In opposition to globalization, they propose "Greekization."[225]

I try to see how Atlas possibly relates to my study of Cretan music. I know his dream is to get rid of his burdens and to rest forever in Ithaca. To meditate more on my thoughts, I compare Atlas to an economist who produces, markets and sells music all over the world. Because of him, non-Greeks know Cretan music. Atlas reaches Ithaca when his products become part of the musical life and tradition of many countries other than Greece. [226]

Cretans often talk negatively about Atlas. They think he does not respect his Greek origins. Atlas tells them about one of his favorite Greek artists, the popular and famous Eleftheria Arvanitaki, who currently represents Greece abroad in festivals such as the WOMAD.[227] Atlas particularly likes the way Eleftheria is "nostalgic about the future." He repeatedly plays her compact disc *E k p o m p í* (*Broadcast)* on which she collaborates with artists from various ethnic backgrounds. After a concert, Arvanitaki tells him: "During my career, I have always been trying to give an updated version of my roots, and to discover new sounds".[228] "Because we are between the West and East, we, Greeks, know very well the music of Europe and America, but we know the music of Asia as well. We are well-positioned to take the best from both worlds, but we keep doing our music in our own way."[229]

Somewhere there is music performed. "Ah! It must be those Cretans again with their music, songs and dances!" Atlas sighs. While talking with Vasilis Stavrakakis I feel Atlas's presence: Stavrakakis often mentions the word "globalization." Through his art, he tries to build a song that will be globally heard. Toward this goal, he uses instruments other than Cretan ones alone. In his group, he includes the Cretan l í r a , but not as the prevailing instrument. Instead, he favors and underscores through his music performances instruments such as the m a n d o l í n o , the t z o u r á s , and the t o u b e l é k i .

Stavrakakis looks at Cretan music as a global art. In my face, he foresees a capable person to present and disseminate Cretan music, first to the United States and then to the rest of the world. "You are the ambassador of Cretan music," he characteristically says to me. At the same time, he somehow contradicts himself: "Whatever you end up doing, when you are done, you should return not only to Greece, but to Crete".

In my opinion, globalization means that, in things of different forms, we may recognize the same human values. Thus, we should not be stuck to outer characteristics of a musical tradition, in our case the Greek one or, even more specifically, the Cretan one. We should view ourselves, or rather, we should view Greek and Cretan music as aspects of the same thing, of musical art.

In one of my conversations with Ross Daly,[230] he talks more about globalization to make clear to me that this term does not imply i s o p é d o s i (equalization; leveling): "Knowing that we are all making artful music does not make us all the same: Instead, it makes us respect our differences, but, at the same time, work from our different bases toward a better musical world."

Atlas cannot read because his arms are occupied with carrying the earth. He has strong memory. He recalls an article in a book I was reading aloud the other day: "Geographical variations in the background, culture, and influences of musicians reflected in their music help to construct particular places and the ways in which people conceptualize them."[231] And he comments: "I see changes in the globe; people talk about globalization. I believe, thus, that the whole relationship between music and locality is constantly changing."

Festivals, conferences, tourist promotions, competitions increase. "When Greece participates and Cretan music is one of the musical scenes the country has to exhibit, who are the musicians, who is the audience, what about Hermes and his media?," Atlas asks.[232] My response to him is that, in such cases, Hyacinth and Zeus, standing tall as the symbol of the place they inhabit, the proud mountain of Psiloritis, come to the forefront to defend their music and dance performances. Though they adopt the "foreign," "western" idea of hosting a series of events or concerts in their land, they also offer mountain tea and p a x i m á d i during the performance, thereby sharing their local flavors.[233]

Atlas comments on the Cretan artists, especially those l í r a players, who day by day become models and idols. He sees them everywhere, on posters, on walls, in newspapers and magazines. While talking with Ross Daly, Atlas recalls Daly saying how much Cretan artists remind him of Hollywood stars. "They behave like them, they wear rings, and they must have a Mercedes or a BMW, it's a must. So, I think that, because their models have changed, the Cretan l í r a players gain afterwards as well as adopt the western model of the artist, who is the one that stands out. Thus, for the whole week they make shoes, and Saturday night, they play the l í r a and we dance, and then Monday, shoes again…".[234]

I stop by a kiosk to buy the magazine *J a z z k a i T z a z*.[235] I look for the issue devoted to "Ethnic Voices and Songs." There, I find interesting articles that express various opinions on globalization viewed basically through economical and communicational lenses. The writers of these articles speak of tolerance. I read some of them to Atlas and we both agree that globalization is just the beginning, especially due to technological developments and the co-existence of many musicians. In other words, we both view globalization as a way of experiencing differences and special emotions each moment gives us.

As I prepare to go home and listen to the compact disc of Cretan music that comes with another magazine I buy, *K o n d i l i é s* (www.kontilies.gr), Atlas interrupts me with one of his complicated, puzzling questions: "Doesn't Cretan music itself have global dimensions?" I read him the first pages of my writings here, which talk about Crete. There, I view it as an island where many people from different countries, cultures and religions have lived and have left their traces. So isn't music in Crete today a product of all these mixtures and cultural elements? Couldn't Crete, by extension, serve as one of the places where musical traditions from other parts of the world interact, come together, and intermingle?

I missed Vasilis Stavrakakis's performance, part of a series of fundraising musical concerts for supporting the Kurdish people.[236] At this event in the Oasis Garden-Theater "Nikos Kazantzakis," he played Cretan music, "his" songs, and then the Kurdish "Grup Yorum" followed. For the closing, members of Stavrakakis's group and the Kurdish group performed together. I asked my parents to attend the event on my behalf. My father recorded it and sent me the discs. My mother took my "other" field notes. While Vasilis's group was onstage, before the performance, Heraklion's politicians gave speeches on "solidarity, mutual aid" — otherwise called — "the 'other' globalization, that of the ideas."

As the world lends an ear: Vasilis Stavrakakis's musical group in performance

Ithaca[237]

> Ethnic: Exotic music. Very much in fashion. Often, folk travesty.
>
> Dimou, *Ironic Modern Greek Lexicon*[238]

3D show

Height

What sort of madness comes over us? What sort of madness comes over us to make us throw ourselves on another man? There was a time when I used to say: "That man's a Turk, or a Bulgarian, or a Greek." Now, when I look at people, I say: "This one's a good fellow, that one's a bastard." They can be Greeks, or Bulgarians, or Turks — it doesn't matter. Is he good? Or is he bad? That's the only thing I ask nowadays. And as I grow older... I feel I shall not even go on asking that! Whether a man's good or bad, I'm sorry for him, for all of them...

Kazantzakis, *Zorba the Greek*[239]

Width

The teaching of the Minoan civilization enters Turkish universities. Psiloritis and Troy claim they are cousins. Similarities we discover between Minoan Crete and Asia Minor: Milatos, a region in Crete, Militos of Ionia. More Turks read Kazantzakis and translate his books into their own language. More Greeks visit Turkey and Turks visit Greece. Both, in their ancient times, believe in the Big Mother and the sacred bull. In Anoya, they still honor Saint Mamas, the protector of shepherds and animals, and celebrate him through music and dances every September 2nd. Turkish-Cretans speak the Cretan dialect and sing by heart excerpts from *E r o t ó k r i t o s*. Many Turks love and listen to Theodorakis's music. Art serves as a connecting bond between the two peoples. Art brings them closer. [240]

Yper-X magazine

Depth

Our songs express our sorrow, our fights and the agonies of our people. The Mediterranean functions as the uterus of all the peoples who live around it. There are many common things in the way these people create and express themselves. The purpose of this music instrument exhibition is to show these similarities — the common points that link these peoples — and to contribute to communication through this common language of music, which is the language of soul. We must say it is apparent that the music of the people in the Mediterranean and Mesopotamia touches and moves each of us.

Daly in *Traditional Music Instruments*[241]

A world music show

The era we live in is modern, built on a past of many histories and a future of many expectations. At this "modern" time, music has its own mythologies: As Martin Stokes proposes, it grows and is nurtured in the same social and cultural worlds as we do, and follows our paths and steps as a very important part of our "modern" life. And though we do not forget our ancestors, we do not ignore our traditions, we do move on musically in the future with lots of creative looks, by taking quick glances at the past.

In this "modern" epoch, on the island of Ithaca, music and dance performances have an educational flavor: Through music-making and dancing people learn how to understand and accept each other. The participants in music and dance events on the island of Crete join, or at least attempt to join, their co-islanders' behaviors. Toward this goal, Cretans expect not only to make more recordings of their music, but also to perform live in various events and occasions.

As a result, Greeks and Cretans wish to present their musical materials in a world music sphere. Many think that Cretans consciously dress up their music with "exotic" clothes to indulge and appeal to larger audiences. Others, among them Cretans themselves, try — through music — to particularly establish and create a notion of "Cretanness" for outside consumption.[242] Thus, today, more contemporary Cretan artists perform music having one more expectation in mind: That their audiences may be of any "ethnic" background.

Vasilis Stavrakakis is thrilled: More young people listen to Cretan music today. He feels that he himself experiences it: members of the audience at his performances, even outside Crete, are young. "Cretan music is a tradition very much alive," he thinks. "It even expands its horizons all over Greece." On May 21, 2001, he performed in Thessaloniki in Northern Greece. During his performance, he was in a great mood: He could not imagine that his music would appeal so much to a non-Cretan audience.

Cretans want everyone to understand that, even though they have their own musical tradition, they perform music as all people of the world do. To make their musical presence obvious to everyone, they record and distribute their music. Recall for a moment the compact disc I played for Hermes, a recording of the Iakinthia festivities of 2001. It was released immediately after that event. In its liner notes, Loudovikos of Anoya feels the need to praise the Cretan m a n d i n á d e s . Looking at them as poetry that applies to everyday situations, he dares compare them to the Spanish flamenco and the Portuguese fados.

A world's music show

People on the island of Crete still honor Nikos Xylouris as the ambassador of Cretan music to the rest of the world, representing it with all of the dignity and ethos worthy of such a noble tradition. In Nikos Xylouris, Cretans see their "archangel" who, with his distinctive vocal timbre, together with its timeless archetypal expressive quality, gave an entirely new dimension to whatever he sang. In Anoya, his birthplace, every summer, in combination with the religious celebration for the Dormition of Virgin Mary, on August 15, and the Anoya holocaust by Nazi forces, on August 13, music, dance and other events take place in commemoration of his name. Why Nikos Xylouris?:

Although very "traditional" in his approach, Nikos Xylouris is also highly innovative, always giving a "fresh" personal sound to whatever he sings. He listens very carefully to all of the great l í r a players prior to himself and absorbs the essence of their music, never simply copying what they were doing. Once this essence becomes part of his very being, he is able to use it in his own unique and creative way. Essentially, this is the way in which all great traditions grow and develop through the medium of remarkable individuals such as Nikos Xylouris.

Daly in *Welcome Crete*[243]

For the Greek people as a whole, he has come to be regarded as a symbol, indeed as an embodiment of the sum total of the virtues of the archetypal Cretan spirit. It was his unique personality which incorporated and balanced the attributes of pride and humility, nobility and simplicity, and which won him a place primarily in the hearts of the Greek people and secondarily in their memories.

Daly in interview[244]

We still hear the sounds of Nikos Xylouris everywhere in Crete. We worship his contributions. We cannot forget the voice of that Cretan man who struggles and finally manages to be heard in difficult political times for Greece. In Nikos, we see another prophet: The one who gets in trouble because of his strong beliefs for freedom, independence and creativity. When Stavrakakis performs Nikos Xylouris's songs[245] — something he does in most of his performances — the audience shivers. Nikos is still alive among us: He "owns" songs and is an idol, a prototype for all Cretan performers.

Next to Nikos Xylouris, who opens my world music show, I add now the picture of Ross Daly. I was born in Athens in May, 1973. I grew up and was nurtured with Xylouris's songs: My parents identify strongly with him. Today, always the eternal student, I constantly move. In my wanderings, I met Ross Daly and experienced his music. Wherever I travel, wherever I decide to set up my gypsy tent, I always carry, besides memories, recordings of the two: Nikos from Anoya, a sound profoundly Cretan, and Ross, a man who loves Crete and its music.

I hear, I feel and I identify with most of Daly's performances and compositions. The so-called Irishman, Ross Daly thinks of himself as an artist of no nation, an eternal traveler. Among the variety of string instruments he plays, he particularly caresses the Cretan l í r a . A man of no specific identity, Daly plays this three-stringed instrument, based on all the experiences he has gained from his classical music training and from his extensive studying with great masters in the Middle East and Asia.

Ross Daly gives to the l í r a his own voice, exceeding its local borders, going "safe" through customs. As a result, both musician and instrument transcend borders. As Xylouris creates his own unique style and makes Cretan music heard all over Greece, so does Daly.

In this spirit, Daly performs and creates his own musical universe, taking his audiences, both with his concerts and his recordings, on magic musical voyages beyond multicultural fashions.[246]

I am not interested in anyone's ethnic civilization. I believe we all have different aspects of the same thing, with some specialties and variations. The differences are superficial enough and it is, like when we say, that I want to study the plants

Psaronikos, the archangelic voice of Crete

of a region, then, I definitely have to study the specific form of the nature, namely, which plants grow here and which there. But, I never forget that my subject is the whole of nature. The same thing happens with music: it is something that unites the whole world, but in different places it exists in different forms.

Daly, quoted by M. Alexakis in *Ostria*

During our interview, Daly recalls the time when his teacher, Kostas Moundakis, went to India to perform as part of a cultural exchange program. He also remembers the time when he joined Moundakis to perform Cretan music in London. There, they happened to be in a house with musicians from Rajasthan and Bengali, musicians of the street. Moundakis had no problem playing with them on his l í r a . In this "informal" music performance, the Indians "heard" something — they found a common place: "Bravo, you are a big guru," they told him.

This example, he tells me, showed him how Indian or any good musicians who may not know anything specific about Cretan music can understand, feel, and ultimately identify with someone who plays well. It shows us how Cretan music can be disseminated, heard, and favored by people all over the world, not with the logic, however, that "we are the best and we will conquer the world with our music." As Daly wishes, "Cretan music should have a place of its own in world music."

Our musician learns from his teacher (and others) that "whoever lives and fully understands one type of music has access to many others of its kind." Musicians who have a good relationship with their civilizations are not closed or opposed to other parts of the world. Instead, they are more open. Automatically, they gain a sense of respect toward everything that is being created and is genuine. "She/he who is closed to the other (civilizations) and sees only hers/his, usually, in her/his relationship with her/his own (civilization) there is some type of a crack."[247]

Always in motion, Ross Daly, after having learned to play instruments and perform music from several traditions, searches for his own sound. And he wonders:

I am not Cretan, I am not even a good sample of an Irishman. I am a little bit a peculiar occasion. I do not have a country I can say that I was born and raised there. However, I want to play music. I can not say that by definition I have any tradition. I like and I love lots of traditions so I am engaged with them. All this engagement, all this work I have been doing for all these years, where does it lead me?[248]

Looking for an answer to the question posed above and having always been interested and in favor of music composition, Ross Daly travels continuously and learns from his travels. He shapes his own playing of the Cretan l í r a , in which he embodies all he knows about the l í r a s that belong, for instance, to the Cretan, the Turkish, and the Bulgarian musical traditions. Moreover, in his wanderings, he embraces all the experiences he has with Indian music as a whole, even though, when in India, he studied the sitar.

As a result, Ross Daly invites Indian musicians and gives concerts with them in Crete and elsewhere in Greece.[249] He sits down and studies: "How am I going to play Indian music with the l í r a ?" He recognizes the different approaches to music that Indians have, and decides that his playing of the l í r a must agree with specific assumptions concerning music. At the same time, as he stresses during our talk, he believes that the Cretan l í r a should enter the Indian musical tradition carrying its uniqueness as an instrument and not by refusing or denying its personality. His own personal attempt is definitely not simply to perform "normal Cretan playing."

In musical journeys-experiments of this type, Ross Daly does not think of himself as a characteristic example of a Cretan l í r a player. For instance — he explains — he embodies his own playing into one Indian piece and performs Indian elements on the l í r a. He takes popular, traditional Cretan melodies, such as from the A n o y a n é s k o n d i l i é s or the p e n d o z á l i s, and he arranges them in ways that match with that specific Indian piece. As a result, Daly improvises using phraseology from Cretan pieces, but even from some Irish ones.[250] In other occasions, Daly plays the rabáb in the style and the technique of an Arab o ú t i and an Indian saród, combined with Greek and Turkish phrasing.

Though Ross Daly views Cretan music as one of many spiritual musical traditions in search of a common origin of nature, he admits that it is not as easy for a foreigner to gain acceptance in Crete as he not only plays a "classical" Cretan instrument, but also performs non-traditional Cretan music on it. At the same time, he does not depart from what makes him feel complete, and he stays because "Crete is quite unlike any other place in the world, for a number of reasons: Its long history and the many powers and cultures which have left their traces here, the special geographic situation, the island and the people have their own very special character." When Daly visited Crete for the first time in 1971, he was so moved, so drawn to the place that, "by some inexplicable stroke of fate," he ended up there and established Crete as "the basis and point of reference" for his musical travels.

Ross Daly stops at no borders. For him, music is not any man's creation; it is not even the creation of mankind as a whole. Rather, it is a gift to mankind:

> Civilization belongs to the realm of lived experience. Inspiration and initiation do not belong to this realm. Instead, they merely leave imprints in the world of experience, which serve as catalysts for the awakening of the search and the longing for the source of inspiration, of music, of experience. It is through the awakening of this longing that we can see the primary and indeed fundamental difference between this music and any other expressive arts, which utilize the medium of sound.[251]

The 1992 album *Ross Daly: Selected Works* is a compilation of some of Daly's most interesting and inspired compositions. Here, we can see both the wide variety of influences as well as the underlying continuity and coherence that unites them, a key characteristic of Daly's music. As I am trying to show, Daly believes that the harmonious meeting and union of apparently different elements of various cultures is not something to be achieved by means of experiments with exterior form; rather, it must inevitably come as a result of the resolution within oneself of the essential internal differences that give rise to external appearances.

After establishing his group in Heraklion around 1982, Daly first concentrated on the many different traditions and cultures that have influenced the music of Crete over the course of the centuries. In his improvisations and compositions, he tried to work out these different cultural tendencies within Cretan music. Later, he moved to Athens with his group and came into contact with musicians from other countries and other cultures, and the range of their music broadened considerably. One of the compact discs they recorded, *Ross Daly & Labyrinth: Mitos (Thread),* indicates some of the musical traditions they worked with, those of Afghanistan, Azerbaijan, and Turkey, to name a few.

The multi-ethnic festival that Daly organized on the island of Rhodes in the summer of 2001, and with which I chose to open this step, is another example of his continuous, living musical acquisitions. For him, music has no boundaries; it does not belong to any given civilization. All its sounds simultaneously contain and transcend civilizations, peoples, places.[252] "Music," for Ross Daly, "is a glance that falls on something that does not take us to the rest, but to what is behind what we see."[253]

Worlds of Music

We hear Cretan music not only in Crete, but also throughout the world. Cretans live in Crete, in Greece, but also in many places around the world as well. And because music is a great part of our tradition and culture, we seek occasions where we can listen to it. Cretans in the United States, for example, invite l í r a players and hold Cretan feasts where we can dance or merely listen to "our" music.

In the liner notes of a series of compact discs devoted to the Cretan music masters,[254] I read about the l í r a player Spyros Sifoyiorgakis, who, at the First Festival of the Young in Helsinki, was awarded the first prize for his performance with Markoyiannis on the l a o ú t o , and a group of Cretan dancers. Following this success, around 1955-56, he toured in Eastern Europe and in the United States where he recorded his first record, *The Beacon.* Even President Truman presented him with the golden key to the U.S.A. during his stay.

A word show

I, the Cretan, not selfishly, consider all of my writings, throughout all these words and pages, as one more performance of world music. As Ross Daly does, I do not wish to view this interest in world music as a manifestation of Western arrogance or racism. I urge you to understand "the first thing about the music: the cultural and human background." Once more I borrow the words of the great musician and master — Ross Daly:

> In a world where lots of sharp producers are churning out a kind of homogenous world music by throwing together fragments of different musical cultures and blending them with all the available technology of contemporary studios, we should see world music as an inner and outer journey, in which any attempt to approach the various musical traditions of the world also has to involve an appreciation of the musicians themselves. In other words, we have to constantly be aware that we are all a part of this planet, learning to understand and accept each other in many different forms of expression.[255]

The five steps of my p e n d o z á l i s are now complete. Pleasantly dizzy, tiring, torturing, dancing, moving: through the past, in the present and onto the future. You have entered and have delved deeply into the labyrinth. But you have not exited it yet: You choose! You may go and get some water, because "everything flows."[256] Everything, like a dance, moves in a circle. Fifth step: future step.

CODA: DA CAPO AL FINE

I-Eye[257]

As a perfectionist, among other things, I cannot state that this work is complete, but at least I dare to claim it is honest. A relativist at most and Cretan, of course — though not a liar[258] — I place my current mythologies at specific times, places, circumstances.

My mythologies, as they move through time, from the past to the present and onto the future, aim to show how musical and dancing identities are locally shaped and that who we are in the end is what we want to be or what we think we are. What the people of Crete are or want to be cannot be "inauthentic." My words speak of the island of Crete, in Greece, but at the same time, I paint, or at least envision them, in contours of worldly dimensions.

I dream and imagine Crete as the place where several musicians from the Mediterranean and surrounding areas gather and perform, in peace — in the same spirit in which Ross Daly dreams of Crete as the place where he can have gatherings of musicians, teachers and students. I hope I can fulfill Stavrakakis's hope and, with my current work, contribute as an ambassador of Cretan music to the world.

Time is I am[259]

We enter the ancient palace of Knossos and the Minotaur's labyrinth with the help of the thread, which I hand to you as Ariadne guides me. On Psiloritis, the tallest mountain on the island of Crete, Zeus is born. Though his father, Kronos, eats his children, Cretans yet dance and perform loudly to cover the baby's cries so that he will survive. To them, Zeus owes his existence; they honor and praise him through their music and dance. Next to Zeus, Hyacinth inspires their performances. Along with many other Minotaurs, Zeus and Hyacinth together playfully shape living cultures that still make music for and dance to them.

According to ancient Greek mythology, Ariadne, my Cretan muse, hands the thread to Theseus so that he won't get lost in the meanders and be eaten by the Minotaur. As a result, Theseus comes out of the labyrinth safely. He marries Ariadne and they invite us to their wedding feast. At a later point in time, more medieval, but in the same place, in Crete, two young people, a man and a woman, Erotokritos and Aretousa, choose to speak out and sing of their passion, their love.

Even later in time, on the high, proud mountain of Psiloritis, near the village of Anoya, Zorba the Greek flirts with a young woman, Erofili. In a dialectic conversation they have, based on relativism, they speak about identity, local and non-local, traditional, national and ethnic. They agree with me — or, perhaps more accurately, I agree with them — that the identity of (and in) the labyrinth is shaped by socio-cultural ideas.

Hermes spreads to the world the rumors and all the aforementioned mythologies about the palace of Knossos.

Many guests and visitors arrive on Crete. While Atlas continues to carry the world on his shoulders, the Odyssey and all the mythologies I choose to present to you reach an Ithaca, to start all over again.

A-mazing Is-Eyes

Ross Daly chose "Labyrinth" as the name for his musical ensemble. For both of us, the labyrinth is a reference to our lives in a mythical sense:

> Between life and death there is this labyrinth, an enormously complex area of situations, experiences and possibilities, in which meaning and direction are determined by a certain goal: The Ariadne thread as a symbol of knowledge, understanding and enlightenment. The main opponent is the Minotaur, the ego. Each of us is working on our own Ariadne thread, with our own Minotaur lurking for any opportunity to devour us. The world of music is also a vast labyrinth, so that anyone seriously involved in "real music" has to deal with both these fundamental principles and their significance for music.[260]

May my mythologies fulfill the expectations of our labyrinthine, a-mazingly performed lives, and that they accomplish and follow the fundamental principles that "real music and dances" carry.

Every time I reach my goal, every time I complete the five main steps of "our" dance, the p e n d o z á l i s , I abandon myself to it — I let it make me dizzy, turn me around in circles. Every single time, I decide to improvise on it solo, with various maneuvers: Its circle never ends. It is a dance of, for and full of life. It makes me feel Cretan and, as such,[261] "I fear nothing, I hope for nothing, I am free."

Accompaniments

Ligature

A) Muses

Aerakis, Nikiforos: Born in 1945 in the village of Anoya, lira player and singer ("Aerakis, Nikiforos" 2002).

Amalthea: The Cretan goat that nurtured Zeus with her milk.

Apollo: The ancient Greek god of light (the sun) and musical harmony (the lyre); he enchanted both immortals and mortals alike.

Aretousa: Erotokritos's love interest.

Ariadne: The daughter of Pasiphae and King Minos of Crete. She helped Theseus escape from the Minotaur's labyrinth by giving him a ball of thread, which he unraveled as he went in, and used to trace his way out after having killed the Minotaur. Ariadne and Theseus then fled, but he deserted her on the island of Naxos, where Dionysus found and married her.

Atlas: Held the pillars that keep the earth and the heaven apart; a punishment Zeus imposed on him for having been the leader of the Titans during their revolt against the Olympian Gods.

Cavafy, Constantine: C. P. Cavafy (1863-1933), celebrated Greek poet. In the words of *The Times Literary Supplement*, "one of the greatest writers of our times."[262]

Daedalus and Icarus: Ingenious technician and his son trapped in the labyrinth by King Minos. To escape by flying away, Daedalus built wings from bird feathers and stuck them to their bodies with wax. Icarus flew too close to the sun and his wings melted away.

Damaskinos, Michael: Major Cretan painter of the second half of the sixteenth century.

Diyenis, Akritas: Medieval epic hero; the biracial knight of the border (ákro), diyenís meaning of two races;

son of an Arab chieftain and an aristocratic Greek lady; the subject of the second part of Kazantzakis's Odyssey.[263]

Elytis, Odysseus: Famous Greek poet, born in Crete in 1911. He received the Nobel Prize in 1979.[264]

Epimenides: (Mythical) Cretan philosopher of the 7th century. One of the Seven Sages of Greek antiquity.[265]

Erofili: The main heroine of the book by Hortatsis with the same title.

Erotokritos: The main hero of the book by Kornaros with the same title.

Euripides: Born in Salamis around 480 B.C. In 406 B.C. he died in Macedonia in King Archelaus's Court. Euripides wrote 92 plays, of which 78 were known by the Alexandrians; of them 19 survived complete. He won five times in dramatic contests, once post humously.[266]

Foustalieris (Foustalierakis), Stelios: Born in 1911. He lived in Rethymnon where he owned a small watch-repair shop. He played an unusual instrument known as the boulgarí, a smaller version of the Turkish saz.[267]

Hainis (Hainides): Guerilla; apostate; fugitive.

Hatzidakis, Manos: Famous Greek composer who is credited with reviving the rebetiko style of music. Hatzidakis established the "Musical August" cultural events in both the village of Anoya and Heraklion, Crete.

Heraclitus: c. 535-c. 475 B.C; Greek philosopher from Ephesus.

Hercules (Heracles): Mythical Greek hero, one of the Idaean Dactyls. When the grown-up Zeus was recognized as the unquestionable God of men — after winning the war against his father — the good gods Kourites, who had meanwhile taught people how to lead a peaceful life in organized societies and had initiated them into secrets of dance and song, left for the holy land of ancient Olympia. There, the oldest one who was called Hercules — just like the one who is referred to as demigod in mythology with his famous labors — came up with the idea of telling his brothers to run into beautiful plains, in order to see who would be the winner. He is considered to be the founder of the Olympic Games. Thus according to the myth, the Olympic spirit was born in Ancient Olympia by a Cretan god.[268]

Hermes: Ancient Greek god of communication; the messenger among gods, but also between gods and humans.

Herodotus: Ancient Greek historian.

Homer: Ancient Greek epic poet, author of the Odyssey and the Iliad.

Hortatsis, Yeorgios: Cretan poet, perhaps the greatest dramatist of the Cretan theater (c.middle of 16th century - c.beginning of 17th century).

Hyacinth: Ancient Greek god who was born and died every year.

Idaean Dactyls: Demons believed to live on Mount Ida and the first metallurgists. Their name is derived from the Greek word for "finger" (dáktilo).

Kallergis, Michalis: Líra player, born in 1957 in the village of Karkadiotissa.

Kazantzakis, Nikos: Born on February 18, 1883, in Heraklion. Among the most prominent and well-known Greek authors worldwide.

King Minos: The legendary King of Crete; the father of Ariadne.

Kondylakis, Ioannis: 1861-1920; Cretan journalist who wrote fiery patriotic articles in the Cretan dialect under the pseudonym "The Passer."

Kornaros, Vitsentzos: He was born in the village of Trapezounta, near Sitia, in 1553. He belonged to the noble Veneto-Cretan family of Cornaro. He was a member of the Council of the Nobles and held various administrative posts.[269]

Kourites: The ancient Cretans.

Koutsourelis, Yiorgos: Mandolin and laoúto player, born in Kissamos, in 1914.

Kronos: The father of Zeus; an alteration of the word Chronos (time).

Leondaritis, Frangiskos: Cretan musician of the Renaissance period.

Loudovikos of Anoya: Mandolin player, composer and singer from the village of Anoya.

Lucian (Loukianos): Ancient Greek theoretician; he wrote the "Dialogues of the Gods."

Lykastos: Name of an ancient Cretan city in the Heraklion region, near Knossos; also, the name of the Cretan hero that came from that city.

Markopoulos, Yiannis: Contemporary Greek composer of Cretan descent.

Minotaur: Beast in the palace of Knossos.

Moundakis, Kostas: Líra player and teacher, born at the village of Alfa in 1926. His contribution to the preservation and dissemination of the líra has been invaluable.[270]

Mousa: Deity of music, poetry, orchestrics, drama; protector of Arts and Letters.

Odysseus: The Homeric hero; symbol of the ingenious man and the eternal traveler.

Papadaki, Aspasia: Cretan líra player and singer; as far as we know, the first woman in the history of Cretan music to play this instrument.[271]

Piperakis, Harilaos: Known as Harilaos the Kritikós (Cretan), he was born in either 1894 or 1895 in Xerosterni, Chania. He founded his own record company in the United States under the name of Fáros (Lighthouse).

Plato: Ancient Greek philosopher (429 or 427-347 B.C.),

student of Socrates.

Prevelakis, Pandelis: Cretan writer; Kazantzakis's disciple.

Procrustes: Mythic figure who offered a "one-size-fits-all" bed to passing travelers, "adjusting" them to the bed by stretching or chopping their limbs.

Psaradonis: Music composer from Anoya, l í r a player and singer. Brother of the Nikos Xylouris.

Psaroyiannis: Cretan l a o ú t o player, brother of Nikos Xylouris and Psaradonis.

Psaroyiorgis: Son of Psaradonis; Cretan l a o ú t o player and singer.

Pythagoras: Philosopher, mathematician and music theorist. He lived between 530 and 497 B.C.; he was born and died at Megapontium, in Samos.

Radamanthis: King Minos's brother, fair ruler.

Rodinos: Born in Rethymnon in 1912. A great performer, creator, and master of folk music.[272]

Sappho: 630-570 B.C. Born at Eresos of Lesbos and lived in the town of Mytilene. The greatest lyric poet of ancient Greece who was also called "the Tenth Muse," "the Mortal Muse," or the "Feminine Homer."

Seferis, George: Greek poet, born in Smyrna, Asia Minor, in 1900. His first volume of poetry, *Strophí (Turning point)*, in 1931, marked a turning point in modern Greek poetry. In 1963, he was awarded the Nobel Prize for Literature.

Sikelianos, Angelos: Greek poet, born on the island of Lefcada in 1884.

Skironas (Skiron): Mythical Greek figure who forced passers-by to wash his feet and then kicked them from a cliff into the sea to be eaten by a giant sea-turtle.

Skordalos, Thanasis: L í r a player born in 1920, in Spili.

Skoulas, Vasilis: Contemporary popular Cretan l í r a player and singer from the village of Anoya.

Solomos, Dionysios: Greek poet; he wrote the lyrics of the Greek national anthem.

Stavrakakis, Mitsos: Cretan folk poet and composer; Cretans consider him as one of the most prominent contemporary Cretan folk poetry (m a n d i n á d a) composers.

Theodorakis, Mikis: Famous Greek composer born in 1925 to a family of Cretan descent.

Theofanis the Cretan: Great artist and iconographer of the 15th century.

Theotokopoulos, Domenicus: Cretan painter who moved and worked extensively in Toledo, Spain; known as El Greco.

Theseus: Ancient Greek hero; one out of the seven young men (besides the six young women) that the Minotaur was supposed to eat.

Tourkokritikoi; Tourkokrites: Turkish-Cretans; Cretan in origin, language and customs, but Muslim in religious beliefs.

Xydakis, Nikos: Composer, born on March 17, 1952 , in Cairo.

Xylouris, Nikos; Psaronikos: Singer, the "Archangel of Crete," born on July 7, 1936, in the village of Anoya.[273]

Zeus (Dias, Kritagenis, Xenios): Jupiter; Jove; the amorous father of the twelve gods of antiquity.

B) Melodies

Acropolis: The ancient citadel in Athens, containing the Parthenon, the Erectheum, and other notable buildings, mostly dating from the 5th century B.C.

A m á n - a m á n: For mercy's sake!; woe is me!; Turkish exclamatory expression that denotes, among other things, sorrow, pain, misfortune.

Amanés (manés): Melodic improvisation, based on the word a m á n . Dancers translate this word into movement(s).

Anáktoro: Palace; court.

Andalusia: The southernmost region of Spain, bordering on

the Atlantic and the Mediterranean; capital, Seville; the region, under Moorish rule from 711 to 1492, was probably named by the Moors after the Vandals, who had settled there in the 5th century.

'Ano; Anóyi: Upper; Loft.

Anthótiros: Cretan salty white cheese.

Anoyanós Pidihtós: Leaping dance from Anoya.

Anthropoloyía: Anthropology.

'Anthropos: Human being; man.

Apollonian: Of or relating to Apollo; orderly, rational, self-disciplined.

Arák: Alcoholic spirit from grapes or dates.

Askomadoúra: Bagpipe; pibroch; a s k ó s (animal skin) and bandura (in Italian, a kind of rough flute [pipe] usually out of calamus); the instrument has been very popular with the shepherds and the inhabitants of the mountainous areas of Crete.

Baglamás: Long-necked type of lute of various sizes.

Bálos: Greek folk dance mainly performed on the islands and by couples.

Bendír: Frame drum.

Brostáris: The leader of the dancing line, the first dancer.

Boulgarí (bourgarí): L a o ú t o; in Turkish, small guitar; smaller version of the Turkish saz or the t a m b o u r á s found in other regions of Greece.

Chania (Khania): A port on the north coast of Crete, capital of the island from 1841 to 1971.

Chaniótis, Chaniótiko(s), Chaniótikos Syrtós: A circle dance from the city of Chania; a dance where dancers hold arms at shoulder height.

Chóra: The closest city to the village; the capital of the district.

Chorós: Dance; dancing.

Chrónos: Time.

Daoúli: Drum; cylindrical, double-headed drum.

Défi: Tambourine; tabor.

Delína: Frolic; madness.

Díktamo (or érondas): Dictamnus; a herb deriving its name from the Greek god Dias (Zeus).

'Embolo: Fine (sterile) sheep, oftentimes selected as a gift for a dear friend.

Egoismós: Ego; pride.

Elefthería: Freedom; liberty.

'Ellinas: Hellene; Greek.

EOT: Initials of E l l i n i k ó s O r g a n i s m ó s T o u r i s m o ú, i.e. Greek Tourism Organization.

Epikrédios: Cretan war-dance (p y r r h í c h e). Nothing definite is known about its characteristic features. [274]

'Erganos: Tool; instrument.

Filótimo: Love of honor, earnestness.

Filótimos: Conscientious.

Filoxenía: Hospitality.

Flogéra: Fife; flute.

Gadoúlka: Bulgarian type of l í r a; three-stringed, pear-shaped folk fiddle.

Gáida: Bagpipe.

Galaktoboúreko: Milk pastry.

Gámos: Marriage; wedding feast.

Geranós: Ancient Greek dance.

Gléndi: Big celebration; feast.

Gýros: Meat cooked in a rotisserie.

Halépa: Extent of stony and infertile ground; region in Chania.

Halépi: Aleppo; Halab in Arabic; a city in northern Syria, formerly an important commercial center on the trade route between the Mediterranean and the countries of the East.

Heráklion (Iráklio): A port and the capital of Crete, on the north coast of the island.

Hypórchema: Sung and danced in honor of Apollo. Hyporchema was also the dance itself.

'Ida ('Idi; Nída): Older, pre-Hellenic name for Psiloritis.

Idaíon 'Andro: Cave in the mountain of Psiloritis where, according to tradition, Zeus was born.

Ithaca: An island off the western coast of Greece in the Ionian Sea, the legendary home of Odysseus.

Kaimós: Sorrow; yearning.

Karagiózis: Figure of the shadow-puppet theater; buffoon; fool.

Kastrinós, Kastrinós Pidihtós, Herakliótikos Kastrinós, Maleviziótis, Kastrinés Kondiliés: Leaping dance from Heraklion; from the district of Malevizi (a West Heraklion province); a lively dance, performed with arms interlinked at shoulder height.

Kástro (Megálo): Castle (Big); Heraklion, the capital of Crete, named Kastro in the past.

Kathimeriní: The name of a contemporary Greek newspaper, meaning "Daily."

Káto Horió; Perahori: "Lower Village."

Kéfi: High spirits; gaiety.

Kementzé(s): Líra type of instrument played especially in the Black Sea region of Turkey; in Persian "keman" means bow, "tze" small.[275]

Kéndro: Club.

Knossos: The principal city of Minoan Crete, the remains of which are situated on the north coast of Crete.

Kondíli: Condyle; node; plectrum or feather.

Kondiliá: Cretan musical phrase.

Kondaromahía: Fight with poles; tourney.

Kouradóvrisi: Drinking fountain for a flock of goats and sheep.

Kri-kri: Ibex.

Kríti: Crete.

Kritikí: Cretan (female, singular); also critique in oral speech.

Kritikopoúla: Cretan woman; Kritikópoula: Cretan children.

Kourá: Sheep's shearing (pl. kourés).

Kouroúpi: Small jar.

Kouzoulós: Crazy; mad; insane.

Laodikía: Latakia; a seaport on the coast of western Syria, across the north-eastern tip of Cyprus.

Laografía: Folklore.

Laoúto: Large lute; its name is quite obviously a derivative of the Arabic word al'oud (namely, the wood).[276]

Lavírinthos: Labyrinth.

Levéndis: Gallant; chappie; corker.

Líra: The pre-eminent national instrument of ancient Greece; the most important and most widely known of all instruments. Associated with Apollo's cult, it was much respected (in this context, known as lyre). Today, the líra is the main folk instrument on the island of Crete. We also find it in other regions of Greece (e.g. the island of Karpathos, in Thrace, in the Dodecanese, and so on) and in its neighboring countries, such as Bulgaria (gadúlka) and Turkey (kementzé).

Logári: Treasure.

Mandináda (matináda): Cretan proverbial saying, poetic form; rhyming distich often imbued with "gnomic" force; in Italian, mattinata is an early morning serenade.

Mandolíno: Mandolin; it first appeared in Crete during the Venetian occupation.

Meráki: Yearning; passion; sorrow.

Meraklís: A man who demands the best and is knowledgeable in the rules of g l é n d i, capable of experiencing and conveying true k é f i; m e r a k l í k i: noun denoting this attitude.

Methistís: Inebriant.

Mezés: Appetizer; served with drinks before the main course.

Mitáto: A shepherd's shack.

Mizíthra: Soft white cheese.

Mousikí: Music; the word m o u s i k í appears for the first time (in preserved texts so far) in the 5th century.

Muwashshahat: Some of the oldest pieces of music in the repertoire of Arabic music, generally attributed to the Arabs of Andalusia who, after being expelled from Spain in the 14th century, settled all over the Arab world, especially in Syria.

Na zis' i Kríti!: May Crete live for ever!

Níki: Victory.

NET: Initials for N é a E l l i n i k í T i l e ó r a s i i.e. New Greek Television.

Oftós: Roast.

Olympia: In ancient Greece it was the site of the chief sanctuary of Zeus, the place where the original Olympic Games were held.

Oneírou Tópi: Dreamlands.

Oréos, ópa-ópa léo!: Nice, ó p a - ó p a I'm saying!

'Ormos: Ancient Greek dance.

Orsítes: A Cretan war-dance; some writers believe that both the o r s í t e s and the e p i k r é d i o s are different names for the same dance.

Orthós Lógos: Right Thought; Logic.

Oud: Short-necked lute.

Oúti: Oud.

Palikári: Brave man.

Paniyíri: Big celebration, feast.

Paréa: Company; gang; party.

Patitíri: Wine press.

Patrís: Homeland, also the name of a major, daily Cretan newspaper.

Paximádi: Rusk.

Pendozáli(s): Characteristic Cretan dance (p é n d e means five and z á l a means steps).

Peloponnese (Pelopónnisos): The mountainous southern peninsula of Greece, connected to central Greece by the isthmus of Corinth.

Pidichtós: Leaping dance.

Pitáki: Small pie.

Póli: City; town; also refers to Constantinople.

Polimíchanos: Ingenious; resourceful; the adjective Homer uses to characterize his hero, Odysseus.

Polítiki líra: Kementzé-type of l í r a mainly used in Istanbul.

Psarós: Grizzly.

Psichagogía: Recreation; amusement; entertainment.

Psilorítis (psiló óros): The tallest mountain in Crete; also referred to as Ida.

Pyrrhíche: The most important and majestic kind (or class) of war-dance.

Pyrrhíchios: Pyrrhic dance; the dance of pyrrhiche; also a metrical foot of two short syllables.[277]

Qanún (kanonáki): A kind of psaltery, or plucked zither.

Rabáb: String instrument belonging to the lute family; it is considered as the most ancient string instrument: a legend says that Adam enjoyed playing it.[278]

Raéti: Good food; excellent meal.

Rakí: Alcoholic spirit distilled from the skin and stones of raisins.[279]

Rebétiko: Urban Greek music with roots from Asia Minor.

Réthymnon (Réthimnon): A port on the north coast of Crete.

Rizítika: Songs of the foothills (in Greek, r í z e s means roots and also foothills) originating in the western mountainous area of the island of Crete.

Saganáki: Ramekin.

Sandoúri: Type of dulcimer.

Sarángi: North Indian instrument, particularly found in Rajasthan, similar to the kementzé.

Saríki: Turban.

Sarikópita: Turban shaped cheese pitas.

Saród: Classical Indian music string instrument.

Saz: Middle-Eastern string instrument; long-necked type of lute.

Sfirohábiolo (thiabóli; fiabóli; chabióli; babióli; flogéra): fife; flute; the faithful companion of shepherds grazing their sheep on the remote mountain slopes of Crete.

Siganós: Slow dance; usually performed during wedding celebrations.

Sitar: String instrument of the northern classical Indian musical tradition.

Skáloma: Deadlock.

Stifádo: Hare stew.

Stiváni: Boots; buskin.

Stráta: Road; street; path.

Soústa: Spring; clasp; a Cretan dance of great delicacy and finesse.

Syrtáki: Popular "invented" Greek dance; the Zorba dance.

Syrtós: Dragging dance; movement of the feet over the ground in a dragging or shuffling motion.

Tabachaniótiko: Cretan genre of vocal music; the name originates from the Tabachanádes (sanatoria), thus, sad and lonely places for those people branded with the stigma of tuberculosis.[280]

Távla: Oblong table for banquets.

Taxími: Middle-Eastern musical improvisational scheme.

Thessaloniki (Salonica; Thessalonica): A seaport in Northern Greece.

Thimári: Thyme.

Tragoúdi: Song.

Trýgos: Vine harvest.

Tsiftetéli: Belly dance.

Toube(r)léki: Darabuka; goblet-shaped drum; tom-tom.

Tzatzíki: Relish of yogurt, cucumber and garlic.

Tzourás: String instrument, long-necked type of lute, of medium size.[281]

Vasilikós: Basil.

Votrydón: Ancient Greek dance.

Vráka: Breeches; trousers.

Xasteriá: Fair weather; starry sky.

Xathéri: The best quality of something.

Xóbli: Pattern for embroidery.

Yiasemí: Jasmine.

Yia sou!; Yia mas!: To your health!; to our health!

Zeimbék(iko): A solo male dance that is found in both Greece and Turkey.

Notes

1 Schechner (1985) talks about anthropology being theatricalized: The process of acknowledging that humans are also jesters and performers, ones who play and perform. We may thus view life as a theater full of performances as well as performers not to be ignored.

2 In the Cretan dialect, the verb "sound" is used to denote "smell." This phenomenon is called lexical-gustatory synaesthesia.

3 There was a church for prophet Havdeu in nearby Kontaria. For more information on the village of Avdou visit http://www.avdou.com/avdou.asp

4 Grandmother Christina passed away on September 12, 2004. She is survived by four daughters and nine grandchildren.

5 As a result, the text has been written so that one can read it with little or no reference to the notes (Geertz 1980: xi). The argument is in the text, together with the essential empirical material supporting it, uncluttered by references or in-group qualifications. Henry Glassie (1982) follows the same technique, namely choosing endnotes instead of straight citations or footnotes.

6 As far as it concerns this structure, I'm influenced by Shelemay (1998).

7 "Demon" is the first song in Stavrakakis's 2001a compact disc.

8 "Light Blue and Green" is fifth song in the Stavrakakis's 2001a compact disc.

9 An excerpt from the seventh song in Stavrakakis's 2001a compact disc.

10 An excerpt from the fourth song in Stavrakakis's 2001a compact disc.

11 For instance, the líra, the instrument-stereotype of Cretan music.

12 Such as Ross Daly, an Irishman but also a main figure on the Cretan music scene.

13 For example, the popular Cretan singer Vasilis Stavrakakis, who is not a líra but a mandolíno player.

14 Although they may not necessarily imply lexical meanings as language does.

15 Such works are, for instance, the tragedy *Erofíli* (Hortatsis 1996), the epic poem *Erotókritos* (Kornaros 1994) and the writings of the Cretan writer Nikos Kazantzakis.

16 At this point, my writings are significantly inspired by Sondra Horton Fraleigh's work (1987). She attempts to develop an aesthetic perspective of dance through existential phenomenology (particularly through the concept of the living body). I make use of her ideas here, but I also expand them beyond dance into music performance. In general, I agree with her that phenomenology is a method which attempts to view any experience from the inside rather than from a distance, often taking the form of first-person description.

17 "The road up and down is one and the same" (in Barnstone 1999: 43).

18 Henry Glassie's (1975) and Oscar Lewis's (1959) works on individual stories are of great use as well as James Clifford's (1988) way of interpreting culture.

19 Martin Stokes suggested this to me during an informal conversation at the 2000 Society for Ethnomusicology (SEM) conference in Toronto, Canada.

20 The works of Herzfeld (1987, 1995) and Eickelman (1998) are telling on this issue.

21 Belonging somewhere is very confusing, especially for ethnographers. My personal notion of belonging relates to human presence. I belong where I have people to love and love me.

22 This question, indeed, about "Zorba's problem" is very crucial. Not only through Zorba the Greek, but also through his other books (*Freedom or Death* and *Christ Recrucified*), Kazantzakis creates an archetypal Crete and a prototype of the Cretan man and woman who, in my opinion, influence not only foreigners but Greeks and Cretans themselves. Further investigating that point might include the question of how much of the "Cretan character" is an invention of Kazantzakis (or even his disciple, Padelis Prevelakis).

23 Ruth Stone (1978, 1982), like Herzfeld, makes use of icons and iconicity in cultural ideologies.

24 Zeimbék(iko) is a mainly solo male dance that is performed in both countries.

25 I do not wish to call the other type of fieldwork "unconscious" and it should not be understood and taken as such.

26 That is why, in the following essays, I talk mostly historically about the past.

27 In "good" translations, the translator is self-effacing. In "good" ethnography, by contrast, the presence of the ethnographer must not be allowed to disappear from view.

28 Thus, I feel flattered by Michael Herzfeld, who maintains that the ethnography of Greece provides a rich source of material for investigation (1987). I, furthermore, feel particularly challenged.

29 Herzfeld's view of ethnography "through the looking-glass" (1987).

30 In the same sense, Michael Herzfeld calls for an ethnography of the ethnographers: "It's time to do some 'fieldwork.' Watch yourself and your friends do the same things too. This is a good exercise in reflexivity, the analysis of one's own role in what he studies. We are all in it together, because we are all participants in a social world" (Herzfeld 1987: 90).

31 In the next Step I comment more extensively on the idea of locality.

32 Geertzian (1988) words.

33 The Epimenides paradox is a problem in logic, named after the Cretan semi-mythical philosopher-poet Epimenides of Knossos (flourished circa 600 BC). The "lie" of the Cretans was that Zeus was mortal, whereas Epimenides considered him immortal.

34 Anthropological interest in Southern Europe often has been converged in a more generalized Mediterranean culture area. The founding of the Society for the Anthropology of Europe appears to have re-centered the area focus to a significant degree. Recent studies, therefore, of moral and symbolic systems have taken for granted the concept of a "Mediterranean culture area" (Herzfeld 1984).

35 Greece is a country that offers Michael Herzfeld many chances to shape his thought in the context of cultural anthropology (Herzfeld 1987). According to him, Europe has been traditionally excluded from ethnography. The ethnography of Greece, however, provides a rich source of material for investigation (Herzfeld 1992b).

36 Relevant Heraclitian saying: "We are and we are not" (in Barnstone 1999: 48).

37 That is during the first third of the nineteenth century, when the Greek state emerges as a unity.

38 This is what Michael Herzfeld terms as the "Hellenic thesis." This thesis, based on Western Europe's perception of ancient Greece, views modern Greek culture — especially folk culture — as what survived of ancient Greek ideals and denies oriental influences on it. On the other hand, there is the "Romeic thesis" which, most characteristically exemplified by linguistic demagoguery, represents the familiar self-image which Greeks entertain about themselves when conversing among themselves (Herzfeld 1986).

39 For more information, one may look at *The Cretan Glance: The World and Art of Nikos Kazantzakis* by Morton P. Levitt, Ohio State University Press, Columbus, OH, 1980.

40 "I Kríti sti zoí...", Psilakis 1977.

41 For instance, scenes in *Freedom or Death* (1956) and *The Greek Passion* (1954).

42 Herzfeld gives a critical account of the birth and development of folklore as a scholarly field in modern Greece (1982). *Ours Once More: Folklore, Ideology and the Making of Modern*

Greece shows how history is important in the making of national and international politics, as well as the construction of an undeniable cultural continuity from ancient to modern Greece.

43 In the same sense, the Brazilian nationalistic movement sees also folklore (or folk music) as the basis upon which to construct its own musical tradition (Reily 1994: 79).

44 Even though the ancient Greek lyre has structurally nothing to do with the Cretan one.

45 This idea is based on the book by Hobsbawm and Ranger (1992).

46 Where we are not going to see our Greek predecessors (heroes), but our reality (downfalls). Or, as Nikos Dimou in his 1975 book says, not Alexander the Great, but... Karagiozis.

47 The title of the first song in this compact disc is "The Murder Knife," basically, a love song, speaking of a man who will commit murder with an old knife, if he is not able to "take" the girl he is in love with.

48 In opposition to the ancient Greek saying "moderation is best," namely, "avoid extremes."

49 In Greek oral speech, "kritikí" may mean a) the female (woman) that comes from the island of Crete and b) critique.

50 Popular Greek song. Music by Yiannis Markopoulos and lyrics by Michalis Stavrakakis or Nidiotis.

51 *Kríti: Istoría kai politismós*, 1987, pp. xiv-xv.

52 These are popular mythologies still found today on the island of Crete. In the following step I talk more about them.

53 *Kríti...*, 1987, pp. 53 (Keftiou), 113 (dancing), 126 (Ariadne), 114 (Lucian), 133 (Greek civilization), 133 (eastern themes), 114 (tension), 179-80 (conservationism).

54 Of or relating to ancient Athens or Attica, or the form of Greek spoken there.

55 *Kríti...*, 1987, pp. 221 (Cretans' interests), 228 (dances), 344 (Hellenistic era), 380 (Arabs), 400 (older speculations), 360 (Byzantine era), 366 (Venetian rule).

56 In 1862, Crete is multi-cultural (polipolitismikí), a place where the Greek element tries to co-exist with the Turks, Jews, Arabs and blacks. Crete is multiracial, a crossroads for people that left their traces on the long history of the island [*Patrís* November 6 2001 (a)]. The architecture on the island reveals this melting pot as well.

57 *Kríti...*, 1987, pp. 134 (village population), 139 (Handakas), 346 (Ottoman rule).

58 Even the converting of the Arabs who remained in Crete after its liberation was a problem for Istanbul (*Kríti...*, 1987, p. 401).

59 *Kríti...*, 1987, pp. 347 (Tourkokrítes), 143 (mixing of techniques), 189 (artistic figures), 387 (Egyptian rule).

60 Ida, Psiloritis's ancient name, means forest, and it is a sign of Zeus's (Dias's) existence on the mountain (*Kríti...*, 1987, p. 92).

61 Xenios Zeus means hospitable Zeus (filoxenía in Greek meaning hospitality) whereas Kritagénis Días means Zeus born in Crete.

62 Friar 1985: 144.

63 This is also the expectation of the first meeting of the "Cretan Youth," as it appears on the brochure that comes out after its first worldwide meeting in Crete, in August 1998.

64 Barnstone 1999b: 73 (154, Incert. 16).

65 This reputation for excellent dancing is also referred to in the Homeric poems (Makreas 1979: 18-22).

66 All quotes in this introductory part are based on my own field-recordings, notes and brochures of July 6, 2001.

67 That Zeus is a work of the sculptor Nicola Zarboni, professor of Fine Arts in Bologna (1.60m by 1.10m); *The Dance of the Stone: Iakinthia; Reference to Zeus* 2001).

68 Hymn by Orpheus dated around the 6th century B.C.

69 Part of the readings devoted to Zeus recited that night.

70 The village of Anoya mourned the unfortunate death of the 34 year-old Sbokos on October 2004 and devoted the 2005 series of Cultural Events to him, while his fellow and director Lefteris Haronitis made a film in the memory of "Atzaroyiorgis."

71 From left to right, as I see them on the stage: Laodikis (toubelêki), Maria Fasoulaki (singing and bendír), Yiorgis Stavrakakis (laoúto), Vagelis Alexakis (líra), Vasilis Stavrakakis (singing and playing mandolin), Vasilis Sygletos (laoúto) and Fanouris Kalemakis (guitar).

72 Again, from left to right, as I see them on the stage: Yiorgis Stavrakakis (laoúto), Michalis Kallergis (líra), Vasilis Sygletos (laoúto) and Fanouris Kalemakis (guitar).

73 Since the ancient times of the Minoan civilization, the inhabitants of Crete seemed to be aware of the value of food like olive oil, olives, green vegetables, herbs and many other products that are found in Crete in great abundance (greens, nuts, grains, legumes, honey, and so on).

74 There are athletic games (weight lifting [ársi varón]) taking place at the same time these events are being held.

75 There is also an exhibition of pottery and weaving, and of xóblia (decorations) of pastries for weddings, baptisms, births, deaths, going on in the village of Anoya. People have the chance to watch theatrical plays and films that relate to all the legends and myths surrounding that area (for example, the film Idaeou míthi –directed by Lefteris Haronitis — where the archaeologist Yiannis Sakelarakis is the protagonist).

76 Flaubert, Gustave. 1854. Dictionary of Accepted Ideas. Translated with an introduction and notes by Jacques Barzun. Connecticut: Norfolk.

77 Dimou 2001: 50.

78 Ideas drawn from Herzfeld (1984, 1992b).

79 I comment on this aspect more on the fifth and last step, particularly on its first essay, Knossos.

80 This is the very last scene of the first film. The book with the same title proceeds further and ends differently.

81 Ideas and words borrowed from Cowan's opening paragraph (2000).

82 The Kazantzakis "Captain Michalis" novel is titled and known in English by the translation of its Greek subtitle, thus, "Freedom or Death".

83 "Fovoú tous 'Ellines" (Beware of Greeks bearing guns"), a 1999 Greek-Australian production.

84 Review entitled "O 'Mítsos' pou égine Mános", Kathimerini newspaper, January 30, 2000, page 47.

85 Syncretism is the attempt to reconcile disparate, even opposing, beliefs and to meld practices of various schools of thought. It is especially associated with the attempt to merge and analogize several originally discrete traditions, particularly in theology and the mythology of religion and thus assert an underlying unity. Cretans united in their differences and came together in alliance when faced with external dangers. The word is a compound of syn, "together", and... "Crete".

86 All phrases published in Yper-X (26):20-1. One may read more on the purpose and the mission of the Pancretan Association of America (PAA) in http://www.pancretan .org/mission/mission.aspx

87 Makreas (1979) discusses and illustrates these issues with more detail throughout her M.A. thesis.

88 These are also Michael Herzfeld's observations described in detail in his 1985a book.

89 One of Henry Glassie's main ideas (1989).

90 These ideas are inspired from Stokes's discussion on music and identity (1994: 3-5).

91 Ideas obviously influenced by Savigliano (1995).

92 Dragging on and "teasing" Levi-Strauss (1986), can mythic thinking be seen in music?

93 Valentine's day, which, in any case, was never part of Greek Orthodox Christian beliefs, is this way locally celebrated in the name day of Saint Iakinthos.

94 This idea is discussed and illustrated in Magowan's essay (1994: 135-155).

95 "Sto Petrokefáli...", Patrís November 22, 2001.

96 "Messara...", Patrís November 2, 2001.

97 "Was the Olympic..." 2000.

98 Inspired by this, in 2004, director Lefteris Haronitis produced the DVD "Cretan Olympic Games Winners".

99 I adopt Cohen's ideas when she talks about the construction of Liverpool-ness (Cohen 1994: 133).

100 "Sto Venerato...", *Patrís* November 1, 2001.

101 Cowan (1990), Dubisch (1986), Herzfeld (1985a) and Loizos and Papataxiarchis (1991) investigate gender issues in Greece whereas other works, such as those of Abu-Lughod (1986) and Nieuwkerk (1995), locate them in other places in the Middle East.

102 Michael Herzfeld (1985a) extensively talks and comments on animal-theft in Crete.

103 Pages 437-442, *Erotókritos*, by V. Kornaros.

104 This friend I met in the summer of 1998. When I saw him again in the summer of 2001, at another wedding feast, he invited me to his own wedding, the one I am talking about here.

105 More specifically, Ruth Stone (1982) states that music is communication and that meaning in music is created by participants in the course of social interaction. Thus, the social relationships among participants are based upon the simultaneous experiencing of the performance in multiple dimensions of time. Being an ethnomusicologist, she makes inferences about music and music event interaction by engaging in interactional behavior. She draws on symbolic interaction and phenomenology, and she is interested in the event. She wants to understand processes of interaction within music and event — those processes that unite behavior and sound.

106 Theaters in Crete are usually named after famous locals. In the village of Anoya, for example, the theater is called Nikos Xylouris and feasts are held annually there to honor him.

107 An example of that is Vasilis's concert in Heraklion, at Oasis or Garden Theater Nikos Kazantzakis, in the memory of his relative Michalos, known among the Anoya locals as Nidiotis, on July 20, 2000.

108 During our meetings, Vasilis oftentimes mentions the notion of paréa (company) and all the atmosphere around such an informal gathering which includes music.

109 For the recordings of Cretan music I talk more in the last step, on the "Hermes's" essay.

110 For more discussion on this point look at "Knossos" in the fifth step.

111 In Greece, more generally, one cannot have a wedding without dance. The dance event and the wedding event are, in a certain sense, integrated, inseparable. Dance begins from the moment one gets married in the church. In the Greek Orthodox church, after the priest gives the newly-weds the Holy Cup to drink from three times in a row, in token of their common life together, and after the pair has partaken, the entire wedding party walks three times around the analóyio (lectern), while among hymns the following is sung: "O Isaiah, dance thy joy: for a Virgin was with child and hath borne a son, Emmanuel, both God and man." The scene described above has begun traditionally called (in the Greek Orthodox Church) "Isaiah's dance." In one of the weddings that I attended, a man, as soon as the "Isaiah's dance" part had begun, said that the wedding was finished, but the dance had just begun. Greek people very often, when they think that it is time for someone to get married, usually ask, whether she/he knows the dance, in order to get married, or they comment saying that the time has come for her/him to "dance the Isaiah."

112 Dawe 1998:41.

113 For example, in *The Cretan* by Prevelakis, Nostos Books (2001), pp. 151-64.

114 This is the first song in *Dreamlands*, lyrics by Mitsos Stavrakakis.

115 Ross Daly is of Irish descent. He was brought up in England, North America (San Francisco mainly), and Japan ("Ross Daly" 2002; Daly, July 13 2001).

116 For a schedule of seminars visit: http://www.rossdalymusic.com/concerts%20and%20%20Seminars%202005EN.htm

117 Rhapsody A, verses 389-404. These verses from *Erotókritos* are oftentimes performed in concerts by Stavrakakis. They compile the third item on the second side of the tape *Dreamlands*.

118 Nidiotis means the one who comes from Nida (or Ida), thus, the plains of Psiloritis.

119 This is the concert where I "officially" first met Vasilis and which I also attended "paying careful attention" for the purposes of this book.

120 Manos Hatzidakis established this festival in 1979. It included performances of local dances and songs. The following year he also initiated "Musical August" in Heraklion.

121 The 2004 double CD *Echo of Time* includes these recordings — the result of 20 years of collaboration with the Cretan lyricist Mitsos Stavrakakis.

122 These lyrics — by Mitsos Stavrakakis again — are an excerpt from the third song in the Stavrakakis 2001 compact disc.

123 Last time I spoke with Laodikis was in January 2007. Though a Greek citizen now, he lives in Athens, and music is not his primary profession.

124 Barnstone 1999b: 113.

125 Erdener, 1987: 3.

126 Ibid. 5.

127 Ibid. 7.

128 Ibid. 81.

129 Ibid. 299.

130 "Black Eagle" is the nickname of a person in the village of Anoya.

131 I pick illustrations and metaphors from memory after long-term, repetitious, and constant exposure to *Erotókritos*.

132 Personal communication by e-mail, January 24, 2001.

133 My father who is one of the invisible contributors to this work, knows through his work a relative of Faragoulitakis. Through this acquaintance, we arranged a Sunday excursion to his house.

134 On June 2006, at my brother's wedding, one of the young musicians who performed was Yiannis Romboyiannakis, a master of the bagpipe and several other Cretan wind instruments. On August 2006, Romboyiannakis participated and represented Crete at a meeting for the bagpipes of the Aegean, which took place and I attended at the village of Gergeri.

135 "If anything, the Cretan example provides a socialist model," Dr. Chris Williams supports. We elaborated more on that idea during our person-to-person conversation in London on January 2, 2002.

136 Daly 1992.

137 "De déhomai…", *Yper-X* (26) 2001.

138 In that spirit of the "unknown Cretan music dance tradition", in 2005, the Pancretan Association of America and the Hellenic Music Archives release the CD "Traditional Dances of Crete", whereas in 2006, Aerakis Seistron Music announces the release of the audiovisual album "When I hear Crete".

139 Its name derives from the city of Heraklion, the capital of Crete, which had the name Kastro — fortress — in the past, and pidihtós, which means leaping.

140 From the district of Malevizi, a west Heraklion province.

141 Leaping dance from the village of Anoya.

142 Cowan 1990: 103.

143 Herzfeld 1991: 46.

144 Herzfeld 1985a: 123-24.

145 Conclusion based on a personal communication with Michael Herzfeld in the fall of 2000.

146 The concert took place on August 13, 2001. Dimitris (Mitsos) Kontoyiannis performs traditional, popular and urban Greek music known as laiká and rebétika. As a student in Athens, where he is based, I participated as a singer in his group.

147 Ideas in this paragraph are based on Stokes, 1994: 6-7.

148 Stokes 1994: 2. With this point, Seeger (1987) also agrees.

149 Moderation is best: Ancient Greek proverbial saying.

150 I have adopted these words from the essay by Magowan, 1994: 135-155.

151 The current essay I base on Herzfeld's discussions on what

"traditional" and "modern(izing)" is. I agree with him that "behind such a sharp division, a series of subordinate, but equally value-laden oppositions, lie: myths versus history, ritual versus science, rural versus urban, metaphor versus literality" (Herzfeld 1992a). Moreover, "the concept of Greek 'tradition' does not simply reproduce an image of Ottoman times nor is it necessarily associated with concomitant images of 'backwardness.' On the contrary, it may be the very hallmark of modernity" (Herzfeld 1995). In this context, history might be a hotly contested word (Herzfeld 1992a).

152 Comment in Strataki 2002.

153 A Cretan friend informed me of this "lore" on November 6 2001. Another mandináda: "You swept my mind as if you were Katrina, my typhoon, and I shall kidnap you one night to Athens". With these examples I do not intend to hurt the feelings of any American people. Instead, we can see the artistic expressions and the worldly dimensions a catastrophe may inspire.

154 In addition, *The Path of the Great: An Adaptation of the Epic Poem Erotókritos* (by Stephen Gargilis, Athena Publishers, Boston Massachusetts, 1945) is a prosaic adaptation of *Erotókritos* in the English language, based on Athenian popular publications, prologued by the author. This curiously informed, updated version around the era of World War II shows how *Erotókritos* and its legend survived through the ages even for Greek-Americans (Kornaros 1994: 548).

155 Ross Daly 1994a: 10-11.

156 Related ideas can be found in Gilroy (1993: 276) and Clifford (1994: 321).

157 Tradition is the nourishment of national identity, just as Hellas is of Europe (main idea in Michael Herzfeld 1997a).

158 Holst-Warhaft 1998: 111.

159 This is the title of another book by Nikos Kazantzakis (1983).

160 All the ideas in this paragraph are based on Bien 1974: 118-9.

161 "Stín Anatolí...", *Patrís* November 8, 2001.

162 Hortatsis composes *Erofíli* around 1595. The discussion here is based on the 1996 edition and publication of his masterpiece.

163 Hortatsis 1996: 161-4.

164 He chooses Jewish-Arabic names for his characters (Hortatsis 1996: 27).

165 Hortatsis came from Asia Minor. Possibly his last name denotes a Byzantine-Asian Minor descent of the family that, according to the local tradition, came to Crete when the well-known establishment of wealthy men and old soldiers of the Byzantine army took place in 961.
The Cortazi (from the Latin *saturo*; to fill, to satiate, to satisfy, to saturate) were among the first, large "Roman," Constantinople families that settled in Crete when given land by Nikiforos Fokas (Hortatsis 1996: 42-3).

166 This continues on several levels until the beginning of the last 30 years of the 16th century (Hortatsis 1996: 56).

167 Kornaros, the writer of *Erotókritos*.

168 Baily 1994: 48

169 Savigliano 1995. In the same sense, Dorothy Sara Lee (1981) talks about understanding music and identity in the social world where cultural knowledge and performance identities are in constant, dialogic negotiation.

170 Daly 1994a: 9.

171 This is Shelemay's main thesis statement and part of her 1998 book title.

172 Personal communication, 2002.

173 2000: 1008.

174 Williams 2002.

175 Ibid.

176 Koutsourelis 2000.

177 Daly 2000.

178 Magrini maintains that the violin was considered a symbol of foreign dominance and "pollution" (Ethnomusicology on Line [EOL] 3).

179 Anoyiannakis 1991: 270-1.

180 "Ross Daly" 2002.

181 Daly in Alexakis 1995.

182 Williams 2002.

183 Ibid.

184 Daly 1994a: 9.

185 Williams 2002.

186 Ibid.

187 Translated by my Turkish friend Suheyla on November 6, 2002.

188 Williams 2002.

189 Translated by my Palestinian friend Khuloud on November 6, 2002.

190 Ross Daly in that e-mail goes into more musical detail and analysis to show me how this piece is Arabic and not Turkish.

191 July 13, 2001.

192 Williams 2002.

193 Daly, July 13, 2001.

194 "Cretan music" 2002.

195 Ibid.

196 People from Alatsata, a region in Asia Minor.

197 Kondylakis 1961.

198 Tsivis 1933.

199 Williams 2002.

200 Greek proverb. It refers mainly to the gypsies who perform music on the streets accompanied by a dancing bear and, as a result, attract audiences and make money.

201 Zorba says these words in one of the most popular scenes of the homonymous movie.

202 Seferis, George. 1976. *Tetrádio Gymnasmáton B* (Exercise Book B). Athens: Ikaros. Excerpt from the poem "Grámma ston Rex Warner pároiko tou Storrs, Connecticut, U.S.A., yia ta exínda tou hrónia" ("Letter to Rex Warner, sojourner of Storrs, Connecticut, U.S.A., for his 60th birthday").

203 Bravo was inaugurated in the summer of 2001.

204 Roussetos Panayiotakis, a local artist, was responsible for the graphics, editing, and printing of this poster.

205 Similar discussion on these topics is also found in Stokes 1994: 16 and 99.

206 Producer, Aerakis, Cretan Musical Workshop, S.A. 014/585, distributed by Kouvidis and Manouras, who own a bookstore in Heraklion which sells postcards, among other things. They both come from the village of Anoya.

207 A r ó l i t h o s meaning small basin (hollow rock) that fills up when it rains (especially in the winter time).

208 Dimitra and Papaheimona 1992.

209 On April 2006, Dr. Nikolaos Scarmeas associated this diet's findings with lower rates of cardiovascular disease, lower oxidative stress and lower inflammation, which have in turn been associated with lower risk for Alzheimer's. ("Mediterranean diet and risk for Alzheimer's disease". *Annals of Neurology* 2006,59: 912-921.)

210 I do not regret my task, however. Not only does it add to my experiences, but it also makes me realize how many mistakes the human ear can make and, more importantly, how different the choices of the producers of such recordings, who are not ethnomusicologists, are. In addition, it is worthwhile to compare the selections I chose to the ones the compact disc producers did.

211 See note 67.

212 Cohen 1994: 118.

213 Williams 2002.

214 "The networks of technology that envelop the world and shrink it, supposedly distorting our sense of space and time so successfully, are at the same time rich with the patterns of intersecting group identities, local and historical significance, in order to construct a sense of difference and distinctiveness, a sense of Liverpool-ness" (in Cohen 1994: 133).

215 In opposition to music "out of place" as Stokes discusses (1994: 98).

216 Daly in Alexakis 1995.

217 *Byzantine Liturgical Chants composed in Crete: Chanted by chanters from the city of Iraklio*, Crete 2001.

218 *Welcome Crete* (9): 11.

219 Not to forget Nikos Mamangakis, another contemporary, significant Cretan composer, who has created music works not only inspired by *Erotókritos*, but also by Cretan heroic epics, as well as several other literary and folk lore.

220 Yet today, at the Cretan daily newspaper *Patrís*, teacher and poet Kostis Lagoudianakis oftentimes writes about the history and the folklore of Crete using the traditional 15-syllable rhyme.

221 Yiannis, one of his sons, is responsible for the webpage.

222 He also has a webpage: http://www.rossdalymusic.com/

223 Dimou, 2001:86.

224 Menuhin and Estrella 1998.

225 "We use the word *ellinopoíisi* (Greekization) only when we talk about giving the Greek citizenship to foreigners. Metaphorically it could be used as "trying to make something appear as Greek" — there is of course a tinge of nationalism…" (Dimou, e-mail: 2002).

226 Dimou 2002.

227 The World of Music Arts and Dance Organization, founded by Peter Gabriel.

228 *Cronicas De Terra* (Portugal) 10/99.

229 Broughton 1999.

230 Daly 1995.

231 Cohen 1994: 117.

232 See a similar discussion in Stokes 1994: 15.

233 Ideas based on Cohen 1994: 133.

234 July 13, 2001.

235 1998: 26-9.

236 September 29, 2001; I left for the United States on September 5, 2001.

237 "Ithaca" (translated by E. Keeley and P. Sherrard):
As you set out for Ithaca / hope your road is a long one, /full of adventure, full of discovery. / Laistrygonians, Cyclops, / angry Poseidon — don't be afraid of them: / you'll never find things like that your way / as long as you keep your thoughts raised high, / as long as a rare sensation/touches your spirit and your body. / Laistrygonians, Cyclops, / with Poseidon-- you won't encounter them / unless you bring them along inside your soul, / unless your soul sets them up in front of you.

Hope your road is a long one. / May there be many summer mornings when, / with what pleasure, what joy, / you enter harbors you're seeing for the first time; / may you stop at Phoenician trading stations / to buy fine things, / mother of pearl and coral, amber and ebony, / sensual perfumes as you can; / and may you visit many Egyptian cities /to learn and go on learning from those who know.

Keep Ithaca always in your mind. /Arriving there is what you're destined for. / But don't hurry the journey at all. / Better if it lasts for years, / so you're old by the time you reach the island, / wealthy with all you've gained on the way, / not expecting Ithaca to make you rich.

Ithaca gave you the marvelous journey. / Without her you wouldn't have set out. / She has nothing left to give you now. / And if you find her poor, Ithaca won't have fooled you. / Wise as you will have become, so full of experience, / You'll have understood by then what these Ithacas mean.

238 Dimou, 2001: 37-8.

239 Bien uses Kazantzakis's words to talk about his activism and the transubstantiation of life into art (1974: 129).

240 "Minoikós…". *Yper-X* (26) 2001.

241 Daly 1994a.

242 My ideas here agree with the whole discussion of world music and ethnicity in Stokes, especially when he says that "there is a more general process of a highly flexible, creative construction of ethnicity, which is increasingly common as tourism, 'world music' events and media bring together unlikely groups of musicians and listeners". (1994: 16).

243 Daly 2000: 40-3.

244 Daly 2001.

245 Nikos Xylouris composed his own songs in addition to singing songs by other composers.

246 "Ross Daly" 2002.

247 Daly in Alexakis 1995.

248 July 13, 2001.

249 I attended one in the summer of 2000 in Crete, and I own the recordings from these collaborative performances.

250 "There is one repeated scheme in Indian music where you play many times and you leave space, and you fill the gap with various improvisations and you return to that base, the basic melody... I got half of a syrtos by Moundakis, and I used it a little bit arranged in order to do a specific type of improvisation of Indian style..." (Daly, July 13 2001). More specifically, "embodiments" of A n o y a n é s k o n d i l i é s, Irish reels and popular melodies from the p e n d o z á l i s performed by Daly on the Cretan l í r a one may listen to in track 5, on the second CD titled Έllines kai Indoí (*Greeks and Indians*).

251 "Ross Daly" 2007.

252 Ibid.

253 Daly in Alexakis.

254 Aerakis 1994.

255 From the liner notes of the CD entitled *Ross Daly & Labyrinth: Mitos.*

256 Heraclitian saying.

257 Title inspired by the "I-witnessing" essay in Geerzt 1988: 73-101.

258 According to... "Epimenides said: all Cretans are liars. But Epimenides is a Cretan."

259 According to Barnstone (1994): "I'm Only Time."

260 See note 255.

261 The following quote is from Kazantzakis's *Ascetics* (1971).

262 Keeley 1984: i.

263 Friar 1985.

264 Keeley and Sherrard 1992: 199-200.

265 Dimou 2001.

266 Michaelides 1978: 117-9.

267 Aerakis 1994.

268 "Was the Olympic ...", *Holidays' Info Crete* 2000.

269 Holton 1991: 4.

270 Aerakis 1994.

271 Ibid.

272 Ibid.

273 Daly 2001.

274 Michaelides 1978: 105.

275 Daly 1994a: 30-1.

276 Ibid. 23.

277 Michaelides 1978: 281.

278 Daly 1994a: 14.

279 Moss 1950: 191.

280 Aerakis 1994.

281 Ibid.

Pictures at an exhibition

In this bibliography, entries between single quotation marks are for descriptive titles or key words for information to be obtained from websources cited in entry.

Abu-Lughod, Lila. 1986. *Veiled Sentiments: Honor and Poetry in a Bedouin Society*. Berkeley: University of California Press.

Aerakis, Stelios (research, compilation, review). 1994. *Cretan Musical Traditions: The Masters; 1920-1955, Original Recordings*. Aerakis, Cretan Musical Workshop. S.A. CD 540.

Alexakis, Manolis. 1995. "Ross Daly: Me ti musikí anakalíptoume ton ánthropo" ["Through music we discover humanity"]. *Ostria* magazine (1): 9, 16.

Alexis Zorbas (alternate title: *Zorba the Greek*). 1964. Motion picture, directed by Michalis Cacoyannis. (2003. DVD, Beverly Hills: Twentieth Century Fox Studio Classics) www.foxmovies.com.au/dvd/zorba-the-greek-121/121/

Anoyiannakis, Foivos. 1991. *Elliniká laiká musiká órgana [Greek Folk Music Instruments]*. (First edition in 1976 from the National Bank of Greece). Athens: Melissa.

Apostolakis, Stamatis A. 1993. *Rizítika: Ta dimotiká tragoúdia tis Krítis. [Rizítika: The folk songs of Crete]*. Athens: Gnosi.

Arvanitaki, Eleftheria. 2001. *Ekpompí [Broadcast]*. Greece: Mercury/Universal Music S.A. A Universal Music Company. CD.

Baily, John. 1994. "The Role of Music in the Creation of an Afghan National Identity, 1923-73." In Stokes, Martin (ed.), *Ethnicity, Identity and Music: The Musical Construction of Place*, pp. 45-60. Oxford/ Providence, USA: Berg.

Barnstone, Willis. 1994. *Meditations in the Yucatan*. Bloomington, Indiana: Sackett & Milk.

—. 1999. *To Touch the Sky: Poems of Mystical, Spiritual & Metaphysical Light*. New York: New Directions.

—. 1999. *Sappho Poems: A New Version*. Kobenhavn, Los Angeles: Green Integer 26.

Baud-Bovy, Samuel. 1984. *Dokímio yia to ellinikó tragoúdi. [Essay for the Greek Folk Song]*. Nafplion (Nauplia): Peloponnisiako Laografiko Idrima [Peloponnesian Folklore Foundation].

Berger, P. and Luckmann, T. 1966. *The Social Construction of Reality: A Treatise in the Sociology of Knowledge*. Garden City, N.Y.: Doubleday.

Bien, Peter. 1974. "The Mellowed Nationalism of Kazantzakis's *Zorba the Greek*." *Review of National Literatures. Greece: The Modern Voice* 5 (2): 113-136.

Blacking, John. 1995. "Music, Culture, and Experience." In *Music, Culture, and Experience*. Chicago: University of Chicago Press.

Byzantine Liturgical Chants Composed in Crete: Chanted by Chanters from the City of Iraklio, Crete. 2001. Heraklion: Cretaphon(e) Ltd. CD.

Caraveli, Anna. 1985. "The Symbolic Village: *Community Born* in Performance," *Journal of American Folklore* (98), no. 389: 259-286.

Caton, Steven Charles. 1990. *Peaks of Yemen I Summon: Poetry as Cultural Practice in a North Yemeni Tribe*. Berkeley: University of California Press.

Clifford, James. 1988 [c1983]. "On Ethnographic Authority." In *Writing Culture: The Poetics and Politics of*

Ethnography, James Clifford and George E. Marcus (eds.), pp. 21-54. Berkeley: University of California Press.

—. 1994. "Diasporas." *Cultural Anthropology* 9 (3): 302-337.

Cohen, Sara. 1994. "Identity, Place and the 'Liverpool Sound.'" In Stokes, Martin (ed.), *Ethnicity, Identity and Music: The Musical Construction of Place*, pp. 117-134. Oxford/Providence, USA: Berg.

Cowan, Jane K. 1990. *Dance and the Body Politics in Northern Greece*. Princeton: Princeton University Press.

—. 2000. "Greece." In *The Garland Encyclopedia of World Music (2)*, Tim Rice, James Porter, Chris Goertzen (eds.), pp. 1007-1032. New York: Garland Publications.

'Cretan Music.' For links on Nikiforos Aerakis, Piperakis, *Erotókritos*, tampachaniótika, Nikos Xylouris biography and discography and other notable Cretan music personalities and album and CD productions, see http://www.cretan-music.gr/index.php (accessed January 2007).

Cretan Traditional Music: Radio Broadcasts. 1996. Heraklion, Crete: The Cretan Musical Workshop. CD.

'Cretaphone.' (also spelled 'Cretaphon'). http://www.cretaphone.gr/shop (accessed January 2007).

Cronicas De Terra (Portugal); 10/99 (under 'Press/Old articles' in http://www.arvanitaki.gr/en/index2.cfm).

Daly, Ross. 1992 [c1986-91]. *Ross Daly: Selected Works*. Athens: Digital Press Hellas. CD.

Daly, Ross. 1992. *Ross Daly & Labyrinth: Mitos [Thread]*. Eurasia (8): World Network. CD.

—. 1994a. *Paradosiaká musiká órgana: Musiká órgana apó tin Elláda, Mési Anatolí, Vória Afrikí, Kentrikí Asía ke India [Traditional Music Instruments: Music Instruments from Greece, the Middle East, North Africa, the Central Asia and India]*. Dimos Patreon [Municipality of Patras].

—. 1994b. "Sinomilóndas me ton Ross Daly" [Talking with Ross Daly]. In *O mítos tis Ariádnis [Ariadne's Thread]*, pp. 36-41. Panepistimiakés Ekdóseis Krítis [University of Crete Publications].

—. 2000. "Cretan Traditional Music: Ross Daly." *Welcome Crete* (5): 40-43.

—. 2001. Interview on July 13th, Houdetsi, Crete.

Daly, Ross and Halkias, Petroloukas. 2000. *'Ellines kai Indoí [Greeks and Indians]*. Saraswati. CD.

Daly, Ross and Stavrakakis, Mitsos. 1982. *Oneírou tópoi [Dreamlands]*. Re-released in 2003 as *Ihó tou chrónou*. Heraklion: Seistron. CD.

—. 2001. *The Dance of the Stone: Iakinthia; Reference to Zeus*. Athens: Líra. CD 4992.

Danielson, Virginia. 1997. *The Voice of Egypt: Umm Kulthum, Arabic Song, and Egyptian Society in the Twentieth Century*. Chicago: University of Chicago Press.

Dawe, Kevin. 1996. "The Engendered Líra: Music, Poetry and Manhood in Crete." *British Journal of Ethnomusicology* (5): 93-112.

—. 1998. "Bandleaders in Crete: Musicians and entrepreneurs in a Greek Island Economy." *British Journal of Ethnomusicology* (7): 23-44.

"De déhomai Kríti horís líra, gléndi, horís choró" ["I do not accept Crete without líra, *gléndi* without dance"]. 2001. *Yper-X* (26): 76-7.

Dimitra, Dimitra and Papaheimona, Marineta. 1992. *Greek Now*. Athens: Nostos [Nostalgia].

Dimou, Nikos. 1975. *I distichía tou na eísai 'Ellinas* [The Misfortune of Being Greek]. Athens: Patakis.

—. 1984. *To apólito kai to távli* [The Absolute and the Backgammon]. Athens: Patakis.

—. 1997. *Apoloyía enós anthéllina* [Apology of an Anti-Hellene]. Athens: Opera.

—. 2001. *Eironikó neoellinikó lexikó* [Ironic Modern Greek Lexicon]. Athens: Patakis.

—. E-mail: personal communication, November 8 2001.

—. E-mail: personal communication, February 4 2002.

"Dokouménto! I Tourkokratoúmeni Kríti tou 1862 mésa apó mia epistolí tou Amerikanoú próxenou" ["Document: Crete of 1862 under Turkish rule, seen through a letter by the American ambassador"]. 2001. *Patris* November 6 (a).

Dubisch, J. (ed.). 1986. *Gender and Power in Rural Greece*. Princeton: Princeton University Press.

Eickelman, Dale F. 1998. *The Middle East and Central Asia: An Anthropological Approach*. Upper Saddle River, N.J.: Prentice Hall.

"Elliniká laiká musiká órgana" ["Greek Folk Musical Instruments"]. *Eptá Iméres* [*Seven Days*], *Kathimeriní*, January 18 1998.

Elytis, Odysseus. 1982 (3rd edition). *O mikrós naftílos* [The Young Navigator]. Athens: Icarus.

Erdener, Yildiray. 1987. "Dueling Singers: Interaction Processes and Strategies Among Turkish Minstrels." Ph. D. dissertation, Indiana University.

Erotokritos: Four approaches to the Cretan Medieval Romance. 2000. Athens: Líra. CD 4966.

Feld, Steven. 1989. *Sound and Sentiment: Bird, Weeping, Poetics and Songs in Kaluli Expression*. Philadelphia: University of Pennsylvania Press.

Fraleigh, Sondra Horton. 1987. *Dance and the Lived Body: A Descriptive Aesthetics*. Pittsburgh, Pennsylvania: University of Pennsylvania Press.

Friar, Kimon. (Translation into English Verse, Introduction, Synopsis, and Notes). 1985. *The Odyssey: A Modern Sequel by Nikos Kazantzakis*. New York: Simon and Schuster.

Geertz, Clifford. 1980. *Negara: The Theatre State in Nine-teenth-Century Bali*. Princeton, Oxford: Princeton University Press.

—. 1988. *Works and Lives: The Anthropologist as Author*. Stanford: Stanford University Press.

Gilroy, Paul. 1993. *The Black Atlantic: Double Consciousness and Modernity*. Cambridge: Harvard University Press.

Glassie, Henry. 1975. *All Silver and No Brass: An Irish Christmas Mumming*. Philadelphia: University of Pennsylvania Press.

—. 1982. *Passing the Time in Ballymenone*. Bloomington and Indianapolis: Indiana University Press.

—. 1989. *The Spirit of Folk Art: The Girard Collection at the Museum of International Folk Art*. New York: Harry N. Abrams, Inc. & Santa Fe: The Museum of New Mexico.

—. 1999. *The Potter's Art*. Bloomington and Indianapolis: Indiana University Press.

'Greece.' In *World Music (1)*, Simon Broughton, Mark Ellingham and Richard Trillo with Orla Duane and Vanessa Dowell (eds.), pp. 126-142. London: The Rough Guides.

Hanna, Judith Lynne. 1979. *To Dance Is Human: A Theory of Nonverbal Communication*. Austin and London: University of Texas Press.

Hatzidakis, Georgios. 1958. *Cretan Music: History, Music Systems, Songs, and Dances*. Athens, Greece.

Herzfeld, Michael. 1974. "Cretan Distichs: 'The Quartered Shield' in Cross-Cultural Perspective." *Semiotica* 12: 203-218.

—. 1980. "On the Ethnography of 'Prejudice' in an Exclusive Community." *Ethnic Groups* 2: 283-305.

—. 1982. *Ours Once More: Folklore, Ideology and the Making of Modern Greece*. Austin: University of Texas Press.

—. 1984. "The Horns of the Mediterraneanist Dilemma." *American Ethnologist* 11: 439-454.

—. 1985a. *The Poetics of Manhood: Contest and Identity in a Cretan Mountain Village*, Princeton: Princeton University Press.

—. 1985b. "I keimenikótita tou ellinikoú dimotikoú tragoudioú" ["The Textuality of Greek Folk Song"]. In *Proceedings [Praktika] of the Fourth Patras Poetry Symposium*, pp. 31-42. Athens: Gnosis.

—. 1986. "Within and Without: The Category of 'Female' in the Ethnography of Rural Greece." In *Gender and Power in Rural Greece*, J. Dubisch (ed.), pp. 215-33. Princeton: Princeton University Press.

—. 1987. *Anthropology through the Looking-Glass: Critical Ethnography in the Margins of Europe*, Cambridge: Cambridge University Press.

—. 1990. "Commentary: Gender, Political Ideology, and Nationalism in Eastern Europe: Challenging Questions and Elusive Answers." *East European Quarterly* 23: 507-516.

—. 1991. *A Place in History: Monumental and Social Time in a Cretan Town*. Princeton: Princeton University Press.

—. 1992a. "History in the Making: National and International Politics in a Rural Cretan Community." In J.K. Campbell and Joao de Pina Cabral, eds., *Europe Observed*: 93-122. London: Macmillan.

—. 1992b. *The Social Production of Indifference: Exploring the Symbolic Roots of Western Bureaucracy*. Oxford: Berg.

—. 1993. "I kritikí mandináda kai i koinonikí ékfrasi tis andipalótitas." In *I kritikí mandináda*—1o Simbósio Parádosis Dímou Anoyíon, pp. 16-21. Anoya: Kriti.

—. 1995. "Hellenism and Occidentalism: The Permutations of Performance in Greek Bourgeois Identity." In *Occidentalism: Images of the West*, James G. Carrier (ed.), pp. 218-233. Oxford: Oxford University Press.

—. 1997a. *Cultural Intimacy: Social Poetics in the Nation-State*. New York: Routledge.

—. 1997b. *Portrait of a Greek Imagination: An Ethnographic Biography of Andreas Nenedakis*. Chicago: The University of Chicago Press.

Hnaraki, Maria. 1999. "Speaking Without Words: Cretan Dance at Weddings as Expression, Dialogue, and Communication." M.A. thesis, Indiana University.

—. 2001. "Kriti: Mousikí, chorós, tragoúdi" ["Crete: Music, Dance, Song"]. http://www.cretaphone.gr/shop/news.php?news=unique&news_id=39 (accessed January 2007).

—. 2002. "Into the Labyrinth; Unraveling Ariadne's Thread: Cretan Music Identity and Aesthetics." Ph.D. dissertation, Indiana University.

Hobsbawm, Eric J. and Terence Ranger (eds.). 1992. *The Invention of Tradition*. Cambridge: Cambridge University Press.

Holst-Warhaft. 1998. "Rebétika: The Double-descended

Deep Songs of Greece." In *The Passion of Music and Dance: Body, Gender and Sexuality*, William Washabaugh (ed.), pp. 111-26. Oxford, New York: Berg.

Holton, David. 1991. *Erotókritos*. Bristol: Bristol Classical.

Homer. 1997. *Odyssey*. Translated by Nikos Kazantzakis. Athens: Organismós Ekdóseon Didaktikón Vivlíon (OEDV) [Publishing Organization of Educational Books].

Hortatsis, Yeorgios. 1996 (2nd edition). *Erofili: Tragedy*. Athens: Stigmi. Editors: Stilianos Alexiou, Martha Aposkiti.

'Iakinthia.' http://www.yakinthia.com / bindexgr.html (accessed January 2007).

Idomeneos, Marinos I. 2006. *Kritikó Glossário* [Cretan Glossary]. Herakleion: Vikelaia Vivliothiki [Vikelaia Library].

Jazz kai Tzaz. June 1998. "Ethnic Voices and Songs." (63): 26-9.

Kaeppler, Adrienne, L. 1992. "Theoretical and Methodological Considerations for Anthropological Studies of Dance and Human Movement Systems." *Ethnographica* 8: 151-157. The Peloponnesian Folklore Foundation.

—. 1995. "Visible and Invisible in Hawaiian Dance." In *Human Action Signs in Cultural Context: The Visible and the Invisible in Movement and Dance*, Brenda Farnell (ed.), pp. 31-43. N.J. and London: Metuchen.

Kallergis, Michalis. 2001. *'Aroma Krítis [Perfume of Crete]*. Heraklion, Aerakis, CD 643.

Kalokyris, M. I. 1970. *Anoya Mylopotamou-Rethymnis: Laografikí Syllogí*. Heraklion.

Kaloyanides, Michael George. 1975. "The Music of Cretan Dances: A Study of the Musical Structures of Cretan Dance Forms as Performed in the Irakleion Province of Crete." Ph.D. dissertation, Wesleyan University.

Karatzis, Yiorgis. 2000. *Emine: Kritikó erondikó tragoúdi [Emine: Cretan Love Song]*. Book and accompanying CD. Heraklion: Aerakis.

Kavouras, Pavlos. 1999. "I viografía enós laikoú organopékti: Ethnografikí epitópia érevna, ermineía kai mithoplasía" ["The Biography of a Folk Instrumentalist: Ethnographic Field Research and Interpretation"]. In *Mousikés tis Thrákis: Mia diepistimonikí proséngisi [Music of Thrace: An Interdisciplinary Approach]: Evros*, pp. 341-450. Athens: Síllogos oi Fíloi tis Mousikís [Club of the Friends of Music], Erevnitikó Prógramma "Thraki" [Research Program "Thrace"].

Kazantzakis, Helen. 1968. *Nikos Kazantzakis: A Biography Based on His Letters*. Translated by Amy Mims. New York: Simon and Schuster.

Kazantzakis, Nikos. 1953. *Zorba the Greek*. New York: Simon and Schuster.

—. 1954. *The Greek Passion*. Translated by Jonathan Griffin. New York: Simon and Schuster.

—. 1954. *Freedom or Death*. Translated by Jonathan Griffin. New York: Simon and Schuster. First Greek-language publication: 1953. *Capetan Michalis [Captain Michalis]*, Athens: Makridis.

—. 1969 (6th edition). *Taxidévondas: Italía, 'Egyptos, Siná, Ierusalím, Kípros, o Moriás [Journeying: Italy, Egypt, Jerusalem, Cyprus, Morias]*. Athens: Ekdoseis [Publications] Eleni Kazantzaki.

—. 1971 (5th edition). *Askitikí [Ascetics]: Salvatores Dei*. Athens: Ekdoseis [Publications] Eleni Kazantzaki.

—. 1983. *Buddha*. Translated by Kimon Friar and Athena Dallas-Damis. San Diego: Avant Books.

Keeley, Edmund and Sherrard, Philip. 1984. *C. P. Cavafy: Collected Poems*. Edited by George Savidis. London: The Hogart Press.

—, eds. and translators. 1992. *A Greek Quintet: Poems by Cavafy, Sikelianos, Seferis, Elytis, Gatsos*. Limni, Evia, Greece: Denise Harvey & Company.

Kondylakis, Ioannis. 1961. *Ta 'Apanda [Collected Works]*. Athens: Aidon [Nightingale].

Kornaros, Vitsentzos. 1994 (3rd edition). *Erotókritos*. Stylianos Alexiou, editor. Athens: Ermís.

'Koutsourelis.' 2006. http://members.tripod.com/~mikepatt/ (accessed January 2007).

Kriti: Istoría kai politismós [Crete: History and Civilization]. 1987. Síndesmos Topikón Enóseon Dímon kai Kinotíton Krítis [Union of Unified Local Cretan Municipalities and Communities]. Epistimoniki Epimélia [Scientific editing]: Nikolaos M. Panayiotakis. Ekdotiki Frontida [Publishing Care]: "Vikelaia Vivliothiki" [Vikelaia Library].

"Kritikí Musikí Parádosi: Klasikés Musikés Ekdóseis apó to Kritikó Musikó Ergastíri" ["Cretan Musical Tradition: Classical Musical Publications by the Cretan Musical Workshop"] 2001. *Welcome Crete* (9): 11.

Kyriakaki, E. "I póli mou htes, símera, ávrio" ["My city yesterday, today, tomorrow"]. Fylládio. [Brochure].

Laodikis. 2001. Interview on July 19, Heraklion, Crete.

Lee, Dorothy Sara. 1981. "Toward an Understanding of Music and Identity in the Social World." *Discourse in Ethnomusicology II: A Tribute to Alan P. Merriam*. Indiana University: Ethnomusicology Publications Group.

Levi-Strauss, Claude. 1955. *Tristes Tropiques*. New York: Penguin Books.

—. 1986. *The Raw and the Cooked*. Harmondsworth: Penguin.

Levitt, Morton P. 1980. *The Cretan Glance: The World and Art of Nikos Kazantzakis*. Columbus, OH: Ohio State University Press.

Lewis, Oscar. 1959. *Five Families: Mexican Case Studies in the Culture of Poverty*. United States: Basic Books.

Loizos, Peter and Euthymios Papataxiarchis (eds.). 1991. *Contested Identities: Gender and Kinship in Modern Greece*. Princeton: Princeton University Press.

Loutzaki, Rena. 1994. "The Local Dancing Repertory: Localization and Transcription in the Region of the Southeastern Aegean." In *Music and Dances of the East Aegean*. Records of the meeting held in the island of Samos in July 1993. Athens.

Magenta: English-Greek/Greek-English electronic dictionary. CD-ROM Golden Version.

Magowan, Fiona. 1994. "'The Land is Our Maerr (Essence), It Stays Forever': The *Yothu-Yindi* Relationship in Australian Aboriginal Traditional and Popular Music." In Stokes, Martin (ed.), *Ethnicity, Identity and Music: The Musical Construction of Place*, pp. 135-156. Oxford/Providence, USA: Berg.

Magrini, Tulia. 2002. "Repertories and identities of a musician from Crete." Ethnomusicology on Line (EOL) 3. http://research.umbc.edu/eol/3/magrini/ (accessed January 2007).

Makreas, Mary Ellen. 1979. *Cretan Dance: The Meaning of Kéfi and Figoúres*. M.A. thesis, Indiana University.

Menuhin, Yehudi and Estrella, Miguel Angel. "I musikí, angeliafóros tis eirínis" [Music, messenger of peace"]. *Kathimeriní*, 22 March 1998.

"M'episimótita t'apokaliptíria stin Athína: Mnimeío yia ton

Kritikó mahití" ["Ceremonial inauguration in Athens: Monument for the Cretan fighter"]. 2001. *Patris* November 6 (b).

"Messara, i patrída tis Evrópis" ["Messara, the home of Europe"]. 2001. *Patrís* November 2.

Michaelides, Solon. 1978. *The Music of Ancient Greece: An Encyclopaedia*. London: Faber and Faber Limited in association with Faber Music Limited.

"Mikis Theodorakis: True patriot and untiring champion of social freedom, faithful servant of Apollo." 2000. *Holidays' Info Crete*: 6-8.

"Minoikós Politismós se tourkikó panepistímio" ["Minoan Civilization at a Turkish University"]. 2001. *Yper-X* (26): 58-64.

Moss, Stanley W. 1950. *Ill Met By Moonlight*. London, Sydney, Toronto, Bombay: George G. Harrap & Co. Ltd.

Ness, Sally Ann. 1992. *Body, Movement, and Culture: Kinesthetic and Visual Symbolism in a Philippine Community*. Philadelphia: University of Pennsylvania Press.

Nettl, Bruno. 1996. "Relating the Present to the Past: Thoughts on the Study of Musical Change and Culture Change in Ethnomusicology." *Music & Anthropology* 1.

Never on Sunday. 1960. Motion picture, written and directed by Jules Dassin (2006. DVD, Culver City: Metro Goldwyn Mayer). www.mgm.com/title_title.do?title_star=NEVERONS

Nieuwkerk, Karin. 1995. *A Trade Like Any Other: Female Singers and Dancers in Egypt*. Austin: University of Texas Press.

"Nikos Kazantzakis." 2001. *Welcome Crete* (9): 58-60.

"Nikos Xylouris." 2001. *Welcome Crete* (9): 4-10.

"O 'Mitsos' pou égine Manos" ["Mitsos who became Manos"]. 2000. *Kathimeriní* January 30: 47.

Pearsall, Judy and Trumble, Bill (eds.). 1996. *The Oxford English Reference Dictionary*. Oxford: Oxford University Press.

Petrides, Ted. 1989. "Greek Folk Dances and Change." In *The Dance Event: A Complex Cultural Phenomenon*, L. Torp (ed.), pp. 151-7. Copenhagen: ICTM STG on Ethnochoreology.

Pring, J. T. 1995. *The Pocket Oxford Greek Dictionary: Greek-English; English-Greek*. Oxford: Oxford University Press.

Psaradonis. 2001. Interview on June 15. Heraklion, Crete.

Psilakis, Nikos. 1996. *Kritikí mithología [Cretan Mythology]*. Heraklion: Karmanor.

—. 1997. "I Kríti sti zoí kai to érgo tou Nikou Kazantzaki: Kritognosía tou Nikou Kazantzaki" ["Crete in the life and work of Nikos Kazantzakis: Nikos Kazantzakis's knowledge of Crete"]. 2001. *Yper-X* (19): 19-26.

—. 2000. "Handsome Hyacinth: The Ancient God Who Became a Flower." *Welcome Crete* (5): 20-3.

Racy, Ali Jihad. 1976. "Record Industry and Egyptian Traditional Music: 1904-1932." *Ethnomusicology* 20 (1): 23-48.

Reily, Suzel Ana. 1994. "Macunaima's Music: National Identity and Ethnomusicological Research in Brazil." In Stokes, Martin (ed.), *Ethnicity, Identity and Music: The Musical Construction of Place*, pp. 71-96. Oxford/Providence, USA: Berg.

Rice, Timothy. 1994. *May It Fill Your Soul: Experiencing Bulgarian Music*. Chicago and London: The University of Chicago Press.

'Ross Daly.' See http://www.rossdalymusic.com (accessed January 2007).

Royce, Anya Peterson. 1977. *The Anthropology of Dance*. Bloomington and London: Indiana University Press.

Sachs, Curt. 1937. *World History of the Dance*. New York: W. W. Norton & Company, Inc.

Said, Edward W. 1999. *Out of Place: A Memoir*. New York: Alfred A. Knopf.

Savigliano, Marta E. 1995. *Tango and the Political Economy of Passion*. Boulder, San Francisco, and Oxford: Westview Press.

Sbokos, Georgios. 1992. *Anoya: I istoría mésa apó ta tragoúdia tous [Anoya: Its History through its Songs]*. Athens.

Schade-Poulsen, Marc. 1999. *Men and Popular Music in Algeria: The Social Significance of Rai*. Austin: University of Texas Press.

Schechner, Richard. 1985. *Between Theater and Anthropology*. Philadelphia: University of Pennsylvania Press.

Seeger, Anthony. 1987. *Why Suya Sing: A Musical Anthropology of an Amazonian People*. Cambridge: Cambridge University Press.

Shand, Angela. 1998. "The Tsifte-teli Sermon: Identity, Theology, and Gender in Rebetika." In *The Passion of Music and Dance: Body, Gender and Sexuality*, William Washabaugh (ed.), pp. 127-32. Oxford and New York: Berg.

Shelemay, Kay Kaufman. 1998. *Let Jasmine Rain Down*. Chicago and London: The University of Chicago Press.

Shiloah, Amnon. 2006 "On Jewish and Muslim musicians of the Mediterranean." http://research.umbc.edu/eol/3/shiloah/(accessed January 2007).

Skoulas, Vasilis. 2001. Interview on September 1. Anoya, Crete.

Stavrakakis, Mitsos and Vasilis. 2001a. *Sti díni ton anémo [In the Winds' Whirlpool]*. Heraklion: Seistron. CD 16555.

Stavrakakis, Vasilis. 2001b. Interview on August 22. Ammoudara, Crete.

Stavrakakis, Yiorgis. 2003. *Thliméni haravgí [Sad Dawn]*. Book and accompanying CD. Heraklion: Seistron.

Stergiou, Anna. 2006. "Diavá ste ti égrapse kápoios yia éna apó ta pio vasiká órgana tis Kritikís mousikís" ["Read what someone wrote about one of the most important Cretan musical instruments"]. http://www.cretaphone.gr/shop/news.php?news=unique&news_id=41(accessed January 2007).

"Stin Anatolí vrísko éna állo ároma zoís" ["In the East I find another aroma of life"]. 2001. *Patris* November 8.

"Stin Kríti zoun móno íroes: Ena grámma apó tin Amerikí tou 1945" ["In Crete only heroes live: A letter from the United States in 1945"]. 2001. *Yper-X* (26): 20-1.

Stokes, Martin (ed.). 1994. *Ethnicity, Identity and Music: The Musical Construction of Place*. Oxford/Providence, USA: Berg.

Stone, Ruth M. 1978. "Communication and Interaction Processes in Music Events Among the Kpelle of Liberia." Ph.D. dissertation, Indiana University.

—. 1982. *Let the Inside Be Sweet*. Bloomington: Indiana University Press.

—. 2000. "The Nature of Inquiry in Ethnomusicology" and "Theoretical Foundation of Comparative Musicology." Unpublished chapters from *Theory in Ethnomusicology Today*.

"Sto Petrokefáli Messarás éginan ta engaínia tou I. Naoú 'To Genésio tis Theotókou'" [In Petrokefali, Messara, the inauguration of the House of God 'The Birth of Virgin

Mary' took place"]. 2001. *Patris* November 22.

"Sto Veneráto me protovoulía tou politistikoú sillógou anaviónei i parádosi tou Ai Yiorgi tou Methistí" ["The tradition of St. George the Inebriant is revived in Venerato by the Cultural Club"]. 2001. *Patris* November 1.

Strataki, Maria. 2006. "Líga lóyia yia tous panémorfous choroús tis Kritis mas" ["A few words on our gorgeous Cretan dances"]. http://www.cretaphone.gr/shop/news.php?news=unique&news_id=40 (accessed January 2007).

Sugarman, Jane. 1997. *Engendering Song: Singing and Subjectivity at Prespa Albanian Weddings*. Chicago and London: The University of Chicago Press.

Tsarouhis, Yiannis. 1978. *Anámesa se Anatoli kai Disi: Pénde Keímena [Between East and West: Five Texts]*: Athens: Ekdoseis [Publications] Agra.

Tsivis, Yiannis, D. 1993. *Chania 1252-1940*. Athens: Gnosi.

Tuohy, Sue. 1988. "Imagining the Chinese Tradition: The Case of Hua'er Songs, Festivals, and Scholarship." Ph.D. dissertation, Indiana University.

"The upbringing of Zeus: Amalthea." *Welcome Crete* (2): 26.

"Was the Olympic Spirit born on Crete?" 2000. *Holidays' Info Crete*: 53-5.

Williams, Chris. E-mail: personal communication, January 24, 2001.

—. E-mail: personal communication: "Why does Music Matter? Questions of Identity in Cretan Music." February 19 2002.

—. 2003. "The Cretan Muslims and the Music of Crete." In *Greece and the Balkans: Identities, Perceptions and Cultural Encounters since the Enlightenment*. Chapter 14, pp. 208-219. Ashgate Publishing Company: England/USA.

Xanthinakis, Antonios. 2000. *Lexikó Ermineftikó & Etimologikó tou ditikokritikoú glosikoú idiómatos. [Monolingual & Etymological Dictionary of the Western Cretan Idiom]*. Heraklion: Panepistimiakes Ekdoseis Kritis [University of Crete Publications].

NOTE: The title of this bibliography is borrowed from *Pictures at an Exhibition* by Modest Mussorgsky, written in 1874 as a group of pieces for piano. The pictures were mainly watercolors, painted by Victor Hartman, a friend of Mussorgsky, who had died the previous year. The piece is a musical description of walking around an exhibition of Hartman's paintings. A recurring "Promenade" movement represents the visitor. Each of the pieces has a movement conjuring up the mood invoked by the picture, or in some cases even painting the picture in music. Unfortunately, many of the original pictures no longer exist and Mussorgsky's music is all we have to remember them by. Although this work was originally written for piano, it owes a lot of its popularity to the orchestral arrangement by Maurice Ravel, who brought different colors to the piece.

Compositions

Ross Daly Selected Discography

Except for the *Mitos* compact disc, which contains live recordings from a concert in Germany, all recordings have been released exclusively in Greece. *Selected Works* (1995), *AN-KI* (1995) and *Eléfthero simeío* (1996) on the Oriente label are the first original releases outside Greece. The concert video *Live in Berlin* has been exclusively released by Oriente.

8 Tragoúdia ki éna semai (*8 Songs and One Semai* 1990, with Spyridoula Toutoudaki)
Abadai
Anádisi (*Breaking surface*, 1987)
AN-KI (1994, with Djamshid Chemirani)
At the Café Amán (with Niki Tramba)
Beyond the horizon
Breath, (1991, with Vasilis Soukas)
Choroi (*Dances*, 1991)
Cross Current
Eléfthero simeío/Ishtar (*Free point*, 1990)
'Ellines kai Indoí (*Greeks and Indians*)
Gulistan
Hrismós (*Oracle*)
Ihó tou chrónou (*Echo of Time*, 2003, incorporating *Oneírou Tópoi* and *Lavírinthos*)
IRIS
Kin-Kin
Kriti (*Crete*, 1990, with Manolis Manasakis)
Kriti 2: O Vourgias (*Crete 2: Vourgias* 1991, with Haralampos Hairetis)
Lavirinthos (*Labyrinth*, 1984)
Live at Théâtre de la ville
Me ti févga tou kairoú (*As Time Goes By*)
Melissókipos (*Bee Garden*)
Mikrókosmos (*Microcosm*)
Mítos (*Thread*, 1992)
Music of Crete
Naghma
O kýklos sto stavrodrómi (*The circle on the crossroad*, 1991)
Oneírou tópoi (*Dreamlands*, 1982)
Ross Daly (1986)
Selected works (Compilation 1986-91, 1992)
Sinávgia (*Fusion*)
Stavrakakides
Sti díni ton anémo (*In the Winds' Whirlpool*, 2001, with the Stavrakakis family)
http://www.studio52.gr/info_en.asp?infoID=00000rnq,ROSSDALY/

Collaborations

Haínides (Several collaborations)
Kondá sti dóxa miá stigmí (*Near Glory for a Moment*, 1987, by Nikos Xydakis)
Manía (1987, by Nikos Xydakis)
My own friends (*Oi dikoí mou fíloi*, by Stelios Petrakis)
Nótios íhos (*Southern Sound*, 1994, by Achilleas Persidis)
Skiá tis thálassas (*Shadow of the Sea*, 1996)
T' aidónia tis Anatolís (*Nightingales of the East*, 1990, with Chronis Aidonidis)
Touliatos

Vasilis Stavrakakis Selected Discography

Astrofengiá (*Starlight*)
Ihó tou chrónou (*Echo of Time*, 2003, incorporating *Oneírou Tópoi* and *Lavírinthos*)
Lavirinthos (*Labyrinth*, 1984)
Oneírou tópoi (*Dreamlands*, 1982)
Stavrakakides
Sti díni ton anémo (*In the Winds' Whirlpool* 2001, with the Stavrakakis family)
Xathéri 2002

Collaborations

O xypólitos príngipas (*The Barefoot Prince*, by Hainides)
Erotókritos & Aretí (by Yiannis Markopoulos)
Mousikí ánoixi (*Musical spring*, by Antonis and Michalis Frangiadakis)
Oi dikoí mou fíloi, (*My own friends*, by Stelios Petrakis)

Laodikis Selected Discography

'Aroma Krítis (2001, with Michalis Kallergis)
Haínides (several collaborations)
Xóblia (with Miltiadis Skoulas) (*Music Frills*)

Index

This is a general thematic index. It includes historical periods, proper names and pseudonyms, geographical names (cities, villages, regions), as well as song, CD, album, event and book titles. Page numbers in italics refer to photographs.

Achilles 54

'Ada sahillerinde bekliyorum' (see 'I am Waiting at the Coast of the Island')

Aegean (Sea) 24

Aerakis, Nikiforos 70, 79, 142

Aerakis Seistron Music 142, 143

Aerakis, Stelios 74, 140

Alexakis, Manolis 84, 103, 111, 112, 152

Amalthea 30, 61, 118

Amanés 98

Amariótika pendozália 71

"Amazing Grace" 24

Ambar 116

Anoya 25, 32, 37, 39, 41, 45, 49, 50, 52, 58, 61, 62, 63, 65, 67, 70, 71, 72, 73, 78, 80, 81, 82, 84, 90, 96, 97, 98, 100, 101, 103, 106, 107, 108, 110, 113, 117, 130, 131, 139, 142, 143, 156

Anoya: I istoría mésa apó ta tragoúdia tous (see *Anoya: Its History Through its Songs*)

Anoya: Its History Through its Songs 52

Anoyanés kondiliés 71, 153

Anoyanós pidihtós 59, 104, 130

Anoyiannakis, Foivos 126

Anthimos, Archbishop of Rethymnon 70

Anthropology Through the Looking-Glass 36

Aphrodite 60

Apollo 68

Apology of an Anti-Hellene 36, 72

Arab occupation 34

Aretousa 58, 73, 74, 75, 120, 124, 156

Ariadne 46, 78, 110, 113, 120, 156

Arkadi 49

Armanoya 31, 70

'Armenochorianós Syrtós' 125

'Arnisi' (see "Denial")

'Aroma Krítis (see *Aroma of Crete*)

Aroma of Crete 44, 142

Arvanitaki, Eleftheria 145

Ascetics 43

Asia Minor 31, 46, 49, 98, 122, 127, 128

Askitikí (see *Ascetics*)

Askomadoúra 59, 91, 100

Atlas 134, 144, 145, 146, 157

Avdou 24

A Place in History: Monumental and Social Time in a Cretan Town 34

Baglamás 127

Bagpipe 100, 116

Bálos 104

Barber, Samuel 24

Barnstone, Willis 34

Battle of Crete 49, 53, 81

Baud-Bovy, Samuel 110

Beacon, The 154

Bedioui, Lamia 116

Bendír 31, 74, 98, 100, 116

Benham, Patrick 87

Berger, Peter 79

Bien, Peter 43

Blacking, John 80

Black Sea 25

Black Sea 128

Boulgarí 100, 130

Bouzoúki 62, 66, 86, 100, 125

Broadcast 145

Brostáris 66, 73, 107

Buddha 43

Byzantine period 42, 45, 48, 121

Candia 45

Captain Michalis 45, 65

Caraveli, Anna 80, 95

Chania 49, 71, 87, 97, 98, 101, 103, 127, 128

Chaniótis (Chaniótikos) dance 71, 103, 110

'Chaniótiko mou yiasemí' 71

Cogan, Rachael 98

Cohen, Sara 139

Constantinople 127

Cowan, Jane 73, 81, 125

Creta Channel 140

Cretan Dance: The Meaning of Kéfi and Figoúres 106

Cretan Epic, The 142

"Cretan Love Song" 143

Cretan music 23, 27, 31, 32, 44, 50, 54, 65, 72, 73, 75, 79, 86, 95, 96, 97, 98, 100, 101, 102, 117, 118, 120, 124, 125, 126, 127, 128, 130, 136, 139, 145, 146, 149, 150, 152, 153, 154

Cretan Musical Tradition, The 142

Cretan Musical Traditions: The Masters, 1920-1955 74

Cretan Mythology 68

Cretan Panorama 139

Cretan Poem 72

Cretan Sun 142

Cretan wedding 74, 78, 81, 82, 96, 103, 104, 106, 107, 108, 110

Cretaphone 143, 144

Crete 25, 27, 32, 33, 37, 38, 53, 65, 66, 73, 118, 122, 124, 136, 138

Crete 45, 46

Crete, Mother of Gallants 142

Crete TV 140

Cultural Club (of Anoya) 59, 61, 71

Cultural Intimacy and the Social Production of Indifference 40

Daedalus 46, 135

Dalgas, Andonis 128

Daly, Ross 27, 30, 31, 40, 54, 66, 67, 72, 74, 81, 82, *83*, 84, 85, 86, 87, 88, 90, 91, 98, 100, 102, 103, 111, 112, 116, 120, 126, 128, 140, 142, 144, 145, 146, 148, 150, 152, 153, 154, 156, 157

Damaskinos, Michael 48

Dancing

    Cretan men's 107, 108, *109*

    Cretan women's 107, 108, *109*

Dance and the Body Politics in Northern Greece 73

Dance of the Stone: Iakinthia; Reference to Zeus, The 139

Danielson, Virginia 80

"Danny Boy" 24

Daraboúka (see Toubeléki)

Daoúli 116

Daskaloyiannis 23, 104

Dawe, Kevin 82

Dawn 139

Défi 98

De la Cypede, Pierre 72

"Demon" 30

"Denial" 24

Dialogues of the Gods 60

Diamandidis Adonis 128

Dictionary of Accepted Ideas 64

Dimou, Nikos 36, 39, 44, 50, 64, 72, 144, 148

Diyenis, Akritas 43

Dreamlands 87, 91, 128

Egyptian rule 48

El Greco (see Theotokopoulos, Domenicus)

Eleftheria-Thisia-Zoi (see Freedom-Sacrifice-Life) 24

Elytis, Odysseus 39

Emine 143

Engendering Song 73

Ephesus 31

Epikrédios 46

Epimenides 39, 61

Erdener, Yildiray 96, 97

Erofili 116, 118, 120, 121, 122, 124, 125, 126, 127, 128, 130, 131, 156

Erofíli 71

'Eros (Cupid) 60, 68

Erotokritos 58, 70, 73, 74, 75, 98, 101, 103, 111, 120, 124, 127, 143, 156

Erotókritos 27, 52, 88, 120, 143

Erotokritos: Four Approaches to the Cretan Medieval Romance 143

Ethnicity, Identity and Music: The Musical Construction of Place 32, 117

Euripides 61, 103

Europe 71

"Everybody asks me why I cry" 92, 127

Exercise Book B 134

Farangoulitakis, Manolis 100

Fasoulaki, Maria 74, 98, 128

Feld, Steven 80

Fermor, Patrick Leigh 128

Fertis, Yiannis 59

Figoúres 74, 107, 108

"Filedém" 65, 128, 130

First Festival of the Young 154
Flaubert, Gustave 64
Flogéra 31, 98
Flute 116
Foustalieris, Stelios 127, 130
Frangakis, Kostas 143, 144
Freedom or Death 45, 65, 113
Freedom-Sacrifice-Life 24
Friar, Kimon 43

Gáida 116
Gadoúlka 101, 116
Geertz, Clifford 25
General Kreipe 128
George the Methistís, Saint 72, 120
Geranós (also géranos) 46
Gialaftis (pseud.) 61
Giraldi, Giambattista 71, 122
Glassie, Henry 25, 33, 38, 94
Gortyna 71, 138
Grappa 24
Greek civilization era 46
Greek Folklore Research Center of the Academy
    of Athens 44
Greek Passion, The 65
Grup Yorum 146

Hainides 92, 140
'Halepianós amanés' 92, 128
Handakas 45, 48

Handax 48
Handel, G.F. 24
Hanna, Judith Lynne 82
Haravgí (see *Dawn*)
Harvard University 39
Hatzidakis, Georgios 53
Hatzidakis, Manos 64, 90
Havdeu 24
Helen of Troy 40
Hellenistic era 46
Heraclitus 27, 34, 112
Heraklion 24, 31, 40, 42, 45, 49, 62, 70, 71, 87, 90, 92, 106,
    111, 120, 134, 135, 136, 139, 142, 143, 144, 146, 153
Herakliótikos Kastrinós 104
Herakliótikes kondiliés 71
Hercules 71
Hermes 139, 140, 142, 143, 144, 145, 146, 149, 156
Herodotus 36
Herzfeld, Michael 34, 36, 39, 40, 42, 52, 66, 73, 82, 108,
    111
Homer 43, 44, 45, 46, 54
Hortatsis, Yeorgios 48, 173 (n165)
Houdetsi 88, 100, 111
Hyacinth 58, 67, 71, 116, 117, 138, 139, 146, 156
Hyacinth, Saint 58, 70, 139
Hymes, Dell 38
Hypórchema 46

Iakinthia 58, 61, 62, 70, 72, 73, 97, 100, 138, 140, 149
"I am Waiting at the Coast of the Island" 127
Ida (see Psiloritis)

Idaean Dactyls 61, 71

Idéon 'Andro 49

Ierapetra 140

Ierapetrítikos 71

"I'm Worshipping Your Beauty, My People" 90

In the Cretan Pathways 140

In the Winds' Whirlpool 30, 31, 84, 90, 91

Ironic Modern Greek Lexicon 44, 64, 144, 148

Ithaca 40

Ithaca 175 (n237)

Ithagéneia 125

Jazz kai Tzaz 146

Journal of American Folklore 80

Journeying 23, 42

Kaeppler, Adrienne 82

Kaimós 23, 98

Kallergis, Michalis 44, 60, 70, 97, 100, 142

Kalomoiris, Lefteris 70, 79

Kamares *141*

Kanavakis, Anakreontas 140

Kantáda 103

Kantiyie 45

Karatzis (pseud.) 143

Kastrinós horós 71, 104

Kastrinés kondiliés 104

Kastrinós pidihtós 104

Kastro 45

Kathimeriní 144

Kazantzakis, Nikos 23, 31, 36, 42, 43, 44, 45, 50, 65, 82, 113, 135, 148

Kéfi 78, 80, 81, 82, 111, 125

Keftiou 46

Kementzé 101

'Kírie' 24

Knossos 24, 30, 44, 46, 54, 58, 64, 80, 120, 134, 138, 142, 144, 156, 157

Knossos FM 139

Knowland, Brent 87

Kondiliés 30, 146

Kontoyiannis, Dimitris 113, 172 (n146)

Kourites 49, 54, 59, 60, 61, 62, 71, 117

Kourites' Hymn 59

Kornaros 48, 135

Koumendakis, Yiorgos 143

Koule 24, *35* (see also Kule 45)

Kourá (also kourés) 80, 136, *137*

Koutsourelis, Yiorgis 125

Kríti (see *Crete*)

Kritikós ílios (see *Cretan Sun*)

Kritorama (see Cretan Panorama)

Kronos 30, 46, 54, 61

Krousonas 24

Labyrinth 25

Labyrinth (music group) 98

Labyrinth (Lavirinthos) 87, 91

Laiká 92

Laodikia 92

Laodikis 27, 58, 60, 67, 72, 74, 81, 84, 85, 92, 93, 94, 98, 100, 102, 127, 134

Laoúto 24, 25, 31, 54, 59, 66, 79, 87, 90, 100, 101, 125, 127, 130, 134, 143, 154

Lavírinthos (see *Labyrinth*)

Leontaritis, Frangiskos 48

Lassithi 71

Lassithiótika pendozália 71

Latakia 92

Lefka Ori (see White Mountains)

Let the Inside Be Sweet 80

Levendogéna Kríti (see *Crete, Mother of Gallants*)

Levi-Strauss, Claude 38

"Light Blue and Green" 30

Líra 24, 25, 27, 30, 31, 42, 44, 59, 60, 62, 66, 67, 70, 72, 73, 74, 75, 78, 82, 84, 86, 87, 90, 95, 98, 100, 101, 102, 103, 110, 111, 116, 117, 120, 125, 126, 127, 130, 136, 142, 143, 146, 150, 152, 153, 154

Livaneli, Zulfu 125

Loudovikos of Anoya 58, 69, 70, 140, 143, 149

Loutzaki, Rena 82

Lucian (Loukianos) 46

Luckman, Thomas 79

Lyre 112

Madares (see White Mountains)

Magrini, Tulia 40, 42, 44, 84, 98

Makreas, Mary Ellen 106

Maleme 49

Maleviziótis 104, 110

Mamangakis, Nikos 175 (n219)

Mamas, Saint 81

Mandináda 25, 31, 42, 54, 61, 62, 66, 70, 73, 79, 81, 90, 95, 96, 97, 104, 117, 120, 125, 130, 135, 143, 149

Mandolíno 54, 59, 62, 67, 81, 84, 98, 100, 102, 103, 145

Manias, Nikos 142

Manouil, Saint 71

'Manousáki' (see "Narcissus")

Markopoulos, Yiannis 45, 99, 125

Markoyiannis 154

Mattinate 54, 130

May it Fill Your Soul: Experiencing Bulgarian Music 80

Mediterranean 25, 34, 36, 40, 45, 46, 64, 101, 116

Meeting Over Midnight 128

Megalo Kastro

Meraklís (also meraklídes, meraklíki) 66, 90

Merkouri, Melina 64

Messara 86

Messarítikes kondiliés 71

Minoan Era 25, 44, 46, 53

Minos 61

Minotaur 78, 156, 157

Monolingual and Etymological Dictionary of the Western Cretan Idiom 50

Moundakis, Kostas 82, 87, 142, 152

Musical Feasts 90, 172 (n120)

Mousikí 53, 94

Music, Culture and Experience 80

"My Cretan Woman" 70

"My Eyes" 128

Mylopotamos 49, 52

"Narcissus" 31

Neolithic era 46

Ness, Sally Ann 82

NET (Nea Elliniki Tileorasi) 140

Nettl, Bruno 44

Never on Sunday 64

Nidiotis (see Stavrakakis, Michalos)

Odysseus 40, 43, 46, 116

Odyssey 43, 45, 50

Old Tunes of Crete 127

Oezgen, Ohsan 87

Olympia 71

Olympic Games 71

Omar, Mohammad 87

O mikrós naftílos (see *The Young Navigator*)

Oneírou tópoi (see *Dreamlands*)

Orbecche 71, 122

Organization of Greek Tourism (EOT) 135

Oriente Musik 88, 142

Ormos 46

Orsites 46

Ostria 84, 103, 111, 112, 152

Ottoman rule 40, 42, 45, 48, 49, 54, 97, 126

Oud (also oúti) 30, 31, 54, 87, 101, 116, 127, 153

Our Crete 140

Palaioí Skopoí tis Krítis (see *Old Tunes of Crete*)

Pancretan Association of America 66, 172 (n138)

Papa-Androulakaki, Alexandra 143

Papadaki, Aspasia 74

Paris at Vienne 72, 124

Patrís 53, 144

Peloponese 124

Pendozális 25, 31, 39, 104, 153, 155, 157

Peskatore, Erikos 48

Petrides, Ted 42

Phaistos 44, 71

Pictures from the History of Crete 143

Pidihtós 61, 103, 117

Piperakis, Harilaos 127

Plato 61

Poetics of Manhood: Contest and Identity in a Cretan Mountain Village, The 67, 73, 82

Polítiki líra 127

Pontos 25

Potter's Art, The 33, 94

Prevelakis, Pandelis 82, 135

Pringiponisa 127

Prince George 48, 49

Procrustes 31

Psaradonis (Andonis Xylouris) 70, 72, *99*, 101, 134, 140, 142, 143

Psaradonis & Ensemble: Son of Psiloritis 142

Psaronikos (see Xylouris, Nikos)

Psaroyiannis (Yiannis Xylouris) 142

Psaroyiorgis (Yiorgis Xylouris) *105*, 134

Psilakis, Nikos 43, 68

Psiloritis (also Ida) 49, 50, 52, 58, 59, 61, 64, 70, 71, 74, 78, 81, 116, 117, *119*, 121, 131, 138, 140, 146, 156

Puccini, Giacomo 24
Pyrrhíchios (also pyrrhíche) 45, 59, 135
Pythagoras 61

'Qadduka 'al-mayyas' (see 'Your flirtatiously swaying figure')
Quinn, Anthony 64

Rabáb 86, 87, 116
Racy, Ali Jihad 142
Radamanthis 61
Rajasthan 101
Rakí 24, 60, 75, 79, 111, 130, 136, 138, 142
Rea 53
Rebetika 92
Refutation of Crete 48
Rethymniótiki soústa 71
Rethymniótika syrtá 71
Rethymnon 34, 49, 52, 98, 127, 130
Rice, Timothy 80
Rizítika 54, 59, 97, 117, 127
Romboyiannakis, Yiannis *105*, 172 (n134)
Rodinos, Andreas 127
Roman conquest 46, 48
Ross Daly & Labyrinth: Mitos 126, 154
Ross Daly: Selected Works 153

Saha, Jachindranath 87
Saints of Crete 142

Samiou, Helen 23
Santoúri 116
Sappho 53, 95, 117
Sarángi 87, 101
Saríki 59, 75, 110
Savigliano, Marta 31
Saz 30, 31, 87, 100, 116, 127
Sbokos, Georgios 52, 169 (n70)
Seferis, George 24, 134
Sfakia 71, 104
Sfirohábiolo 91
Shankar, Ravi 85
Shiloah, Amnon 84
Sifoyiorgakis, Spyros 75, 154
Siganós 25, 104
Singritismós (see Syncretism)
Sitár 87
Sitiakés kondiliés 71
Skironas 31
Skordalos, Thanasis 75, 130
Skoulas, Vasilis 70, 101, 110, 142, 143
Social Construction of Reality, The 79
Society for the Dissemination of National Music 44
"Song of Nida" 71
Sounds and Pictures of Crete: Cretan Traditional Instruments; Instrumental Songs 136
Soústa 104
Speaking Without Words: Cretan Dance at Weddings as Expression, Dialogue, and Communication 32
Spirit of Folk Art, The 33, 38

Stavrakakis, Mitsos 30

Stavrakakis, Michalos 90

Stavrakakis, Nikiforos 90, 111

Stavrakakis, Vasilis 27, 30, 31, 50, 54, 58, 60, 67, 70, 71, 72, 74, 81, 82, 84, 85, 88, *89*, 90, 91, 92, 97, 98, 100, 102, 111, 120, 134, 140, 145, 146, *147*, 149, 150, 156

Sti díni ton anémo (see *In the Winds' Whirlpool*)

Stivaktakis, Christos 143

Stivánia 59, 71, 110

Stokes, Martin 32, 117, 148

Stone, Ruth 79, 80

"Stop Living with Dreams" 79

Sugarman, Jane 73

Swedish Nyckelharpa Orchestra 116

Syncretism 65, 170 (n85)

Syrtáki 62

Syrtós 103

Tabachaniótika 55, 98, 117, 127

Tar 87

Távla 97

Taxidévondas (see *Journeying*) 23

Taxími 128

Tetrádio gymnasmáton B (see *Exercise Book B*)

"The Rose Bush Leaves" 128

Theodorakis, Mikis 24, 64, 125, 148

Theofanis the Cretan 48

Theotokopoulos, Domenicus 48, 71, 135

Theseus 78, 84, 94, 110, 113

Thomas, Kelly 75, 100

Thucydides 84

'Tis triandafiliás ta fíla' (see "The Rose Bush Leaves")

Tkatcheva, Angelina 100

Toubeléki (daraboúka) 60, 74, 92, 94, 100, 145

Toud 'Sames 116

To Touch the Sky 34

Toutoudaki, Spyridoula 98, 143

Traditional Music Instruments 148

Tsarouhis, Yiannis 44

Tsiftetéli 42, 94

Tristes Tropiques 38

Trocchia-Taiganides, Anna 24

Turkish occupation 34, 104

Tzobanakis, Manolis 53

Tzourás (long-necked lute) 100, 145

University of Crete 82, 94

Venetian occupation 34, 43, 44, 45, 48, 54, 126, 127

Venizelos, Eleftherios 48

Vererakis, Dimitris 25

Vidalis, Stavros 70

Violin 44, 59, 100, 101, 116, 126

Voice of Egypt, The 80

Voriza 100

Votrydón 46

Vráka 110

Wedding events 81-82, 171 (n111)
Welcome Crete 54, 67, 86, 142, 150
White Mountains 97
Williams, Chris 73, 101, 102, 107, 125, 126, 127, 128
Within and Without: The Category of "Female" in the Ethnography of Rural Greece 42
WOMAD 145

Xanthinakis 50
Xydakis, Nikos 143
Xylouris, Nikos 42, 50, 60, 70, 90, 125, 130, 140, 149, 150, *151*

Young Navigator, The 39
"Your flirtatiously swaying figure" 128
Yper-X 95, 148

Zeimbék(iko) 36
Zeno 46
Zervakis, Vangelis 111
Zeus 30, 42, 46, 49, 50, 54, 58, 61, 62, 64, 67, 70, 71, 73, 97, 116, 117, 120, 121, 138, 139, 140, 146, 156
Zeus' Hymn 58
Zorbas, Alexis 31, 36, 65, 66, 116, 121, 122, 124, 125, 126, 127, 128, 130, 131, 136, 156
Zorba the Greek 36, 43, 62, 64, 125, 135, 148

CRETAN MUSIC:
UNRAVELING ARIADNE'S THREAD

WAS PUBLISHED BY
KERKYRA PUBLICATIONS LTD.

PRINTED AND BOUND BY
TYPOS HELLAS LTD.

IN 2,000 COPIES, ATHENS, GREECE

MARCH 2007